Oxford A Level
Religious Studies
for OCR

Christianity, Philosophy and Ethics

Revision Guide

 RECAP   APPLY   REVIEW   SUCCEED

Libby Ahluwalia

OXFORD
UNIVERSITY PRESS

OXFORD
UNIVERSITY PRESS

Great Clarendon Street, Oxford, OX2 6DP, United Kingdom

Oxford University Press is a department of the University of Oxford.
It furthers the University's objective of excellence in research,
scholarship, and education by publishing worldwide. Oxford is a
registered trade mark of Oxford University Press in the UK and in
certain other countries

British Library Cataloguing in Publication Data
Data available

978-0-19-842375-1

10 9 8 7 6 5 4 3 2

MIX
Paper from
responsible sources
FSC
www.fsc.org   FSC® C007785

Paper used in the production of this book is a natural, recyclable
product made from wood grown in sustainable forests. The
manufacturing process conforms to the environmental regulations
of the country of origin.

Printed in Great Britain by Bell and Bain Ltd, Glasgow

Please note that the practice questions in this book allow students a
genuine attempt at practising exam skills, but they are not intended
to replicate examination papers.

With thanks to Robert Bowie, and to Julie Haigh for reviewing this
Revision Guide.

We are grateful to the authors and publishers for use of extracts
from their titles.

Scripture quotations from the Holy Bible, New International
Version, Anglicised © 1979, 1984, 2011 Biblica, used by permission
of Hodder & Stoughton Ltd, an Hachette UK company. All rights
reserved. 'NIV' is a registered trademark of Biblica, UK trademark
number 1448790.

We have made every effort to trace and contact all copyright holders
before publication, but if notified of any errors or omissions, the
publisher will be happy to rectify those at the earliest opportunity.

Cover image: iStock.com;

p10: Adam Eastland / Alamy Stock Photo; p12 (T): Adam eastland/
Alamy Stock Photo; p12 (B): Okcamera/Shutterstock; p14: Adam
Eastland / Alamy Stock Photo; p17: Gomberg/iStockphoto; p19:
Anythings/Shutterstock; p21: Scientifica/Corbis Documentary/Getty
Images; p22: DustyPixel/iStockphoto; p23: Sanjeri/iStockphoto;
p26: Dale O'Dell/Alamy Stock Photo; p28: Ovchinnikova Irina/
Shutterstock; p30: Vold77/iStockphoto; p32: CoreyFord/iStockphoto;
p36: MaLija/Shutterstock; p41: Colin Underhill/Alamy Stock Photo;
p42: ChristianChan/Shutterstock; p45: James A. Sugar/National
Geographic/Getty Images; p46: Banana Pancake/Alamy Stock Photo;
p48: Jon12/Stockimo/Alamy Stock Photo; p51: Lebrecht Music and
Arts Photo Library/Alamy Stock Photo; p53: SolStock/iStockphoto;
p54: Pal Szilagyi Palko/Alamy Stock Photo; p55: FrankyDeMeyer/
iStockphoto; p57: Martin Anderson/Alamy Stock Photo; p59: Andriy
Lipkan/Shutterstock; p63: Aloysius Patrimonio/Alamy Stock Photo;
p73: Ian Rolfe/Alamy Stock Photo; p75: XiXinXing/Alamy Stock
Photo; p77: JP Wallet/Shutterstock; p78: Miriama Taneckova/Alamy
Stock Photo; p81: Tommaso Altamura/Alamy Stock Photo; p85: Scott
Olson/Getty Images; p87: SolStock/iStockphoto; p89: AHowden -
New Zealand Stock Photography/Alamy Stock Photo; p90: Peter
Cade/ The Image Bank/Getty Images; p91: Chrisdorney/Shutterstock;
p93: DisobeyArt/Shutterstock; p94: Claire Norman/Shutterstock;
p95: Ugis Riba/Shutterstock; p101: © James Darling Photography;
p102: Justin Kase zsixz/Alamy Stock Photo; p105: B Christopher/
Alamy Stock Photo; p106: FredFroese/iStockphoto; p109: Steve
Pyke/Contributor/Getty Images; p111: Benoit Daoust/Alamy Stock
Photo; p115: IanDagnall Computing / Alamy Stock Photo; p117:
DEA/Veneranda Biblioteca Ambrosiana/De Agostini Picture Library/
Getty Images; p121: Rawpixel.com/Shutterstock; p131: Jorisvo/
Shutterstock; p152: Ian Dagnall/Alamy Stock Photo; p165: Ullstein
Bild/Getty Images; p175: Mila Supinskaya Glashchenko/Shutterstock;
p187: Avalon_Studio/iStockphoto; p195: Pat Greenhouse/The Boston
Globe/Getty Images; p197: Tim Graham/Alamy Stock Photo; p199:
FatCamera/iStockphoto; p207: RichVintage/iStockphoto; p211: GL
Archive / Alamy Stock Photo.

Artwork by Aptara and Q2A Media Pvt. Ltd.

Contents

Introduction

How to use this book

This book is designed to help you in your revision for OCR A level and AS level Religious Studies. If you are doing AS level, not all the chapters will be relevant to you. We have indicated on the Contents pages which topics you will need to cover for AS. If you are doing A level, all the chapters will apply to you.

Many people think of revision in terms of memorising all the facts they have been taught during the course. This is important, but it is only one aspect of revision – you need to go further than this. There is a real emphasis in Religious Studies on demonstrating thinking skills through making critical judgements and giving evaluation; without practising these skills, your essays will be overly descriptive and list-like, and will not score very high marks.

Work through the 🔵 **RECAP** sections for each chapter, reminding yourself of key points, thinkers and details. You could use these pages as a guide for making your own memory aids such as flashcards or mind maps. Then try the 'Test yourself' questions under ⚙️ **APPLY** to see how much you have remembered; go back over the RECAP section afterwards to fill in any gaps in your knowledge. These sections help you to gain marks for Assessment Objective 1 (AO1), which is about **demonstrating knowledge and understanding.**

Further APPLY sections of the book help you to develop your thinking skills, to help you gain marks for AO2, which is about critical judgement. In the exam, you will be asked for a **critical, evaluative judgement** about a topic you have studied. The questions will not simply ask for description but will ask you what you think. Use the questions on these pages to think really deeply for yourself. Work out your own perspective on different issues and try to articulate your reasoning, so that you do not have to think about the issues for the first time on the day of the exam.

The 'Practice Exam Questions' and 'Mark schemes' will help you to use your knowledge and critical judgement in response to essay questions. When you are confident that you have revised a section carefully, have a go at a practice question and, if possible, write it against the clock. Use the mark scheme at the back of the book to see what examiners might have expected from candidates answering this question and ⏺ **REVIEW** your work – but don't worry if your answer is different from the one suggested. The mark scheme is not a checklist; examiners will credit any reasonable response to the question, even if you have used different material to formulate your argument.

AS and A level

The skills required for AS in Religious Studies are the same as the skills needed for A level; however, the 'weighting' of the marking is slightly different. In A level, a higher percentage of the marks are for your evaluative skill than in AS. However, AS candidates still need to present consistent, analytical arguments in their answers and not just description.

Types of essay question

Essay questions can be worded in a variety of different ways; these are some of the most common ways a question might be phrased:

To what extent...?
For these questions, you are being asked whether a claim is completely true, completely untrue, or true only up to a point. It might ask to what extent Hume is

successful in his criticisms of the cosmological argument, or to what extent feminism is right in accusing Christianity of patriarchy, for example. You need to think about your own position as well as considering views different from your own.

How fair is the claim...?

Similarly, you need to think whether the claim that follows is very fair, not fair at all, or only fair up to a point. It might ask how fair is the claim that Plato's theory of Forms is enlightening, or how fair is the claim that all religions lead to the same goal, for example. You need to think about your own position as well as considering views different from your own. Similar questions might ask **'How convincing is...'** or **'How effective is...'** or **'How helpful is...'**

'Statement.' Discuss.

These questions ask you to consider whether or not you agree with the statement, and also to consider what others with different opinions might say. You still need to arrive at a conclusion and not just stop when you have presented different possibilities. The question is asking, what is your view on the truth of this statement and how does it compare with the views of others?

Discuss critically issues arising from the belief that...

For these questions, you need to decide what the issues are, and then comment on them. For example, you could be asked about the issues arising from the belief that God can be known through the natural world, or the belief that God is omniscient, or the belief that situation ethics is the best response to dilemmas of euthanasia. These questions can be quite straightforward to structure, because once you have chosen some issues to consider, you can write a paragraph on each.

All the questions will require you to formulate an argument. They will never ask for a simple description or presentation of possible points of view.

Essay writing in exams

This is *not the only way* of writing A-level essays, but it is a way that can work well.

Plan your essay

This is essential if you want to score well – it helps you to write with confidence, once you have decided where you are going with the question, and it helps you plan your time if you can see from the start how much ground you want to cover.

You don't have very long in exam conditions, so your planning needs to be brief.

Read the question carefully and then think, **what am I going to *argue*?** Think AO2 first. This makes all the difference to your scores.

Then think, **how am I going to support my argument**, what reasons will I give and which thinkers and/or quotations and/or examples could I use? Use your knowledge and understanding as a part of your argument, rather than simply presenting it. These are your AO1 marks.

Which counter-arguments and/or different perspectives am I going to consider and how am I going to argue against them – **what reasons will I give to explain why I reject those and prefer my own view?**

Your plan should map your argument, rather than simply be a list of the information you want to include. Think of it like packing a suitcase – you need to know where you are going with your essay before you can put the right things in it. Remember essentials and don't bother carrying ideas you won't need to use.

Writing an introduction

Start by telling me what is the issue in the question and why it matters.

'To what extent is analogy an effective method of conveying religious ideas?'

Example opening:

Religious ideas can be difficult to convey using everyday language, because our normal language relates to a shared world available to the five senses, whereas religious belief, some argue, is subjective, intensely personal, other-worldly and not open to empirical testing. Therefore, if religious language is to be effective in conveying ideas, a method has to be found for doing so, and some have suggested that analogy is a possible way forward.

Why include this?
Because it helps you, as a writer, to clarify in your mind what you are being asked (if you realise you don't really know what you are being asked, you've still got time to choose a different question!). It also helps your examiner to have confidence that you've read the question and plan to answer this question rather than writing generally about the topic.

Also, tell me what you're going to argue, right from the start.

This introduction could continue in the following ways:

... In my view, however, analogy has its limitations, and I would argue that religious language needs to combine the use of analogy with other methods such as univocal language, symbol and myth in order to be considered effective.

Or

...I will argue, however, that the logical positivists are right in their claim that religious language is essentially meaningless, and therefore analogy is ineffective because it attempts to convey empty ideas.

Why include this?
Because it helps you to think straight away 'what am I going to argue?' rather than letting your mind run away with all the information you want to include, and so it helps to avoid your essay becoming a list. It also helps your examiner to see that you recognise the importance of demonstrating AO2 skills of critical evaluation.

Exercise

Now try writing some introductions to these exam-style questions:

4. To what extent are a posteriori arguments convincing in demonstrating the existence of God? (AS and A level)

5. 'Individual religious experiences are best understood as the products of over-active imaginations.' Discuss. (AS and A level)

6. How convincing is Boethius' response to the philosophical issues raised by the belief that God is omniscient? (A level)

First section of the body of the essay

Present the side of the argument that you disagree with, and tell me why it's unconvincing.

Who thinks these ideas that you disagree with? What are their ideas? Explain them clearly. Give examples to illustrate their point of view. These are your AO1 marks for knowledge and understanding.

Say what you think of this position – although it has some strengths, which are X and Y (if you think there are any strengths), it's unconvincing because … Outline its flaws. Perhaps it makes assumptions you don't accept (such as that the Bible is literally true, or that the existence of God can be demonstrated), perhaps there are flaws in the reasoning, perhaps the evidence is not strong, perhaps there is a more plausible and compelling case to be found elsewhere. These are your AO2 marks for evaluative, critical argument.

'Augustine presents a stronger response than Irenaeus to the problem of evil.' Discuss.

It could be argued that Augustine's response to the problem of evil has strengths. He works hard to support the view that God cannot be held responsible for natural and moral evil, by placing all the blame on humanity in Adam and Eve's decision to disobey God and fall from grace. In Augustinian theodicy, variety in the world is one of the beauties of creation, and God made angels in variety, giving some of them less grace than others. As a result, some of the angels fell away from God because of their lack of grace and turned to evil. They in turn tempted Adam and Eve, resulting in the Fall. Augustine argued that the Fall was catastrophic on a cosmic scale, causing all future generations to be born with Original Sin and disrupting the natural world to the extent that natural disaster and natural evil was introduced into a previously perfect world. Augustine's theodicy does not try to suggest that God wanted evil in the world, and so he avoids the problems of Irenaean theodicy and the more developed theodicy presented by Hick, who seem to be suggesting that evil is some kind of disguised goodness because it is all part of God's plan. In Augustine's theodicy, the goodness of God is maintained and there is no suggestion that God might allow evil as a means to an end.

However, despite this strength, there are serious flaws in Augustine's theodicy. He does not give a convincing account of why Adam and Eve chose to Fall, if they were created without Original Sin. There should have been nothing in their natures to make them give in to temptation like this. He does not explain why angels, supposedly perfect beings, would fall away from God nor why God did not prevent this. Augustine does not explain why an omniscient God did not anticipate the Fall happening, or why an omnipotent God could not have undone the harm caused. The theodicy is therefore unconvincing because it leaves too many questions unanswered and appears logically inconsistent. His theodicy also assumes a literal interpretation of the Genesis stories which could be difficult for people in a post-Darwinian era to accept.

Practise writing about an opinion different from your own – present it and say why you are rejecting it. Write that part of the essay for the following questions:

7. To what extent are a posteriori arguments convincing in demonstrating the existence of God? (So if you think they are convincing, write about a view that says they are not, and why you reject that. Continue the essay you began in exercise 4.) (AS and A level)

8. 'Human beings have minds which are functions of the brain; there is nothing non-physical about human persons.' Discuss. (AS and A level)

9. How far is Wittgenstein's theory of language games successful in addressing questions of the meaningfulness of religious language? (A level)

> At the end of this exercise, you should be about halfway through your essay.

Second section of the body of the essay

Present your preferred way of looking at things.

Who thinks these ideas that you agree with? What are their ideas? Explain them clearly. Give examples to illustrate their point of view. Again, these are your AO1 marks for knowledge and understanding.

Say why this view is better. Perhaps the evidence is firmer. Perhaps it doesn't rely on us also accepting something shaky. Perhaps it's more consistent with other beliefs and so presents a more coherent picture. This critical comment and evaluation is where you will earn AO2 marks.

You could have a third section of middle ground which might be where your own opinion lies. If so, make sure that you thoroughly present both sides before explaining what makes your view fall between them.

Conclusion

Summarise what you've said with reference to the question.

The conclusion does not have to be long, and should wrap up the essay rather than introducing new ideas. In many ways it should echo your introduction and include a brief summary of your reasons.

Example conclusion:

...therefore it is clear that position X has serious weaknesses, whereas position Y is more convincing because position X is based on unfounded assumptions whereas position Y is well-supported by the evidence.

Successful essays give a balance between demonstrating knowledge and understanding, and demonstrating critical, evaluative skill. It is possible to write a list-like essay with all the information you know, without giving much in the way of argument, but this will not score very well. It is also possible to write something that looks like an argument without knowing very much, just giving vague opinions without supporting them with any kind of knowledge or understanding, but these essays score even less well as they tend to be very superficial and basic.

Keep practising and remember to start every encounter with an essay question by thinking **'What am I going to argue?'**

Reviewing your essay

Use this table once you have written your practice essays to check whether you are demonstrating the skills necessary to gain high marks.

Check your essay...	✓ / X
Did you read the question carefully and make sure you knew what you were being asked before you began? **(AO1 and AO2)**	
Did you have a clear idea in your mind of which opinion you were going to defend before you began to write? **(AO2)**	
Did you make a brief plan, to give your ideas some structure? **(AO1 and AO2)**	
Did you think about your knowledge on the topic and select the most relevant information and ideas for this question (rather than including everything you know whether relevant or not)? **(AO1)**	
Does your introduction make clear you have understood the question? **(AO1 and AO2)**	
Does your introduction indicate what you plan to argue? **(AO2)**	
Have you used appropriate key terminology correctly and confidently in your essay? **(AO1)**	
Is the knowledge you have demonstrated accurate and detailed? **(AO1)**	
Have you used (where appropriate) a good range of scholarly views and/or references to sources of wisdom and authority such as biblical texts or reputable thinkers? **(AO1)**	
Have you got a clear line of argument? **(AO2)**	
Have you supported your argument with reasons (rather than simply asserted that this is what you believe)? **(AO2)**	
If you have referred to the thinking of different scholars, have you given it critical analysis and evaluation by saying what you think of their views? **(AO2)**	
Have you shown that you understand different points of view and counter-arguments? **(AO2)**	
If appropriate, have you given examples to clarify your meaning? **(AO1 and AO2)**	
Is your answer balanced, rather than one-sided? **(AO2)**	
Have you answered the question – when it asked what you thought about an issue, did you explain what you think, or did you just give a range of possible opinions without committing yourself? **(AO2)**	
Does your conclusion successfully summarise your argument and clearly state your position? **(AO2)**	

RECAP

Plato

Plato was a **rationalist** – he thought we gain knowledge primarily through our reason.

Plato was also a **dualist** – he thought reality can be divided into two: the physical world of phenomena and the ideal, or conceptual, world of the Forms.

Plato points upwards, to show his belief in an ideal world 'above' this one

Plato's understanding of reality

- Reality consists of the physical world of phenomena, and the world of concepts (the world of Forms or Ideals).

- The physical world is known through sense experience ('empirical observation') but the senses can be misleading; the world of the Forms is known through reason which gives more certainty.

- The physical world is always changing but the world of the Forms is unchanging, so knowledge about the world of Forms will have a lasting certainty that knowledge about the physical world can never have.

- The physical world is given its reality by the Forms; physical phenomena 'participate in' their Ideal Forms.

The Forms

- The Forms are concepts. They are ideals and universals that we can use to help us understand the world. If we know the Form of Justice, then we can recognise examples of justice when we see them in the physical world. If we understand whiteness as a concept, then we can recognise white things when we see them.

- Phenomena in the physical world 'participate in' their Forms. A domestic cat 'participates in' the Form of Cat, and so does a lion.

- The Forms are superior to physical phenomena, because they are unchanging.

- The Forms can be the objects of certain knowledge, because they are unchanging.

- The Forms are known through reason.

- Plato thought that the Form of the Good was the highest of all the Forms, and that it illuminates them.

- Philosophy leads us to a recognition of true goodness, and so philosophers should rule the state.

- We know about the Forms from birth ('innately') and so we must have encountered them before we were born. Therefore we must have immortal souls that are capable of living without being in our physical bodies.

The Analogy of the Cave

- Plato invents a scenario which he uses as an analogy and an allegory, to show how he understands the importance of philosophy.
- He uses it to illustrate how knowledge gained through experience of the senses (empirical knowledge) is inferior to knowledge gained through knowledge of the Forms.
- The analogy is part of Plato's political work *Republic*.
- Plato compares the physical world with a dark shadowy cave, and the world of the Forms with a sun-filled 'real world'.
- He asks us to imagine prisoners in the cave who have never known anything else but their imprisonment. They have sense experiences which are only shadows of the truth, but they accept these at face value because they do not know any better and never question their senses.
- A prisoner leaves the cave and is enlightened by the Form of the Good, giving him knowledge about the world as it really is.
- The physical 'cave' world demonstrates how knowledge gained through the senses is often partial or misleading.
- People who never question the information they gain through their senses are 'imprisoned' by their own ignorance.
- We mistake the information we gain through our senses as being 'truth', but real truth is found through philosophy which leads us to the Forms.

Key terms

Forms: a name Plato gave to ideal concepts

Rationalist: someone who thinks that the primary source of knowledge is reason

Dualism: the belief that reality can be divided into two distinct parts, such as good and evil, or physical and non-physical

Possible criticisms of Plato's thought

- Some people, such as Richard Dawkins, argue that it makes no sense to talk of another world beyond this physical one. We cannot possibly know or make any meaningful statements about other worlds.
- There is no evidence to support the existence of a world of Forms.
- This physical world is worth studying even if the knowledge we gain from sense experience is not completely certain.
- The theory of Forms is unclear. We do not know if each species of plant has its own Form, or if there is one Form of Plant in general, or if there is a Form of Living Things, or a Form of Forms.
- Plato is not clear about how phenomena 'participate in' their Forms.
- Not everyone would agree that we all recognise 'Goodness' in the same way. Philosophers do not always reach an agreement. Goodness is not only available to the intellectually gifted.
- Plato's recognition that our senses can sometimes mislead us could be seen as valuable.
- Plato could be commended for encouraging people to look beyond surface appearances in order to gain understanding.
- Some critics welcome Plato's assertion that there is more to reality than the physical world.

Aristotle

Aristotle was an **empiricist** – he thought we gain knowledge primarily through our experience of the world, and we have this experience through our senses.

Aristotle's understanding of reality

- We learn about reality through observation of the physical world.
- If anything other than this physical world exists, we have no way of knowing about it.
- Reality can be explained in four different ways – the 'four causes' – which can account for and explain the phenomena of the physical world around us.

Aristotle gestures towards the earth, to show his belief that we gain knowledge through our experience of the physical world

Key terms

Empiricist: someone who thinks that the primary source of knowledge is experience gained through the five senses

Aetion: an explanatory factor, a reason or cause for something

Telos: the end, or purpose, of something

Aristotle's four causes

Aristotle used the term 'aetion', which means 'cause' or 'explanation'. He thought cause could be understood in four different ways:

1 The **material** cause: this explains what something is made from.

The material 'cause' of this chair is wood and glue.

2 The **formal** cause: this explains what shape something takes, or what its identifying features are.

The formal 'cause' of this chair is a square seat and straight back.

3 The **efficient** cause: this explains the activity that makes something happen. It brings about change and 'actualises potential', turning something from what it could be into what it is.

The efficient cause of the carpenter's activity has realised the potential of the wood to become this chair.

4 The **final** cause: this is something's purpose, or reason for existing at all. Aristotle used the term 'telos' or 'end'. He thought something was good if it achieved or fulfilled its telos.

This chair is a good chair if it is sturdy and comfortable to sit on.

Aristotle and the Prime Mover

- Aristotle thought there must be some kind of Prime Mover (or Unmoved Mover) to account for the fact that everything in the physical world is changing.
- He did not think that an endless chain of cause and effect was possible.
- The Prime Mover is the first of all substances and depends on nothing else for its existence – it exists necessarily.
- Because the Prime Mover exists necessarily, it must also be eternal.
- It causes change or motion in everything else by attraction – everything in the universe is drawn towards its perfection.
- The Prime Mover must have no potential for change, but must be pure actuality.
- It must be perfectly good, because it is unchangeable and cannot be corrupted.
- It must be immaterial, because it is not capable of being acted upon.
- It is transcendent and the ultimate reason (telos) for everything: the Prime Mover is the final cause of the universe.

Possible criticisms of Aristotle's thought

- Aristotle's writing often lacks clarity, partly perhaps because we only have fragments of it.
- Aristotle could be criticised for dismissing too readily Plato's belief in another world beyond this one, and for depending too heavily on sense experience.
- Many thinkers, such as Bertrand Russell and Dawkins, reject the view that the universe has a telos (final cause). They argue that it just exists, without any explanation or purpose.
- Perhaps the universe came about by chance rather than because of any Prime Mover.
- Aristotle only succeeds in suggesting a possible explanation for the universe, but it is not the only possibility so he does not arrive at a certain conclusion.
- Many critics admire Aristotle for giving confidence to the idea of scientific investigation through observation.
- Aristotle is often credited with laying the groundwork for later philosophers with his ideas about cause and effect.
- Aristotle's use of a combination of reason and sense experience to gain knowledge could be seen as the best way of learning about the world.

APPLY

Test yourself on key knowledge (AO1)

1. In which book does Plato's Analogy of the Cave appear?
2. What does it mean, to call Plato a 'rationalist'?
3. What does it mean, to call Plato a 'dualist'?
4. Why does Plato think that we can gain certain knowledge of the Forms but cannot gain certain knowledge of the physical world?
5. Which does Plato think is the highest of all the Forms?
6. In the cave allegory, what is represented by the prisoner arriving in the daylight of the outside world?
7. What does it mean, to call Aristotle an 'empiricist'?
8. What does Aristotle mean by the 'material cause' of something?
9. What does Aristotle mean when he says that the Prime Mover must exist 'necessarily'?
10. What does Aristotle mean by the 'efficient cause' of something?
11. How does Aristotle's Prime Mover bring about chains of cause and effect in the physical world?
12. Why did Aristotle think that the Prime Mover must be perfectly good?

If you are unsure about any of the questions, look back over the key points on pages 10–13. You can check your answers on page 217.

13

Develop your skills in critical argument and evaluation (AO2)

For high marks in AO2, you need to think about the ideas in this chapter and develop your own perspective, so that you can produce critically evaluative arguments rather than just describing and presenting the views of others. At AS level, 50% of your marks are awarded for your skills in critical evaluation, and at A level, 60%.

Use the following questions to help you formulate your own views.

» Discuss them with friends, making sure you articulate your own view and listen to the views of others.

» Try writing your answers to these questions, to familiarise yourself with expressing your ideas in an academic style.

» Remember to give reasons for your views.

» Think about counter-arguments – what might someone say who held a different view from your own, and why do you think they are wrong?

1. **Which understanding of reality do you find more convincing: 1) Plato's view that there is a world of Forms more real than this physical world, or 2) Aristotle's view that this physical world is the only reality we can know anything about? How would you support your opinion with reasons? Can you think of any examples you could use to clarify your position? If you don't agree with either of them, what is your own position?**

Here is an example of the kinds of ideas you might explore in formulating your analysis and evaluation:

You might agree with Plato and think that there is more to reality than the physical world we can observe with our senses. This might be because you have a religious belief, and/or it might be because you can see no reason for assuming that there is no more to reality than the physical. You might give examples of things that have reality but are not physical, such as love or emotion or beauty. You might want to agree with Plato that another world could be more real than this one, or you might argue that there are different kinds of reality. Perhaps you might give the example of mathematics, which can give knowledge but comes from reason rather than from sense experience. You might want to agree with Aristotle and argue that the physical world is the only one available to knowledge and that we should concentrate our efforts on studying things that are material and that can be observed, especially if they can be tested by different people so that conclusions are not just subjective.

Now use your critical and evaluative skills to explore these questions on your own.

2. How useful do you think Plato's theory of Forms might be to help us understand reality? Does seeing individual things in terms of 'universals' help us to make sense of the world? Is the theory of Forms useful but only up to a point, or only in some contexts, or not at all? Can you think of any examples? What reasoning could you use to support your opinions?

3. Do you agree with Aristotle that we can gain valuable knowledge through sense experience (empiricism)? How would you justify your view?

4. How helpful do you find Aristotle's understanding of causality (his understanding of how things are caused) when he gives his four causes? Do you agree that everything has a final cause (telos) to explain why it exists at all? Or do some things exist for no reason? Do you think that the universe itself must have a final cause (reason for its existence)? Do you think that you as an individual exist for a reason, or are you just here by chance?

5. Aristotle draws the conclusion that the universe must have a final cause, and that there must be a Prime Mover to account for the existence of the universe. How convincing do you find this view? Must the universe have a cause? Are there alternatives to Aristotle's ideas, and if so, are they more or less convincing than Aristotle's?

6. How do you think Plato's Form of the Good compares with Aristotle's Prime Mover? Which features do they have in common, and where are the differences? Is either concept more plausible, or more attractive, than the other? Do you think Plato and Aristotle might be describing the same being, seen from different perspectives? Give reasons for your responses.

 **REVIEW**

Practice Exam Questions

Try these practice questions. You could:

» write plans for each of them, to practise your skills in structuring an essay
» use them for practice in writing introductions and/or conclusions
» write the whole essay, perhaps against the clock.

1. Discuss critically the philosophical views presented by Plato in his Analogy of the Cave.

2. 'Aristotle is wrong to think worthwhile knowledge can be gained through sense experience.' Discuss.

Use page 9 to review your essay and make sure you have met the assessment objectives. See page 221 for a mark scheme.

Soul, mind and body

 RECAP

The philosophical language of soul, mind and body

'Soul' is a difficult word to define as people use it loosely. Sometimes they use mind and soul interchangeably, but not always.

It is often used to refer to the 'self' or essential part of a person.

Christians and other religious believers see the soul as the most important aspect of a person.

Religious believers often see the soul as non-physical, capable of having a relationship with God and capable of living independently from the body.

Plato's ideas about the soul, mind and body

- Plato had a dualist understanding of the soul and body: he saw them as two separate entities.
- He thought the soul had the capacity to leave the physical body and move on after death, returning to the world of the Forms.
- The demands of the body can impede the progress of the soul.
- He thought life and death come from each other in an endless chain where souls are reborn.
- He had a tripartite view of the soul – that the soul is made of three parts: reason, appetite and emotion.

- He used the analogy of two horses pulling a chariot. Reason is the charioteer, guiding and directing the horses of appetite and emotion to stop them running off wildly.
- In *Meno*, Plato says that an uneducated person such as a slave boy can still work out the answers to geometry and logic problems, because their souls must have encountered ideas before birth in the world of Forms.
- In the *Myth of Er*, Plato describes the immortality and rebirth of souls.

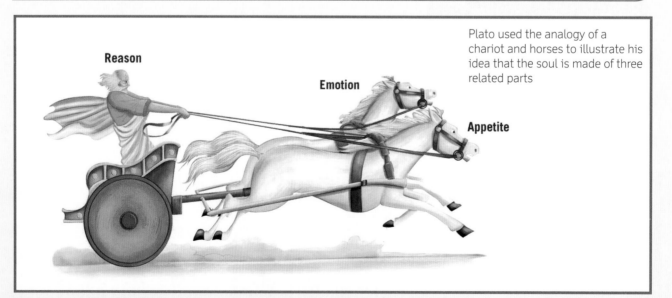

Reason

Emotion

Appetite

Plato used the analogy of a chariot and horses to illustrate his idea that the soul is made of three related parts

Aristotle's ideas about the soul, mind and body

- Aristotle disagreed with Plato.
- He thought the soul was a substance, meaning 'essence' or 'real thing'.
- The soul is that which gives a living thing its essence. The capabilities of living things constitute their souls.
- The soul is not distinct from the body. It is the capacities that the body has to do whatever it is meant to do.
- The soul gives bodily matter its form, efficiency and telos.
- Aristotle gives the analogy of the shape made when soft wax is pressed with a stamp. The shape is inseparable from the wax, as the soul is inseparable from the body.

Aristotle used the analogy of wax with a stamp in it to illustrate his idea that the soul could not be separated from the body

Metaphysics of consciousness

The mind–body problem is the problem of whether the mind (or soul) and body are two separate things, or whether the mind (or soul) is a function of the body and inseparable from it.

Substance dualism

- This is the view that the mind and body are two distinct substances with two distinct sets of properties.
- The body is material and has properties of extension (it takes up space and has measurements). The mind/soul is immaterial and has properties of thought and emotion.
- René Descartes arrived at a substance dualist view through a process of hyperbolic scepticism. He could not be certain he had a body, but he could be certain he had a mind, because he was thinking with it: 'I think, therefore I am'. If the existence of the body is uncertain but the existence of the mind is certain, then the body and mind can't be the same.
- He thought the mind and body must somehow be attached to each other, perhaps through the pineal gland, but he was hazy about how this worked.
- Substance dualism allows the possibility of life after death. The soul or mind could continue after the death of the body, if they are separable.

Property dualism

This is the view that there is only one kind of substance, which is matter, but that matter can have two distinct kinds of properties: physical and mental.

Emergent materialism

This is the view that new properties emerge from physical matter as it becomes more complex, and the mind and body are different but not completely distinct. It was the view of John Stuart Mill.

Reductive materialism (identity theory and type physicalism)

- The mind is not distinct from the body but is identical with it.
- Mental states, e.g. memory, fear and guilt, correspond to different activities in the brain.
- Chemical reactions are the same thing as mental events, not just caused by them.
- Materialism does not allow for life after death. The death of the body necessitates the death of the mind.

Gilbert Ryle: *The Concept of Mind* (1949)

- Ryle argues that the mind is not a distinct part of the body but an aspect of the way the body behaves, just as the 'team spirit' is an aspect of the way the cricket team behaves.
- There is no 'ghost in the machine' – there is no non-physical 'soul' in the matter of the body. Thinking of the mind and body as distinct involves a 'category mistake'.

Richard Dawkins: *The Selfish Gene* (1976) and *River Out of Eden* (1995)

- Dawkins argues that humans are entirely material. They are 'survival machines'.
- He rejects the idea that we need to think of a supernatural soul if we are explaining what it means to be human.
- He calls Platonic ideas of a supernatural soul 'soul one', and Aristotelian ideas of the soul as the essence of a material being 'soul two'.

Richard Dawkins talks about humans as 'survival machines'

Possible criticisms of dualist approaches to the mind–body problem

- Our experience of ourselves does not seem to support a dualist approach. We feel ourselves to be a unity, with mental and physical aspects, rather than two very separate substances (although what we feel to be the case does not necessarily make it true).
- Dualist approaches cannot explain how the mind and the body work together, for example why feeling afraid mentally makes a person's heart race physically.
- The 'problem of other minds' arises – how can we be certain that other people have minds, if they are completely separate from the physical bodies we perceive?
- The distinction between mental and physical properties is not always clear-cut.

Possible criticisms of materialist approaches to the mind–body problem

- The way we use language suggests that we feel ourselves to be more than just a physical body (although what we feel to be the case does not necessarily make it true).
- Descartes' observation that the mind and the body have different properties and so cannot be the same substance is a valid point.
- Materialism cannot explain how a chemical reaction can cause consciousness and mental events.
- Richard Swinburne and Keith Ward argue that losing belief in the soul could have a damaging effect on ethics.

Key terms

Soul: often, but not always, understood to be the non-physical essence of a person

Consciousness: awareness or perception

Substance dualism: the belief that the mind and body both exist as two distinct and separate realities

Scepticism: a questioning approach which does not take assumptions for granted

Reductive materialism: otherwise known as identity theory – the view that mental events are identical with physical occurrences in the brain

Category error or category mistake: a problem of language that arises when things are talked about as if they belong to one category when in fact they belong to another

 APPLY

Test yourself on key knowledge (AO1)

1. What did Plato think happened to the soul after death?

2. What did Plato think were the three different parts of the soul?

3. What example did Plato use to justify his belief that the soul must have lived before the body, in the world of the Forms?

4. What does Aristotle's analogy of wax stamped with a seal illustrate?

5. What did Aristotle understand the soul to be?

6. What is meant by 'the mind–body problem'?

7. What do substance dualists think are the properties of the mind?

8. Why did Descartes think that he could be certain of the existence of his own mind?

9. What is the name given to the idea that there is only one kind of material which has two distinct sets of properties, mental and physical?

10. Why do reductive materialists reject the notion of life after death?

11. In which book does Ryle write about his rejection of the idea of 'the ghost in the machine'?

12. What does Dawkins mean when he talks about 'soul one' and 'soul two'?

If you are unsure about any of the questions, look back over the key points on pages 16–19. You can check your answers on page 217.

Develop your skills in critical argument and evaluation (AO2)

For high marks in AO2, you need to think about the ideas in this chapter and develop your own perspective, so that you can produce critically evaluative arguments rather than just describing and presenting the views of others. At AS level, 50% of your marks are awarded for your skills in critical evaluation, and at A level, 60%.

Use the following questions to help you formulate your own views.

» Discuss them with friends, making sure you articulate your own view and listen to the views of others.

» Try writing your answers to these questions, to familiarise yourself with expressing your ideas in an academic style.

» Remember to give reasons for your views.

» Think about counter-arguments – what might someone say who held a different view from your own, and why do you think they are wrong?

1. **What do you think are the main differences between Plato's view of the soul, and Aristotle's view of the soul? Do you think the two views have any similarities? Which view (if either) do you find more convincing? Give reasons to support your answer.**

Here is an example of the kinds of ideas you might explore in formulating your analysis and evaluation:

You might think the main differences include things like: Plato thinks the soul is part of a person that can be separated from the physical body after death, whereas Aristotle thinks the soul and body are inseparable. Aristotle thinks the soul is the capacities of the body to do the things it does, whereas Plato thinks the soul can be held back by the physical body; in some senses, Plato sees the soul and the body as working in opposition. Plato talks about the possibilities of the soul living in the realm of the Forms whereas Aristotle grounds the soul firmly in the physical world. Plato thinks the soul has abilities, whereas Aristotle thinks the soul is the abilities. Both think that the soul is in some way the 'essence' of a person. You might find Plato's views more convincing, as they allow for the possibility of life after death and see human beings as more than merely physical creatures. Plato's ideas seem more consistent with Christian thought. Perhaps you think that our experiences of ourselves having struggles between physical desires and more spiritual concerns are better reflected by Plato's ideas about a soul being distinct from the body. On the other hand you might be more convinced by Aristotle's less supernatural understanding of the soul. You might think this is more consistent with modern scientific views and does not expect us to believe in other worlds without evidence to support these beliefs. Alternatively you might find neither idea convincing; perhaps you think that talk of 'souls' is misleading and inappropriate now that we have a better understanding of how the human mind works.

Now use your critical and evaluative skills to explore these questions on your own.

2. Do you think Descartes was right to say that we can doubt the existence of our physical bodies but not doubt the existence of our minds? How would you justify your view?

3. Some people might argue that the idea that we have immortal physical souls is much more attractive than the view that we just stop existing when we die. Discuss whether you find the idea more attractive, or not.

4. Do you think that machines could ever be developed to have minds and consciousness just like our own? If so, do you think we then ought to give such machines 'human rights'? If not, what do you think would be the aspects of human consciousness that cannot be created artificially from matter?

5. How far do you agree with Ward's claim that we need to continue to believe in the existence of the human soul in order to treat each other ethically? If you believe that a person is no more than material and does not have an immortal soul, do you therefore have less respect for that person than if you believed they had an immortal soul?

6. How might belief in the immortality of the soul affect beliefs about the sanctity of life?

7. To what extent would you agree with Ryle's claim that a mind–body distinction is no more than a 'category mistake'?

8. Some people might argue that talk of the 'soul' is metaphorical; a poetic way of describing the special qualities of human existence. Do you think this is a helpful way of understanding the soul, or does it make the subject more obscure? Give reasons for your answer.

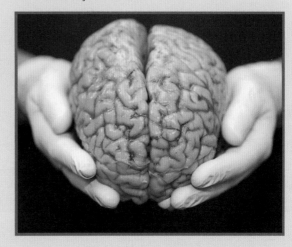

REVIEW

Practice Exam Questions

Try these practice questions. You could:

» write plans for each of them, to practise your skills in structuring an essay

» use them for practice in writing introductions and/or conclusions

» write the whole essay, perhaps against the clock.

1. How convincing is Plato's view that the soul is distinct from the body?

2. 'People are no more than complex physical matter.' Discuss.

Use page 9 to review your essay and make sure you have met the assessment objectives. See page 222 for a mark scheme.

Chapter 1.3 | Arguments based on observation

A posteriori arguments depend on experience and observation, using them to draw conclusions. They look at different possible explanations for whatever it is that we are observing or experiencing, and draw conclusions about which explanation provides the best fit.

Teleological arguments use observation of order, beauty and complexity to draw the conclusion that God exists. Teleological comes from the Greek word 'telos' which means 'tail' or 'end', because the argument uses the end results as a basis for drawing its conclusions.

Cosmological arguments use observation of the fact that the universe exists at all to draw conclusions that it must have been brought into existence by God.

Natural theology seeks to understand the existence and nature of God through observation of the world around us.

Ockham's razor is a principle which says that the best explanation is usually the one which requires the fewest extra assumptions.

Aquinas' teleological (design) argument

- Thomas Aquinas lived in the thirteenth century when Aristotle's ideas were new to the Christian world. Aquinas used Aristotelian ideas extensively in his Christian theology.

- Aquinas thought God gave us our reason so that we could learn about him.

- In his Five Ways, Aquinas gives five ways in which we can use reason to conclude God exists.

- The Fifth of the Five Ways is a short teleological argument.

- He uses the example of an arrow heading for a target. If we saw the arrow in flight we would conclude it must have been shot on purpose because arrows can't move on their own. When we see the planets moving in an orderly way, we can therefore conclude that a divine mind must have put them in motion on purpose, because planets can't move on their own.

Paley's teleological argument

- William Paley lived in the eighteenth century.

- He set out his teleological argument in his book *Natural Theology*.

- Paley used the analogy of someone finding a watch on a heath, to show that when we see things working in an orderly and purposeful manner, we know they must have been designed.

- He said we see order and purpose in the world too, in the structure of animals and plants, and can conclude they must have been designed by God.

- We can tell from the care God put into creation that God must care for us.

Paley observed that order and purpose are visible in the structure of insects, suggesting deliberate design

Aquinas' cosmological argument

- Cosmological arguments address the question of why the universe exists at all, and conclude that it must be because of God.
- The first three of Aquinas' Five Ways are variations of his cosmological argument:
  1. The First Way is the Unmoved Mover – we observe motion and change in the world. There must be a reason for it, which must be God.
  2. The Second Way is the Uncaused Causer – we observe chains of cause and effect in the world. There must be a reason for it, which must be God.
  3. The Third Way is Contingency – we observe that everything in the universe depends on something else for its existence. There must be something that doesn't depend on anything else, otherwise nothing would ever have started, and this must be God.

Leibniz and the principle of sufficient reason

- Gottfried Leibniz argued that there must be a 'sufficient reason' or explanation for everything.
- The universe requires a sufficient reason, and the only reason sufficient to explain the existence of the universe must be God.

Aquinas used the example of an archer shooting an arrow to illustrate his view that things are set in motion by an intelligent mind

The anthropic principle

This is a principle that says the universe seems expertly fine-tuned to allow for human life to exist. It seems more likely that this fine-tuning is a result of deliberate design, than that it happened by chance against enormous odds.

Hume's criticisms of teleological and cosmological arguments

- David Hume was an eighteenth-century sceptic philosopher.
- In *Dialogues Concerning Natural Religion*, Hume criticised teleological and cosmological arguments for the existence of God.
- Hume argues that the analogy between the world and a watch is weak; the world is not very obviously like a watch in its mechanisms.
- Order in the world does not necessarily mean that someone must have had the idea of the design – it is an essential part of the world's existence. It could have come about by chance.
- The universe is unique, so we cannot know how universes are usually made or whether ours is unusually orderly.
- Just because the things in the universe have causes, it does not follow that the universe as a whole must have some kind of universal cause.
- Perhaps the universe is its own cause.
- We cannot look at the effects (the world) and confidently infer the cause (God):
  - it might not be the God Christians describe
  - it might be a God who is stupid, arriving at this design only after countless mistakes or copying someone else's ideas
  - it might be a whole committee of gods, or angels or even demons.

Possible criticisms of teleological arguments

- The argument might be considered to have strengths because we can all see the world around us and appreciate elements of beauty, order and purpose. Such beauty, order and purpose on a global scale could be best explained by the existence of God.
- Darwin's theory of evolution through natural selection provides an alternative explanation for the characteristics of living things. Chance is another possibility. This might be considered a better fit than the God hypothesis.
- Not everyone sees the world as orderly and beautiful and purposive. Some see it as chaotic and full of ugliness and pointlessness.
- As an a posteriori argument, it can only lead to a probable conclusion and does not prove anything.

Possible criticisms of a posteriori arguments

- They can be appealing because they usually use evidence that we can all see for ourselves.
- We don't always see the same things when we look at the world, and our experiences are not always the same as other people's, so a posteriori arguments do not appeal to everyone.
- A posteriori arguments try to find the 'best fit' explanation, but they can never be certain.
- They cannot prove, they can only suggest strongly probable conclusions.
- Some new evidence might come along which forces a need for a new explanation.
- The need for constant review of a posteriori reasoning can be considered a strength as well as a weakness, as it discourages arrogance and encourages questioning.

Possible criticisms of cosmological arguments

- The argument might be considered to have strength because we all share the experience that the universe exists. God could be the best available explanation.
- Other theories suggest different explanations for the existence of the universe, such as the Big Bang theory, or chance. These might be considered a better fit than the God hypothesis.
- Not everyone thinks the universe requires any explanation or reason.
- As an a posteriori argument, it can only lead to a probable conclusion and does not prove anything.

Key terms

A posteriori arguments: arguments which draw conclusions based on observation through experience

A priori arguments: arguments which draw conclusions through the use of reason

Teleological: looking to the end results (telos) in order to draw a conclusion about what is right or wrong

Cosmological: to do with the universe

Natural theology: drawing conclusions about the nature and activity of God by using reason and observing the world

Principle of Sufficient Reason: the principle that everything must have a reason to explain it

Necessary existence: existence which does not depend on anything else

 APPLY

Test yourself on key knowledge (AO1)

1. What is an a posteriori argument?
2. What kind of arguments depend entirely on reasoning and logic?
3. What is 'natural theology'?
4. Why are design arguments often called 'teleological'?
5. Who used the example of an arrow heading for a target to illustrate his teleological argument?
6. What was the name of the book in which Paley set out his teleological argument?
7. What did Paley think was evidence that God must not only exist but must also care for us?
8. Which philosopher argued that there must be a 'sufficient reason' to account for the existence of the universe?

9. What did Hume think of the analogy between the universe and a watch?
10. Hume suggests that the world might not have been made by the Christian God but that there are other possible explanations. What other possibilities does he offer?
11. Which principle suggests that the best explanations demand the fewest assumptions?
12. What does the 'anthropic principle' mean?

If you are unsure about any of the questions, look back over the key points on pages 22–25. You can check your answers on page 217.

Develop your skills in critical argument and evaluation (AO2)

For high marks in AO2, you need to think about the ideas in this chapter and develop your own perspective, so that you can produce critically evaluative arguments rather than just describing and presenting the views of others. At AS level, 50% of your marks are awarded for your skills in critical evaluation, and at A level, 60%.

Use the following questions to help you formulate your own views.

» Discuss them with friends, making sure you articulate your own view and listen to the views of others.

» Try writing your answers to these questions, to familiarise yourself with expressing your ideas in an academic style.

» Remember to give reasons for your views.

» Think about counter-arguments – what might someone say who held a different view from your own, and why do you think they are wrong?

1. **Do you think that questions about the existence of God can ever be resolved by looking at the evidence available to our senses? What sort of experiences, if any, might successfully persuade you that there is a God, or that there isn't?**

Are there fewer assumptions to be made if we consider the universe was created in a natural way, such as through the Big Bang?

Here is an example of the kinds of ideas you might explore in formulating your analysis and evaluation:

You might think that any kind of belief demands evidence to support it – perhaps you agree with Hume, that 'a wise man proportions his belief to the evidence'. You might think that there is insufficient evidence to support belief in God, as God cannot be seen or heard or experienced in the way that other existent things can be experienced. You could argue that there is evidence of the non-existence of God, perhaps in the problem of evil or in the apparently random operations of the quantum world. You might, however, think that there is sufficient evidence of God in the world: perhaps the existence of the universe as a whole is evidence of God (the cosmological argument) or features of the world might strike you as evidence for God (teleological arguments). You might think that religious experience counts as evidential experience of God; or you might want to argue that religious belief depends not on sufficient evidence but on a commitment to faith.

Now use your critical and evaluative skills to explore these questions on your own.

2. Do you think that the world around us does seem orderly and beautiful and purposive? Does your experience lead you to think that there must be some explanation for this?

3. Paley thought that the more we learn about the natural world, the more clearly we can see the designing hand of God. Do you think this is true? For what reasons would you agree or disagree with Paley?

4. How far would you agree with the principle of Ockham's razor? Is it a universally good principle, or does it apply better in some contexts than others? Do scientific explanations for order in the world (such as Darwinism) or for the existence of the universe (such as the Big Bang theory) require fewer assumptions than the existence of God?

5. What do you think is the best explanation for the fact that we have a universe? Is chance the best explanation? Is God the best explanation? Can science provide the best explanation? Give reasons why your choice of explanation is, in your view, the most likely hypothesis.

6. How convincing do you find Hume's criticisms of teleological and cosmological arguments? Do you think all of his criticisms are equally strong, or equally weak, or are there some criticisms that are stronger than others? Give reasons for your answer.

7. The anthropic principle suggests that it is extraordinary that the universe should be fine-tuned such that it is capable of sustaining human life. It suggests that the best explanation for this is God. Do you think there is strength in this argument, or does it fail to persuade you? Give reasons for your views.

REVIEW

Practice Exam Questions

Try these practice questions. You could:

» write plans for each of them, to practise your skills in structuring an essay

» use them for practice in writing introductions and/or conclusions

» write the whole essay, perhaps against the clock.

1. 'Hume presents insurmountable challenges to a posteriori arguments for the existence of God.' Discuss.

2. Discuss critically the view that the existence of God is the best explanation for the existence of the universe.

> Use page 9 to review your essay and make sure you have met the assessment objectives. See pages 222–223 for a mark scheme.

Chapter 1.4 : Arguments based on reason

Ontology is the branch of philosophy which explores the nature of existence.

The ontological argument claims that by thinking about the definition of God and its implications, we can work out through reason that God must exist.

It is an **a priori** argument – it depends on logic rather than sense experience.

A priori and a posteriori arguments

- Some people argue that a priori arguments are more persuasive because they rely on deductive logic. If the premises are true then they lead to certainty.

- A posteriori arguments can only lead to strong probability because they rely on sense experience, and new evidence or a better explanation could be found. However, they might be more persuasive than a priori arguments because people can see the evidence for themselves.

Analytic and synthetic propositions

- An analytic proposition is true by definition and needs no experience or evidence to support it. 'Bachelors are unmarried men' is an analytic proposition.

- A synthetic proposition needs evidence and experience to support it. 'There is a red car outside my house' is a synthetic proposition.

Anselm believed that faith was more important than argument

Anselm's ontological argument

- Anselm lived in the eleventh century and was a Benedictine monk who became Archbishop of Canterbury.
- His argument was written for 'faith seeking understanding', not as an attempt to convert unbelievers.
- He made reference to the 'fool' who does not understand that God must exist: 'The fool says in his heart, "There is no God."' (Psalm 53:1, New International Version).
- His ontological argument appears in his writings called *Proslogion*.

Anselm's argument takes two closely related forms:

First form

- God is 'that than which nothing greater can be thought'.
- A real, existent being is greater than an imaginary being.
- Therefore God must exist because the concept of God is not as great as the real existent God.

Second form

- God is 'that than which nothing greater can be thought'.
- Contingent beings, which are beings that depend on other things for their existence, are inferior to necessary beings, which depend on nothing and exist eternally.
- God is inferior to nothing else, and so must have necessary existence.
- Therefore God exists necessarily.

Descartes' ontological argument

- Descartes was a seventeenth-century mathematician and philosopher.
- He gave his ontological argument in his book *Meditations*.
- He argued that people are born with some ideas already imprinted in their minds, including the idea of God.
- We know God to have all the perfections as his attributes. God is the supremely perfect being.
- Existence is a perfection, therefore God must exist as he cannot lack any of the perfections.
- Existence cannot be separated from God, just as three angles adding up to 180° cannot be separated from a triangle, or a mountain cannot be separated from its valley.

Key terms

Ontological: to do with the nature of existence

A priori arguments: arguments which draw conclusions through the use of reason

Contingent: depending on other things

Necessary existence: existence which does not depend on anything else

Predicate: a term which describes a distinctive characteristic of something

Criticisms of ontological arguments: Gaunilo

Gaunilo was a French monk and eleventh-century contemporary of Anselm.

- Gaunilo said that the flaws in Anselm's argument are obvious if we replace 'God' in the argument with 'lost island'.

- We can imagine the most excellent island – such an island would not be the most excellent unless it existed in reality – therefore our imagined island must exist.

- By using the island instead of God we can see the flaws of the argument. Just defining something as superlative doesn't make it exist.

- Anselm replied to Gaunilo, saying that the ontological argument works only for God, because God exists necessarily whereas an island exists contingently.

Criticisms of ontological arguments: Aquinas

Aquinas was an Italian monk from the thirteenth century.

- Aquinas said that God cannot be demonstrated through a priori argument, because it is not self-evident that God is 'that than which nothing greater can be thought'.

- People have different ideas about what God is, and they are able to conceive of God not existing. The human mind cannot comprehend God.

- 'Non-existent God' can't be a contradiction in terms because people manage to imagine a world with no God.

- Anselm's argument, thought Aquinas, only shows that many people have a concept of God, but it does not show that there is an existent reality which matches that concept.

Gaunilo argued that if we replace 'God' with 'island' in Anselm's argument, we can see how the argument falls down

Criticisms of ontological arguments: Kant

Immanuel Kant was an eighteenth-century German philosopher.

- Kant addressed his criticisms of the ontological argument mainly to Descartes.
- Kant criticised the ontological argument in his book *Critique of Pure Reason*.
- He argued that existence is not a predicate.
- A predicate is a descriptor or characteristic.
- Existence is not a characteristic of something. If we know something exists, we do not know anything about its characteristics. We know, instead, that there is an actual example of this thing.

Criticisms of ontological arguments: Russell

Bertrand Russell was a twentieth-century British philosopher.

- Russell criticised the logic of the ontological argument by using the example that 'the present king of France is bald'.
- Statements about the present king of France can be neither true nor false because there is no present king of France.
- Likewise making statements about the attributes of God are only meaningful if there is an actual God; the statements themselves do nothing to answer this question.

 APPLY

Test yourself on key knowledge (AO1)

1. Is the ontological argument an a priori argument or an a posteriori argument?
2. What does Anselm think is a definition of God that we would all accept?
3. What does the fool say in his heart?
4. What does 'contingent existence' mean?
5. How do the two forms of Anselm's argument differ?
6. What is an 'analytic proposition'?
7. What was Gaunilo's objection to the ontological argument?
8. How did Descartes use the analogy of a triangle in his ontological argument?
9. What is a 'predicate'?
10. In which century did Kant live?
11. What is Aquinas' main objection to the ontological argument?
12. Who used the statement 'the present king of France is bald' to illustrate his objection to the ontological argument?

If you are unsure about any of the questions, look back over the key points on pages 28–31. You can check your answers on page 217.

Develop your skills in critical argument and evaluation (AO2)

For high marks in AO2, you need to think about the ideas in this chapter and develop your own perspective, so that you can produce critically evaluative arguments rather than just describing and presenting the views of others. At AS level, 50% of your marks are awarded for your skills in critical evaluation, and at A level, 60%.

Use the following questions to help you formulate your own views.

» Discuss them with friends, making sure you articulate your own view and listen to the views of others.

» Try writing your answers to these questions, to familiarise yourself with expressing your ideas in an academic style.

» Remember to give reasons for your views.

» Think about counter-arguments – what might someone say who held a different view from your own, and why do you think they are wrong?

Gaunilo argued that it is impossible to bring something into existence simply by describing it

1. **Would you agree with Anselm's definition of God? Is God 'that than which nothing greater can be thought'? Might there be other, different ways of defining God? Do you think everyone shares the same idea of what God is, whether or not they believe in God?**

Here is an example of the kinds of ideas you might explore in formulating your analysis and evaluation:

You might want to agree with Anselm's definition of God. If you are doing A level, you could refer to the work you have done on religious language here, showing how Anselm uses positive terms while avoiding making God seem too small. You could argue that Anselm's definition is broad enough to encompass the attributes of God. Alternatively, you might disagree with Anselm; you might think that God cannot be defined, for example, or you might think the whole concept of God is meaningless, or you might think that our idea of God needs to be limited to take account of God's self-limiting of his omnipotence (if that is a view you hold). You might agree that everyone shares the same idea of God whether they believe in God or not, or you might disagree; if you are doing A level, you could use ideas about God and gender, or you could refer to pluralist ideas about the nature of 'the Real'.

Now use your critical and evaluative skills to explore these questions on your own.

2. Anselm says that his argument is for 'faith seeking understanding' rather than an attempt to convert unbelievers. Do you think he is successful in helping people of faith to understand more about the nature of God and the way in which God exists? Do you think his argument might convert unbelievers? Give reasons for your answer.

3. Gaunilo suggests replacing the idea of God with the idea of an excellent island, to show the flaws in Anselm's ontological argument. How convincing do you find his criticism? Anselm replies that the ontological argument only works when applied to God. Do you think he has successfully overcome the criticism Gaunilo made?

4. Aquinas disagrees with Anselm and says that we do not all share the same idea of what God is, so we cannot use a shared understanding as a starting point for argument. Is Aquinas right?

5. Kant argues that existence is not a predicate, so we cannot use it to describe the nature of God and demonstrate, a priori, that God exists. Is Kant right?

6. Some people (such as Norman Malcolm) think that, although Kant might in general be right in saying that existence is not a predicate (characteristic), perhaps necessary existence *is* a predicate. This is because only God has necessary existence, so if you are saying that a being has necessary existence then we know which one you mean – necessary existence works like a characteristic. So Kant's criticism of the ontological argument would fail. Do you agree with this criticism of Kant? Why, or why not?

7. Do you think that a posteriori arguments (which rely on experience) are more convincing than a priori arguments (which rely on logic)? Or are a priori arguments more convincing? Give reasons for your answer.

 **REVIEW**

Practice Exam Questions

Try these practice questions. You could:

» write plans for each of them, to practise your skills in structuring an essay

» use them for practice in writing introductions and/or conclusions

» write the whole essay, perhaps against the clock.

1. 'The ontological argument fails because it rests on a logical fallacy.' Discuss.

2. How persuasive are ontological arguments for the existence of God?

> Use page 9 to review your essay and make sure you have met the assessment objectives. See pages 223–224 for a mark scheme.

Chapter 1.5 : Religious experience

What is distinctive about religious experience?

Religious experience can be difficult to define, and difficult for people to put into words to describe it if they have had such an experience.

It is often understood to be some kind of encounter between people and the divine.

It is often solitary but can be corporate (shared by a group of people).

Forms of religious experience

Mystical experience

- The term 'mysticism' refers to a sense of connection with God at a deep personal level, where God is beyond the boundaries of reason and knowledge.

- It is a relatively modern term, used to convey the idea that all religions share in common a sense of the divine, expressed in different ways.

- Mystical experiences are difficult to describe in ordinary, everyday language.

- F.C. Happold's book *Mysticism: A Study and an Anthology* looks at this kind of religious experience in different religious traditions, including Christianity.

- Mysticism conveys the idea that this physical world is not all that there is, and that God is the foundation of everything.

- God is known not through reason but by intuition, through the soul rather than the rational mind.

- Mystical experiences often arise through prayer and contemplation.

- They can involve seeing visions or hearing voices.

- The recipient of the numinous experience is filled with a sense of awe and wonder.

- Well-known mystical experiences include the visions of Julian of Norwich, Teresa of Avila, Francis of Assisi and Bernadette Soubirous.

- Mystical experiences are described in the Bible, for example the vision of Isaiah in the Temple (Isaiah 6) and the voices heard by the boy Samuel (1 Samuel 3).

Key terms

Mystical experience: experiences of God or of the supernatural which go beyond everyday sense experience

Numinous experience: an indescribable experience which invokes feelings of awe, worship and fascination

Conversion experience: an experience which produces a radical change in someone's belief system

Corporate religious experience: a religious experience which happens to a group of people 'as a body'

Conversion experience

- Conversion experiences involve abandoning an old way of life and adopting a new one, based on an inner experience.
- Sometimes conversion experiences are dramatic and sometimes they are gradual.
- H.D. Lewis' book *Our Experience of God* describes a pattern found in many conversion experiences:

> The individual is dissatisfied with their current 'system of ideas'.

↓

> The person searches for answers e.g. by reading scripture or trying out going to church.

↓

> There is a point of crisis, which can be emotional, with a sense of the presence of God. The person might see a vision, hear a voice or have a strong sense of forgiveness.

↓

> There is a following sense of peace and joy, and a keenness to tell others about the experience.

↓

> In the long-term, there is a change of direction for the person.

- Conversion experiences have been the focus of psychological studies.
- William James says that in conversion experiences, something which was once on the edge of a person's consciousness becomes at the centre, and religious aims become a habitual focus of energy.
- Well-known conversion experiences include the conversion of St Paul on the road to Damascus (Acts 9).

Corporate religious experience

- A corporate religious experience is when several different people all have the same religious experience at the same time.
- Some people think these have more evidential force as there are more witnesses to the experience.
- Others think that people could be carried along by others' emotion and that they do not have more evidential force.
- Well-known corporate religious experiences include the story of Pentecost (Acts 2) and modern experiences of the Toronto Blessing.

Near-death experience

- Near-death experiences are sometimes reported by people whose hearts have stopped beating or who have been comatose.
- Similarities in descriptions include a sense of being 'out-of-body', feeling a loving presence or a sense of great peace, and feeling as if travelling through a tunnel towards a bright light.
- Some people see these as evidence of life after death, whilst others are more sceptical and think they are more likely to have a natural, scientific explanation.

Key thinkers in the study of religious experience

William James

- William James wrote a book called *The Varieties of Religious Experience* (1902).
- He aimed to take an objective, scientific approach to religious experience and explore it through collecting people's own accounts of their experiences.
- He thought that religious experience could be tested for validity by its long-lasting effects, just as a medicine can be tested by seeing whether it makes the patient better.
- James' approach to understanding truth is pragmatist – he thought that the truth of something could be established by its practical results.
- He identified four main qualities of religious experience:

1. **Ineffability** – difficult to express in normal everyday words.

3. **Transience** – the experiences do not last long although the effects may last a lifetime.

2. **Noetic quality** – recipients feel they have learned something they didn't know before.

4. **Passivity** – the person feels the experience is happening to them rather than that they are doing it.

- James noticed that religious experiences feel very convincing to those who have them.
- He concluded that religious experience does not prove anything but that it should be taken seriously.

Rudolf Otto

- Rudolf Otto wrote a book called *The Idea of the Holy* (1917).
- He aimed to explore the nature of the divine as encountered through religious experience.
- He thought it was central to religion that people should experience God or the divine.
- He thought that the divine could be described as 'mysterium tremendum et fascinans' – an awe-inspiring, fascinating mystery.
- Otto thought the divine has three main characteristics in religious experience:

1. A quality of mystery making the individual realise that God can never be fully understood.

2. A quality of ultimate importance.

3. A quality that is both attractive and dangerous.

Swinburne's principles of credulity and testimony

- Swinburne wrote a book called *Is There a God?* (1979). He argued that people should take religious experience just as seriously as other kinds of experience.

- In his principle of credulity, he said that we should be prepared to trust our own experiences unless we have good reason not to. If it seems to us that we are experiencing God, then we should be prepared to believe that we really are experiencing God.

- In his principle of testimony, he said that if people tell us they have had an experience, we should be prepared to believe them unless we have good grounds not to.

Non-religious understandings of religious experience

Psychological interpretations of religious experience

- Ludwig Feuerbach was very influential in psychological interpretations of religious experience. He argued that God was an invention of the human mind.

- Feuerbach thought that people transfer all their highest ideals and hopes on to this made-up God and imagine him to be all the things they wish they were themselves.

- Sigmund Freud, a founder of modern psychology, used similar ideas in his interpretation of religion.

- He thought the mind was made up of the ego, the id and the superego.

- He thought the subconscious layers of the mind lead people into believing that there is a God, but this is an 'infantile neurosis'. They cannot cope with being adults in the world so they make up an imaginary parent figure.

- Religious experience happens when this sub-conscious invention takes over the imagination. For Freud, people who have religious experiences need psychological treatment.

Physiological interpretations of religious experience

- Neurophysiology is the study of the brain and nervous system.

- Some neurophysiological studies of religious experience suggest that such experiences could have a natural cause rather than a supernatural one.

- 'Persinger's helmet' is a device invented by Michael Persinger in the 1980s which induces feelings similar to those of a religious experience. It could suggest that religious experience is caused by magnetic fields rather than by God.

- Studies of near-death experiences sometimes show that these sensations can be created artificially. The findings could suggest that near-death experiences are caused by endorphins or other emotion-altering hormones in the body rather than by God.

 **APPLY**

Test yourself on key knowledge (AO1)

1. Who described the divine as 'mysterium tremendum et fascinans'?
2. Give an example of a well-known conversion experience.
3. What is meant by a 'numinous experience'?
4. What is Swinburne's 'principle of credulity'?
5. What did James mean by 'noetic quality'?
6. Apart from noetic quality, what did James think were the other three key features of religious experience?
7. What did James think could be a reliable test of the validity of religious experience?
8. James was a pragmatist. What does this mean?
9. What is meant by 'corporate religious experience'?
10. What did Freud think of God?
11. What was Persinger trying to discover with his experiments involving a helmet?
12. How might a neurophysiologist understand near-death experience?

> If you are unsure about any of the questions, look back over the key points on pages 34–37. You can check your answers on page 217.

Develop your skills in critical argument and evaluation (AO2)

For high marks in AO2, you need to think about the ideas in this chapter and develop your own perspective, so that you can produce critically evaluative arguments rather than just describing and presenting the views of others. At AS level, 50% of your marks are awarded for your skills in critical evaluation, and at A level, 60%.

Use the following questions to help you formulate your own views.

» Discuss them with friends, making sure you articulate your own view and listen to the views of others.

» Try writing your answers to these questions, to familiarise yourself with expressing your ideas in an academic style.

» Remember to give reasons for your views.
» Think about counter-arguments – what might someone say who held a different view from your own, and why do you think they are wrong?

1. **James thought that religious experience could be tested by its long-lasting effects – if the experience has a positive influence on the individual and makes them a better person, then the experience itself is valid. Do you agree with James about this? Are there any other ways of testing religious experience that might be better? Is it necessary for religious experience to be capable of being tested?**

Here is an example of the kinds of ideas you might explore in formulating your analysis and evaluation:

You might think that James' test is a good one, because it is practical and easy for other people to observe, as long as they know the individual both before and after the religious experience and can readily see whether they have become more kind or more charitable in their giving. However, you might disagree with him and think that there is not uniform agreement about what a positive effect looks like. Some people might argue that becoming more religious can be negative, making the individual more judgemental perhaps, or less inclined to look at things scientifically.

It could also be argued that the change in a person does not show anything more than that they believe the experience came from God, but they could still be mistaken. Children might behave better if they believe in Father Christmas, but this does not give evidence that Father Christmas is real. You might think that religious experience is better tested in other ways, such as by comparing the details of the experience with details given in the Bible or by Christian saints to see if they match; but you might think that religious experiences do not have to match in order to be valid or you might think that even if they do, it doesn't prove that they come from God. Perhaps you would agree with Schleiermacher, who argues that religious experience does not need to be capable of being tested but is 'self-authenticating' — it speaks for itself. However, you might disagree and argue that if the experience cannot be tested in any way, then it is meaningless or at least need not be taken seriously.

Now use your critical and evaluative skills to explore these questions on your own.

2. Are there some features that help us to distinguish between a religious experience and a disturbance of mental health, in your view? Or do you think religious experiences are always examples of disturbances of mental health? If you had a religious experience yourself, would you be inclined to think it must have come from God, or would you interpret it differently? If you were trying to discover whether a religious experience genuinely came from God, what kind of features would you look for? Give reasons for your answers.

3. James characterises religious experience in terms of its qualities of ineffability, its noetic quality, its transience, and the sense of passivity experienced. Do you agree with his choice of key features, or do you think religious experience has different features instead, or as well? In what ways might classifying the features of religious experience be useful?

4. Do you think that a natural (rather than supernatural) explanation for religious experience is always going to be more persuasive that the explanation that this was a genuine encounter with God? Are some natural explanations more persuasive than others? Do you think that a religious experience could have a natural explanation and yet still come from God? Give reasons for your answer.

5. Swinburne argues that we should take religious experience as seriously as we take other kinds of experience. Is he right? Should we believe someone who says they have heard the voice of God, in just the same way as we might believe them if they said they heard someone knock at the door? Give reasons for your answer.

6. One of the problems of religious experience is that it is so personal and private that it can't usually be tested by others. We only have someone's word that they really did experience the sensations they describe. Do you think the private nature of most religious experience makes it meaningless? Can it be considered as evidence for the existence of God if several people report similar private experiences? If people have a corporate religious experience, does this carry more evidential force than a private experience? Give reasons for your answer.

REVIEW

Practice Exam Questions

Try these practice questions. You could:

» write plans for each of them, to practise your skills in structuring an essay

» use them for practice in writing introductions and/or conclusions

» write the whole essay, perhaps against the clock.

1. 'Conversion experiences present powerful evidence for the existence of God.' Discuss.

2. How convincing are William James' conclusions about religious experience?

Use page 9 to review your essay and make sure you have met the assessment objectives. See page 224 for a mark scheme.

Chapter 1.6 | The problem of evil

Different presentations of the problem of evil

The problem of evil is both a **logical problem** and an **evidential problem**. Attempts to defend God despite the existence of evil and suffering in the world are called **theodicies**.

The problem of evil as a logical problem

- The inconsistent triad argument says that these three beliefs cannot all be held at the same time without contradiction:

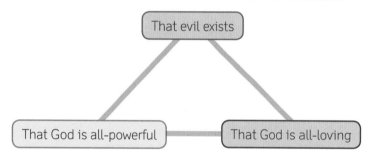

- The logical formulation of the problem of evil assumes that an all-loving and all-powerful God would not want any evil and suffering in the world.
- It therefore concludes that if there is evil and suffering in the world, a God with these attributes cannot exist.
- It is an a priori argument – if the premises are true then the conclusion follows.
- Solutions to this logical problem might include suggesting that God is not totally powerful, that God is not totally loving, or that evil is an illusion or is actually good for us in spite of appearing to be bad.

The problem of evil as an evidential problem

- As an evidential problem, this involves a posteriori reasoning.
- The argument says that there is too much evil and suffering in the world for the belief 'there is an all-good, all-powerful God' to be the best explanation of the evidence.
- A better explanation might be that good and evil simply happen by chance, without the agency of God.
- John Stuart Mill argued that the extent of evil and suffering in the world does not suggest a good God, but instead suggests that if there is a creator behind the world, it must be a malevolent creator.

Natural and moral evil

- Natural evil is said to be that which causes suffering but does not come from any human wrongdoing, for example many diseases and extreme weather conditions such as hurricanes and floods.
- Moral evil is said to be that which causes suffering as the result of human wrongdoing, for example murder, war and poverty.

Responses to the problem of evil: theodicies

The theodicy of Augustine (fourth century)

- Augustine's theodicy was influenced by his earlier Manichee beliefs that the world was divided between forces of good and forces of evil.

- Augustine argued that evil is a 'privatio boni', or absence of good, and not a force in its own right.

- He thought variety is part of the rich goodness of God's creation. If things are varied then naturally some things will have more abilities and strengths than others.

- Augustine believed that God created angels (perfect spiritual beings), who were varied in their characters.

- Some angels received less grace than others and so were less able to worship God without falling into sin.

- Some angels fell away from God and became sinful because they misused their free will.

- Adam and Eve, the first people, were tempted away from God by a fallen angel. They also misused their free will by choosing to disobey God and commit sin.

- This sin was so catastrophic that it corrupted the natural world as well as the human soul. Natural and moral evil came into the world.

In Augustine's theodicy, the sin of Adam and Eve brought natural and moral evil into the world

Possible criticisms of Augustinian theodicy

- The idea of evil as just an absence of good does not seem an adequate explanation of terrible crimes, genocides and natural disasters.

- Augustine fails to explain adequately why the angels and then humanity fell from grace if they were created perfect – surely there would have been no temptation, and they would not have given in to it.

- Augustine's theodicy calls into question the omniscience and wisdom of God, if God did not anticipate the misuse of free will.

- It calls into question the omnipotence of God, if God could not simply undo the damage that had been done.

- Augustine's theodicy depends on a literal belief in angels and a belief that the Fall was an historical event, which can be difficult beliefs for people in the twenty-first century.

- Augustine could be admired for presenting a response to the problem of evil which maintains the idea that God is all-good and all-powerful.

- Augustine makes use of biblical text as an authority to support his view.

- Augustine makes humanity face up to its role in causing evil and suffering in the world.

The theodicy of Irenaeus (second century)

- Irenaeus was a very early Christian.
- He accepted that evil and suffering exist and that God appears to allow them to continue.
- He argued that God allows evil and suffering so that people can develop into freely chosen, mature relationships with God.
- He said there has to be evil in the world for us to appreciate good.
- There have to be fewer good things in the world in order for virtues such as kindness, bravery and generosity to exist at all.
- We are made in God's image but we have to grow into God's likeness.
- Free will is an important part of being made in the image of God.
- We could not have a free relationship with God unless we have genuine options to choose otherwise. Evil has to be a real option for us.
- We cannot grow totally into the likeness of God in this world, and there is a life after death in which we can complete our spiritual development.

John Hick's soul-making theodicy (twentieth and twenty-first centuries)

- Hick took an Irenaean approach to the problem of evil.
- He described the world as a 'vale of soul-making', using words from the poet John Keats.
- He explores his theodicy in his book *Evil and the God of Love* (1966).
- Hick saw the world as a place where our characters and souls are shaped.
- Evil and suffering are not an unfortunate accident but a part of God's loving plan to help us grow into a free relationship with him.
- God deliberately keeps himself partly hidden from us so that there is 'epistemic distance' – we can make free choices if God does not force himself on us in an immediate way.
- Through tackling challenges and hardships we can learn to turn to God through free choice.
- Hick thought that after death, we continue in our spiritual journeys towards a free choice for God, and this option is open to people of any belief.

For Irenaeus and Hick, humans can make a free choice to turn from evil towards good, and therefore grow into a free relationship with God

Possible criticisms of Irenaean theodicies, including Hick

- The idea that evil exists in the world for our own good can seem self-contradictory – if evil (including moral evil) is really good for us then there is confusion between good and evil, making concepts such as sin and salvation difficult to comprehend.

- The idea that God put evil in the world in order to help us develop and grow can become unacceptable when the suffering is great, for example when there is childhood cancer or an act of terrorism or genocide.

- The idea that God's love is difficult for us to comprehend can present problems if we are trying to be more Godlike and do not understand what that means.

- The argument that God has to allow evil in order for us to have free will suggests limitations on God's omnipotence.

- Tackling challenges and hardships makes some people lose faith rather than gain it. An omniscient God should know this in advance of making such people suffer.

- This kind of theodicy does not give an adequate explanation of why animals, very small babies or people with severe learning difficulties suffer.

- These theodicies could be comforting to those who suffer because they suggest that there is a plan and it will turn out well in the end.

- We can relate to the idea that facing challenges helps us to develop.

Key terms

Theodicy: an attempt to justify God in the face of evil in the world

Natural evil: evil and suffering caused by non-human agencies

Moral evil: the evil done and the suffering caused by deliberate misuse of human free will

Privatio boni: a phrase used by Augustine to mean an absence of goodness

Omnipotent: all-powerful

Omnibenevolent: all-good and all-loving

Epistemic distance: a distance in knowledge and understanding

 APPLY

Test yourself on key knowledge (AO1)

1. Which three beliefs does the inconsistent triad argument say are incompatible with each other?

2. What is meant by 'natural evil'?

3. Who argued that we are made in God's image but we have to grow into God's likeness?

4. In which century did Augustine live?

5. What did Augustine mean when he talked about a 'privatio boni'?

6. What was Augustine's explanation for why some angels received less grace than others?

7. How does Augustine account for natural evil in the world?

8. What did Irenaeus think was the reason why there is evil in the world?

9. What does the term 'epistemic distance' mean?

10. Which poet described the world as a 'vale of soul-making'?

11. What reason did Hick give for thinking that there must be evil in the world if we are going to have free will?

12. What did Hick think happens to us after death?

> If you are unsure about any of the questions, look back over the key points on pages 40–43. You can check your answers on page 217.

Develop your skills in critical argument and evaluation (AO2)

For high marks in AO2, you need to think about the ideas in this chapter and develop your own perspective, so that you can produce critically evaluative arguments rather than just describing and presenting the views of others. At AS level, 50% of your marks are awarded for your skills in critical evaluation, and at A level, 60%.

Use the following questions to help you formulate your own views.

» Discuss them with friends, making sure you articulate your own view and listen to the views of others.

» Try writing your answers to these questions, to familiarise yourself with expressing your ideas in an academic style.

» Remember to give reasons for your views.

» Think about counter-arguments – what might someone say who held a different view from your own, and why do you think they are wrong?

1. **Do you think that the logical problem of evil presents serious challenges to religious belief? Is it really impossible that God could be all-powerful and all-loving even though there is evil in the world? Is the assumption that an omnipotent, omnibenevolent God would want no evil in the world a reasonable one to make?**

Here is an example of the kinds of ideas you might explore in formulating your analysis and evaluation:

You might think that the inconsistent triad does present a serious problem; you might argue that it is impossible for a God of power and love to want evil in the world, just as a loving parent would not want their child to encounter evil if they could stop it. You might, however, argue that we cannot expect to know what God might want, as our minds and our understanding are too limited for us to be able to make such judgements. You might want to argue that God could have motives that we can't understand. You could argue that it is wrong for people to question God's reasons. You might argue that perhaps God does not have the characteristics ascribed to him by Christians but could still exist in a different way, or you might want to argue that the inconsistent triad clearly demonstrates the non-existence of God.

Now use your critical and evaluative skills to explore these questions on your own.

2. On balance, do you think that the world is mainly good, or mainly bad? Do you think there is sufficient evidence of evil to justify the view that the world must have been created by a malevolent God? If this is not a perfect world, what do you think would be the qualities of a perfect world instead – what kind of a world would you expect an omnipotent, omnibenevolent God to create?

3. Some people, for example John Hick, argue that God has to make the world ambiguous, otherwise God would be too immediately obvious and we would have no free choice about whether or not to believe in him. Do you agree with this line of argument? What sorts of counter-arguments might be put forward in criticism of it?

4. Is there a clear distinction between natural and moral evil, in your view? Are there examples of evil and suffering that could be both natural and moral, or neither? Which do you think presents the more serious challenge to religious belief, if either, and why do you think it is more serious?

5. Many religious believers argue that we need to have evil and suffering in the world in order for free will to be possible. Do you agree? Do you think that evil and suffering is a price worth paying for free will? If God is omnipotent, could he not have created a world in which people had free will but no suffering? If God had to create evil in order for there to be free will, should he have decided against making a world at all?

6. How convincing do you find Augustine's theodicy? If it is only partially convincing, which parts are more persuasive than others? Could modern people, who might not believe literally in angels, still find Augustine's ideas helpful in understanding the problem of evil? Do you think Augustine is successful in demonstrating that God is not to blame for the existence of evil in the world?

7. Is Irenaeus' theodicy plausible? Do you agree that we need to face challenges and suffering if we are to become mature human beings? Are people who have encountered great suffering in their lives usually more mature than those who have not? How do you think Irenaeus might have answered the question of why people do not all suffer an equal amount?

Some people argue that evil and suffering allow the development of virtues such as compassion

8. What do you think are the main similarities and differences between the theodicies of Augustine and Irenaeus? Do they both present a plausible understanding of the role of free will in the problem of evil, or is one more plausible than the other? Do you think either of these theodicies, or both or neither, would be of comfort to someone who has endured great suffering?

REVIEW

Practice Exam Questions

Try these practice questions. You could:

» write plans for each of them, to practise your skills in structuring an essay

» use them for practice in writing introductions and/or conclusions

» write the whole essay, perhaps against the clock.

1. How convincing is the claim that it is necessary for there to be evil in the world if we are to have genuine free will?

2. 'Irenaeus' theodicy gives a more satisfactory response to the problem of evil than Augustine's theodicy.' Discuss.

Use page 9 to review your essay and make sure you have met the assessment objectives. See page 225 for a mark scheme.

RECAP

Christians traditionally believe that God is omnipotent, omniscient, omnibenevolent, and eternal or everlasting.

Omnipotence

- Omnipotence, or all-powerfulness, is a classical attribute of God.
- The Bible attributes omnipotence to God, for example in the creation stories in Genesis, at the end of the book of Job and in miracle stories.
- There are discussions about whether omnipotence means God can do absolutely anything (including the logically impossible), or whether this has other meanings.

Key terms

Omniscient: all-knowing

Omnibenevolent: all-good and all-loving

Omnipotent: all-powerful

Eternal: timeless, atemporal, being outside the constraints of time

Everlasting: sempiternal, lasting forever on the same timeline as humanity

Descartes' view of omnipotence

- Descartes argued that God must be omnipotent in the sense of being able to do even the logically impossible, because God has all the perfections so therefore God has no limitations at all. This means that God can create a stone too heavy for himself to lift.

- Most scholars disagree with Descartes. Things that are logically impossible, such as square circles and stones too heavy for God to lift, are not really 'things' at all, because they are impossible. God can do anything, but not the logically impossible.

- They also disagree because a God who could do anything at all would be able to do things that go against his loving nature, such as acts of cruelty.

- Descartes' view of a totally powerful God who can do the logically impossible makes it difficult to find an acceptable theodicy.

A stone too heavy for God to lift is a logical impossibility. Most scholars believe omnipotence means God can do everything possible; Descartes, however, thought omnipotence meant God could have no limitations

Aquinas' view of omnipotence

- Aquinas argued that God's omnipotence means God can do everything that is within his nature and does not imply a contradiction.
- So God cannot be cruel or fail or be unwise.
- Some people might argue that if there are things God cannot do and he is limited by his own nature, then he cannot be omnipotent.

Swinburne's view of omnipotence

- Swinburne argued that God can do everything, but logical impossibilities are not things.
- Square circles are not things, and neither are stones too heavy for God to lift or knots that God cannot untie. They could never exist.
- God can do everything possible.

Vardy's view of omnipotence

- Peter Vardy argues that God deliberately limits his own power.
- God created the world in such a way that his own power would have to be limited as a result.
- This does not reduce or undermine God because God chose to do this in order to create a world suitable for free and rational human beings.
- The letter to the Philippians in the Bible suggests the same idea. When God came to the world as Jesus Christ, he deliberately limited his own power in order to be accessible to humanity.
- The Christian doctrine that God deliberately empties himself of his own power is called kenosis.

Other ideas about omnipotence

- There are discussions about whether omnipotence is compatible with other attributes traditionally ascribed to God.
- There are also discussions about whether omnipotence makes sense as a concept. Perhaps an all-powerful being could not possibly exist.
- Perhaps omnipotence is a problem of religious language where we do not have the words to frame an adequate concept of the power of God.
- Whitehead and Hartshorne argue that a totally omnipotent God would not be as impressive as a God who could meet resistance.

Omniscience

- Omniscience, or all-knowingness, is a classical attribute of God. It includes ideas such as being unfailingly wise as well as knowing everything.
- Ideas about the omniscience of God raise issues about God's relationship with time and with human free will.
- If God knows with absolute certainty and is never mistaken, then God's knowledge of people's future actions could be seen to 'fix' those actions and remove freedom of choice. People can't do anything except the action God already knows they will do, so perhaps their free will is compromised.
- Friedrich Schleiermacher argued that God can know us as close friends know us, so he can know what we will do without forcing our choices. But his critics argue that God's knowledge is not like the knowledge friends have because God never guesses or makes mistakes.

The relationship between God and time

- Many classical Christian thinkers, such as Augustine, Anselm and Aquinas, argue that God is eternal in a timeless way – God created time and is not bound by it but exists in the past, present and future.

- Others, such as Swinburne, argue that God is everlasting in a way that moves along the same timeline as we do. This gives us genuine free will and allows us to have a relationship with God who responds to our behaviour and prayers. The past is past for God as well as for us, and the future has not yet happened for God as well as for us.

- Boethius questioned whether an omniscient God could justifiably reward and punish. He concluded that God can see time 'as from a lofty peak' and can observe us making free choices in our lives whilst being outside time himself. We live inside time, on a timeline with a past, a present and a future, but God is timeless and sees all things in a simultaneity (all at once).

Boethius suggested the past, present and future do not exist separately for God

- Anselm took a four-dimensionalist approach to God's relationship with time. The past, present and future all 'exist'. God can be in all times at once, and all times are 'in God', because God created them. We are restricted to being in one place at one time, and we have genuine free will, but God has no restrictions and can be in all places and at all times.

Possible criticisms of the view that God is eternal

- If God is timeless then he does not change so he does not respond to people's behaviour, for example with anger or love.

- God knows everything for all time so our freedom is restricted, for example God knows whether we will go to heaven before we are even born.

- God cannot interact with the universe in a meaningful way at a particular time.

- God is not omniscient because, as he is eternal and outside time, he does not know what day it is.

Possible criticisms of the view that God is everlasting

- It makes God seem less impressive because God is restricted by time and has to wait for things to happen.

- It puts limits on God's omniscience as he cannot know the future with certainty.

- It raises questions of what God was doing before he created the universe.

Omnibenevolence

- The Bible is clear that the nature of God is love. This is a consistent theme throughout the Old and New Testaments. God is described as 'good' and 'perfect' in the Bible.
- When God creates the universe in Genesis, everything is 'very good' (Genesis 1:31, New International Version), suggesting God only does good.
- Unlike Plato's Form of Good, the God of the Bible is interested in moral behaviour.
- When God chooses Israel as his people, he sets them a standard to follow, for example the Ten Commandments.
- When God is angry with people, it is not because of their failure to perform religious rituals, but because of the way they treat each other, especially the poor and the weak.
- For Christians, God's goodness is exemplified in the person of Jesus and his sacrifice on the cross.
- Love is seen as an attribute of God and also as the creation of God. God is found wherever love is found.

Possible criticisms of the idea of God as omnibenevolent

- Some argue that the God of the Bible, especially in the Old Testament, is not particularly good, e.g. he asks Abraham to sacrifice his son as a test, he can be jealous and angry, and in the story of Noah he regretted the flood, suggesting that God can make mistakes.
- The problem of evil raises questions of whether a God of omnipotence can also be all-loving when there is evidence of evil in the world (the inconsistent triad).
- Omnibenevolence might be considered incompatible with other attributes of God, for example if God is omnibenevolent then he cannot do evil but if he is omnipotent then he can do anything.

 APPLY

Test yourself on key knowledge (AO1)

1. What is meant by the word 'omnibenevolence'?
2. Which French philosopher argued that an omnipotent God should be able to do anything, even the logically impossible?
3. How does Aquinas understand the idea of God's omnipotence?
4. Who took a four-dimensionalist approach to God's relationship with time?
5. Who argued that God might know us in the same way that close friends know us, so our actions can be predicted without compromising our free will?
6. Who argued that God is eternal and can see us as if from 'a lofty peak'?
7. What is Swinburne's view about God's relationship with time?

8. What do Christians believe is the ultimate expression of God's goodness and love?
9. Why might God's omnipotence be seen to be incompatible with God's omnibenevolence?
10. Why might God's omniscience be seen as a threat to human free will?
11. Give an example of a thinker who claims that God deliberately limits his own omnipotence for our benefit.
12. Why might some people reject the idea that God is everlasting rather than eternal? (Give two reasons.)

If you are unsure about any of the questions, look back over the key points on pages 46–49. You can check your answers on page 217.

Develop your skills in critical argument and evaluation (AO2)

For high marks in AO2, you need to think about the ideas in this chapter and develop your own perspective, so that you can produce critically evaluative arguments rather than just describing and presenting the views of others. At AS level, 50% of your marks are awarded for your skills in critical evaluation, and at A level, 60%.

Use the following questions to help you formulate your own views.

» Discuss them with friends, making sure you articulate your own view and listen to the views of others.

» Try writing your answers to these questions, to familiarise yourself with expressing your ideas in an academic style.

» Remember to give reasons for your views.

» Think about counter-arguments – what might someone say who held a different view from your own, and why do you think they are wrong?

1. Aquinas argued the omnipotence of God means that God can do anything within his nature that does not imply a contradiction. However, Descartes argued that to call God omnipotent is to recognise that God can do absolutely anything at all, even the logically impossible. Anything less than this is not omnipotence because omnipotence has to mean total power. Which of these two views do you find more convincing as an understanding of omnipotence?

Here is an example of the kinds of ideas you might explore in formulating your analysis and evaluation:

You might think that Aquinas is right and that the omnipotence of God is not compromised by saying that God can only do things which are within his own nature and which do not involve logical contradiction. You could argue that the omnipotence of God is unique and that any difficulties arising from this concept are difficulties of human understanding and of the limitations of human language. You might argue that instead of calling God omnipotent, it might make more sense to think of God in terms of 'maximal greatness' in recognition that there are some things God cannot do. Alternatively you might support the idea that omnipotence should mean an ability to do absolutely anything at all, including the logically contradictory, on the grounds that God is in control of logic and reason and is not limited by anything. You might want to argue that the whole idea of omnipotence does not work and that this demonstrates an omnipotent God cannot exist.

Now use your critical and evaluative skills to explore these questions on your own.

2. Swinburne answers the question of whether God can create a stone too heavy for himself to lift by arguing that such a stone would be an impossibility and therefore not a 'thing' – God can still do every thing. Do you think he is making a strong argument? Give reasons for your answer.

3. Vardy, amongst others, argues that God deliberately limits his own powers in order to allow human beings the freedom to make genuine choices, including choices of belief and faith. Do you think a God who has deliberately limited his own power could still be called 'omnipotent'? Give reasons for your answer.

4. Theodicies (responses to the problem of evil) often use the argument that God could not give us genuine free will without also allowing evil and suffering to exist. Do you think that this argument casts doubt on the omnipotence of God? Should God be able to create a world in which evil and suffering do not exist and yet there is human free will, if God is omnipotent?

5. How convincing do you find the views of Boethius and Anselm when they argue that God exists outside time and can see us at every point in time without compromising our free will? Do their opinions make sense as possible solutions to the problem of God's omniscience and human free will?

6. One of the arguments against the idea that God is eternal is that a timeless God would not be able to have relationships with people, because an eternal God would be incapable of change and therefore could not respond when people behave in different ways. It would be impossible for God to have emotions such as anger or compassion or love, because emotions are feelings that come and go. Do you find this argument persuasive? Give reasons for your answer.

The story of Abraham and Isaac is cited by many who argue that God does not always appear benevolent in the Bible

7. Some critics of Christianity argue that the God of the Bible does not consistently display the all-loving qualities that are necessary for God to be called 'omnibenevolent'. They point to examples such as the story of Abraham and Isaac, and places where God commands the Israelites to go to war, in order to demonstrate that the Bible does not support belief in an omnibenevolent God. How do you think a Christian might respond to such criticism? How persuasive do you find this criticism?

8. Some people argue that the idea of an omnipotent God is incompatible with the idea of an omnibenevolent God, because an omnipotent God can do anything but an omnibenevolent God cannot do evil. How might a Christian respond to this criticism? Do you find the criticism persuasive?

REVIEW

Practice Exam Questions

Try these practice questions. You could:

» write plans for each of them, to practise your skills in structuring an essay

» use them for practice in writing introductions and/or conclusions

» write the whole essay, perhaps against the clock.

1. How fair is the claim that an omnipotent God should be able to do absolutely anything, even the logically impossible?

2. Discuss critically issues arising from the belief that God is omniscient.

Use page 9 to review your essay and make sure you have met the assessment objectives. See pages 225–226 for a mark scheme.

Chapter 1.8 : Religious language: negative, analogical or symbolic

 RECAP

Religious language issues are issues of whether the ordinary language of the everyday physical world can be used to convey ideas or make truth-claims about God, the afterlife or other spiritual issues.

Uses of religious language

Religious language can be used in many different ways, including:

- to make truth-claims
- to evoke feelings of worship
- to express emotion
- to solemnise occasions
- to pray.

The *via negativa* or apophatic way

- Supporters of the *via negativa* claim that in order to say things that are literally true of God, it is important to use only negative terms.
- Negative terms might include things like 'invisible', 'incorporeal' and 'timeless'.
- This is because using positive terms of God makes God seem too small, as if God is like a human father or judge and as if God has only human wisdom or strength.
- Pseudo-Dionysius the Areopagite lived in the sixth century and was influential in developing the *via negativa*, arguing that people need to go beyond the need for understanding and enter a 'cloud of unknowing'.
- Moses Maimonides lived in the twelfth century and gave the example of describing a ship by explaining what it is not, to illustrate how knowledge of God could be communicated.
- The *via negativa* can produce statements which are literally true rather than requiring interpretation.
- Statements made using the *via negativa* can be meaningful across different times and cultures.

Possible criticisms of the *via negativa*

- It could be argued that the *via negativa* is not of much help to someone who knows nothing of God.
- Defining God in negative terms might not be very different from claiming that God is nothing at all.
- The Bible uses positive terms of God, and so does Jesus in the Bible.

The *via positiva* or cataphatic way

Two of the ways in which religious believers might use positive terms to communicate ideas about God are through the use of analogy and symbol.

Analogy

Analogy is a comparison made between one thing and another in an effort to aid understanding.

- Analogical language contrasts with univocal language (where words are used in exactly the same way) and equivocal language (where words have completely different meanings).

- Aquinas argues that whenever we speak of God we use analogy, whether we mean to or not.

- Aquinas thought that recognising that we are using analogy helps to avoid the problem of making God too small.

- Aquinas divides analogy into two kinds: analogy of attribution and analogy of proportionality.

  - Analogy of attribution is where there is a causal relationship between the two things described. When we speak of God as loving we should remember that God is the cause of love. When we speak of God as wise we should remember that God is the cause of wisdom.

  - Analogy of proportionality is when the analogy relates two things that are different in proportion. We need to remember when we speak of God that his attributes are on an infinitely greater scale.

- Ian Ramsey wrote in 1957 about analogy using 'models' and 'qualifiers'. We can take an idea from this limited physical world and use it as a model. We can use other words such as 'infinitely' or 'holy' to indicate that the word is being applied analogically to an infinite being who will always remain beyond human comprehension.

The Bible uses symbolic language for God, for example by describing him as a shepherd

Symbol

Symbol is a word or other kind of representation used to stand for something else and to shed light on its meaning.

- All language is symbolic in that words stand for the things they represent.

- We use metaphor in many contexts to aid understanding and add vividness.

- Using symbolism can be a way of saying positive things about God without making God too small.

- The Bible uses symbolic language of God, for example saying that 'the Lord is my Shepherd' (Psalm 23:1) or that God is a 'father'.
- Paul Tillich was a Protestant theologian of the twentieth century. He had a 'theology of correlation', showing the relation between the questions raised in philosophy, the arts, psychology and history, with the answers offered by theology.
- Tillich argued that all religious language is symbolic.
- Symbols, Tillich thought, 'participate in' the things to which they point.
- Tillich thought that understanding religion as symbolic helps us to understand God as the 'ground of all being'.

Possible criticisms of analogy and symbol as ways of speaking about God

- Using ideas from the limited, imperfect physical world to express ideas about God might make God seem too small.
- Using positive terms to speak of God might wrongly suggest that human beings can come to an understanding of God.
- If we use analogy and symbol knowing that the terms we use are only a partial, smaller shadow of the greatness of God, then we still do not come to a very clear understanding.
- Analogies and symbols require interpretation and we do not always know if we are interpreting them correctly.
- Some symbols can change in meaning over time or between different cultures, for example the swastika symbol.

A swastika is a symbol that has very different meanings in different cultures. In India, it is a symbol of good fortune.

The symbol of light is used in many religious traditions

Key terms

Via negativa **or apophatic way:** a way of speaking about God and theological ideas using only terms that say what God is not

Via positiva **or cataphatic way:** a range of ways of speaking about God and theological ideas using only terms that say what God is

Analogy: a comparison made between one thing and another in an effort to aid understanding

Symbol: a word or other kind of representation used to stand for something else and to shed light on its meaning

APPLY

Test yourself on key knowledge (AO1)

1. The apophatic way is another name for what?

2. Which sixth-century thinker wrote about describing what God is not and leaving behind reason to enter a cloud of unknowing?

3. Which twelfth-century writer used the example of a ship to demonstrate the *via negativa*?

4. What is the main reason suggested for using the *via negativa* to communicate religious ideas?

5. What is another name for the *via positiva*?

6. What is an analogy?

7. What is univocal language?

8. What did Aquinas mean when he referred to analogy of attribution?

9. What did Aquinas mean when he referred to analogy of proportionality?

10. Who argued that symbols 'participate in' the things to which they point?

11. Give an example of a way in which God is symbolised in Christianity.

12. Give an example of a criticism that could be made of communicating ideas about God using symbol.

If you are unsure about any of the questions, look back over the key points on pages 52–55. You can check your answers on page 218.

Develop your skills in critical argument and evaluation (AO2)

For high marks in AO2, you need to think about the ideas in this chapter and develop your own perspective, so that you can produce critically evaluative arguments rather than just describing and presenting the views of others. At AS level, 50% of your marks are awarded for your skills in critical evaluation, and at A level, 60%.

Use the following questions to help you formulate your own views.

» Discuss them with friends, making sure you articulate your own view and listen to the views of others.

» Try writing your answers to these questions, to familiarise yourself with expressing your ideas in an academic style.

» Remember to give reasons for your views.

» Think about counter-arguments – what might someone say who held a different view from your own, and why do you think they are wrong?

1.   **People who support the *via negativa* often claim that using ordinary language to say what God is makes God seem too small. Do you think this is always true? Can you think of any examples of positive language used of God which can convey the infinity or power or mystery of the God of Christian belief?**

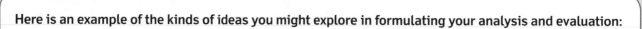

Here is an example of the kinds of ideas you might explore in formulating your analysis and evaluation:

It might be argued that there are some ways of expressing Christian beliefs which avoid the problem of making God seem too small, for example terms like omnibenevolent or omnipotent convey that God is unsurpassable and that his love and power are infinite. Perhaps terms such as 'holy' or 'eternal' also successfully convey the nature of God. You might also want to argue that metaphor, poetry and other kinds of symbol or analogy help to avoid the problem of making

God too small because they convey ideas and impressions rather than attempting to say anything literal. On the other hand, it could be argued that all ordinary language used of God makes God seem too small because even terms like omnibenevolence and omnipotence bring to mind human love and human power. They could convey a concept of human love or power on a big scale rather than successfully communicating the nature of God.

Now use your critical and evaluative skills to explore these questions on your own.

2.   Religious language raises the issue of whether it is possible to communicate anything about a spiritual, eternal being unavailable to the senses, using the ordinary language of this physical world. Some people argue that the task is impossible. How far would you agree?

3.   People who support the *via negativa* claim that by saying what God is not instead of trying to say anything positive about God, some of the difficulties of religious language can be overcome. Do you think this is correct? Give reasons for your answer.

4.   Why do you think analogy is used so often in the communication of scientific understanding? Do you find analogies such as understanding the atom as a kind of mini solar system helpful in your understanding? In what ways do such analogies help and in what ways do they mislead?

5.   Tillich wrote about the power of symbols in helping individuals come to an understanding of the meaning of human existence. What do you think he might have meant by this? Do you think he was right?

6. Symbols can be evocative and help make an idea more vivid and intelligible, but they can also be misinterpreted and change their meaning over time and between cultures. On balance, do you think symbols are an effective or an ineffective way of communicating religious ideas?

7. It could be argued that the *via negativa* is appropriate in some contexts when communicating religious ideas, and the *via positiva* is more appropriate in other contexts. How far would you agree with this claim?

The Alpha Omega symbol has been used in Christianity since its earliest days and is recognisable across language and culture amongst Christians

 **REVIEW**

Practice Exam Questions

Try these practice questions. You could:

» write plans for each of them, to practise your skills in structuring an essay

» use them for practice in writing introductions and/or conclusions

» write the whole essay, perhaps against the clock.

1. How effective is analogy in communicating religious ideas and beliefs?

2. 'Symbol is too often misleading for it to be useful in religious language.' Discuss.

Use page 9 to review your essay and make sure you have met the assessment objectives. See pages 226–227 for a mark scheme.

Chapter 1.9

Religious language: twentieth-century perspectives and philosophical comparisons

 RECAP

Analytic and synthetic statements

An **analytic statement** is a statement of definition; it tells us how words are being used. It does not need any experience to support it.

A **synthetic statement** adds something to our knowledge, and experience can be used to support it.

In the context of religious language, there are questions about whether religious truth-claims have to be supported by **empirical experience** if they are to be meaningful.

Cognitive and non-cognitive uses of language

- Cognitive uses of language involve things that can be known and that could be either true or false.

- Non-cognitive uses of language are not about things that can be known, but instead work in other ways. For example they might express emotions, ask questions, give commands or make associations.

- In the context of religious language, there are questions about whether religious statements should be understood as cognitive or non-cognitive.

Logical positivism

- Logical positivism began in the early twentieth century, with discussions amongst the Vienna Circle.

- The Vienna Circle wanted to clarify the kinds of statements that have meaning, and the kinds which only sound meaningful but are in fact 'empty'.

- The logical positivists presented a challenge to religious believers by claiming that religious language is not true nor false but meaningless.

- A.J. Ayer led the challenge in his book *Language, Truth and Logic* (1936).

- According to logical positivists, a proposition is only meaningful if it is analytic, or if it is capable of being tested using the five senses (empirical testing). This rule is known as the verification principle.

- Religious language is dismissed as meaningless by logical positivists because claims such as 'God made the world' cannot be tested empirically, and are not analytic.

- Many people reject the verification principle because it fails its own test – it cannot be tested for meaningfulness using the five senses.
- The verification principle classifies as meaningless a lot more than religious language – ethical statements, for example, cannot be verified empirically.
- Weak versions of the verification principle have been suggested.

Wittgenstein and language games

- Ludwig Wittgenstein was a twentieth-century philosopher who aimed to work out the limits of what can be known, conceptualised and expressed in language.
- He explored the ways in which language can have meaning.
- His earlier work inspired the Vienna Circle.
- Wittgenstein thought that we can understand how language can be meaningful if we think of it using the analogy of a game.
- Language is meaningful to people who use it when they are participating in a shared 'language game' such as chess or train-driving.
- A 'Lebensform' or 'form of life' is a context in which language might be used. Language has meaning in context, and people outside that context might not understand it so easily.
- Within the Lebensform, there are rules for language usage and everyone understands them.
- Propositions are not simply 'meaningful' or 'meaningless' to everyone, they can be meaningful to some but not to others. Meaning is subjective.
- Religious language can therefore be meaningful to those who are in the Lebensform of religion, even if they are meaningless to those outside it.
- Later thinkers have adopted aspects of Wittgenstein's thought to suggest that religious language could be non-cognitive.

Flew and the falsification principle

- Antony Flew's ideas were presented at a symposium in Oxford in a paper called 'Theology and Falsification' in 1950. He wanted to take the debate about the meaningfulness of religious language into new territory.
- Flew used a parable by John Wisdom to illustrate his argument. A Sceptic and a Believer have different views about the existence of a gardener who visits a clearing in a jungle, because the gardener cannot be detected using the five senses.

Flew used a parable of two people in a jungle to set out his views on religious language

- Nothing the Sceptic offers as evidence against the existence of the gardener will convince the Believer, who in response to the Sceptic keeps qualifying his statements about the characteristics of the invisible gardener to accommodate each challenge.
- Flew argues that religious believers behave in the same way, refusing to accept any counter-evidence to their claims about God.
- Flew says that religious truth-claims end with a 'death by a thousand qualifications'. The assertions are modified until they assert nothing.
- He says that a statement must be in principle falsifiable if it is to be meaningful. We have to know what evidence, if any, would count against our assertions if they are to be meaningful assertions at all.

Responses to Flew

- R.M. Hare responded to Flew by saying that we all have unfalsifiable 'bliks'. 'Blik' was a word he made up to mean a way of framing and understanding the world. Theism is unfalsifiable but so is atheism.
- Hare gave a story of a paranoid 'lunatic' in order to illustrate his argument and show that we all have subjective ways of understanding the world.
- Hare is suggesting that religious belief and religious claims are non-cognitive expressions of preference.

- Basil Mitchell responded to Flew by saying that we have to make commitments to trust and believe in things even when the evidence is ambiguous or lacking.
- Mitchell told a story of a partisan in wartime to illustrate his point and show that sometimes it is necessary to have faith despite the existence of some counter-evidence.
- Mitchell argues that religious language is cognitive even if people do not have readily available facts to support their beliefs.

Comparing Wittgenstein with Aquinas

- Wittgenstein and Aquinas are similar in that they are both addressing problems of religious language.
- Both take a position that does not dismiss the possibility that religious language has meaning.

Differences include the following:

- **Aquinas** tackled issues raised in the thirteenth century of how religious language could be meaningful without making God too small.
- Aquinas proposed thinking in terms of analogy.
- Aquinas took a cognitive approach to religious language, believing that religious language refers to factual truth.

- **Wittgenstein** tackled issues in the twentieth century of whether religious language could be meaningful without being empirically verifiable.
- Wittgenstein proposed thinking in terms of language games.
- Wittgenstein took a more non-cognitive approach to religious language, concentrating on how it is used in context.

The influence of non-cognitive approaches to religious language on the interpretation of sacred texts

- Non-cognitive approaches to religious texts became more popular in the twentieth century.

- They suggest that instead of interpreting texts such as the Bible as factual, historical accounts, it is more helpful to understand them in other ways, as tools for learning and coming to a personal decision about spiritual matters.

- Rudolf Bultmann suggested demythologising the Bible, by which he meant looking past stories with magical or miraculous content and seeing the Bible as calling people to make a personal decision.

- Other thinkers have suggested seeing the Bible in other non-cognitive ways, emphasising the decisions and attitudes people might take in their lives.

- Books such as *Honest to God* and *The Myth of God Incarnate* caused controversy in their suggestions that ideas such as Jesus as God incarnate need not be understood as factually true.

- Cognitive approaches to biblical texts have continued to be more popular amongst Christians than non-cognitive approaches.

Key terms

Empirical: available to be experienced by the five senses

Cognitive: having a factual quality that is available to knowledge, where words are labels for things in the world

Non-cognitive: not having a factual quality that is available to knowledge; words are tools used to achieve something rather than labels for things

Logical positivism: a movement that claimed that assertions have to be capable of being tested empirically if they are to be meaningful

Verification: providing evidence to determine that something is true

Falsification: providing evidence to determine that something is false

 APPLY

Test yourself on key knowledge (AO1)

1. Who accused religious language of dying a 'death by a thousand qualifications'?

2. What does 'Lebensform' mean?

3. In what ways did Wittgenstein think that language is similar to a game?

4. What did Mitchell use as a parable in order to illustrate his response to Flew?

5. What is the name given to the movement that claimed that assertions have to be capable of being tested empirically if they are to be meaningful?

6. What does it mean if someone calls religious language 'non-cognitive'?

7. What is an analytic statement?

8. What name did Hare give to unfalsifiable convictions when he was writing his response to Flew?

9. Give an example of a way in which Aquinas and Wittgenstein took similar approaches to religious language.

10. Who inspired the Vienna Circle to discuss the meaningfulness of language?

11. What was the name of the book in which Ayer set out his verification principle?

12. What is 'empirical testing'?

If you are unsure about any of the questions, look back over the key points on pages 58–61. You can check your answers on page 218.

Develop your skills in critical argument and evaluation (AO2)

For high marks in AO2, you need to think about the ideas in this chapter and develop your own perspective, so that you can produce critically evaluative arguments rather than just describing and presenting the views of others. At AS level, 50% of your marks are awarded for your skills in critical evaluation, and at A level, 60%.

Use the following questions to help you formulate your own views.

» Discuss them with friends, making sure you articulate your own view and listen to the views of others.

» Try writing your answers to these questions, to familiarise yourself with expressing your ideas in an academic style.

» Remember to give reasons for your views.

» Think about counter-arguments – what might someone say who held a different view from your own, and why do you think they are wrong?

1. **Do you think that the Bible, and other religious texts, should be considered non-cognitively, rather than as factual accounts? What are some of the advantages and disadvantages in taking a non-cognitive approach to sacred texts?**

Here is an example of the kinds of ideas you might explore in formulating your analysis and evaluation:

You might want to argue that the Bible should be considered as factual, written with the intention of giving explanations and stories about events that really happened. You might support this view by saying that the Bible often gives no indication that it should be interpreted in any other way, and sometimes it is quite specific about the date or the place of an event. It could be argued that if the Bible is not considered in a cognitive way, it becomes very much diluted and misses the whole point of the idea that God really did create the world, give commandments and come into the world as a man. You might want to argue that the Bible should be understood as cognitive but that the facts are not necessarily true; the writers meant for readers to understand them cognitively whether or not they are credible for modern people. You might, however, want to argue that a non-cognitive approach is more appropriate for modern people, avoiding clashes between science and religion and allowing people to develop their own attitudes and decisions.

Now use your critical and evaluative skills to explore these questions on your own.

2. Logical positivists claim that if propositions are to be meaningful, they must be capable of being verified using the senses. What do you think are the main strengths and weaknesses of this claim? Do you think that, on balance, it is a good rule for deciding whether or not a proposition is meaningful?

3. How convincing do you find Wittgenstein's idea that people operate within different language games, and that language can be meaningful within the game but meaningless outside it? Do you think that someone playing a game such as football understands the meaning of football terms better than someone who observes but does not play? Do you think it is possible to gain meaning from truth-claims made by a religion when you are not part of that religion yourself?

4. Flew argues in 'Theology and Falsification' that religious claims such as 'God loves us' are empty ones, if the speaker cannot give us any possible circumstances that would induce them to withdraw the claim. Do you think Flew is right? If religious believers are unshakeable in their faith in a loving God regardless of the circumstances,

does this mean that their claims about God have no real content?

5. Flew argues that religious believers always make excuses for God when faced with challenges, by saying things like 'God's love is not like human love' or 'God works in mysterious ways'. Do you think this is a fair accusation? How might a Christian respond to Flew?

6. Mitchell and Hare both responded to 'Theology and Falsification' with their own defences of religious language. Which of the two responses do you find more convincing, if either? What do you think are the strengths and weaknesses of their responses?

7. Aquinas and Wittgenstein consider religious language in terms of analogy and in terms of language games respectively. Which of the two approaches do you find more persuasive, if either? Is there another approach (for example, logical positivism) that you think is more persuasive? Give reasons for your answer.

Can someone who does not play football, but observes it, understand the meaning of football terms as well as someone who does play?

REVIEW

Practice Exam Questions

Try these practice questions. You could:

» write plans for each of them, to practise your skills in structuring an essay

» use them for practice in writing introductions and/or conclusions

» write the whole essay, perhaps against the clock.

1. To what extent can Wittgenstein's theory of language games help to resolve the issues raised by religious language?

2. 'A non-cognitive approach to religious language provides valuable insights into the interpretation of religious texts.' Discuss.

Use page 9 to review your essay and make sure you have met the assessment objectives. See pages 227–228 for a mark scheme.

Sample student answers

1. To what extent does Plato's Theory of Forms provide a useful way of understanding the world?

According to Plato, an ancient Greek philosopher, the world is divided into two realms: the realm of appearances (the physical/material world) and the realm of ideas or Forms. The realm of appearances is the physical world we live in. We see, feel, smell, and hear things in this physical realm, basically, everything in this realm is accessible through our senses.

In the realm of Forms, however, things are only accessible through our intellects, our minds. The things in this realm are universal, unchanging and perfect. The things in the realm of appearances are just copies of things in the realm of Forms. Plato's analogy of the cave explains the Theory of Forms.

In Plato's cave, there are a few prisoners chained together. These prisoners are seated together and facing the back wall of the cave and cannot turn their heads sideways. Behind them is a fire that casts shadows of objects on the wall that they face. These prisoners have supposedly stayed like this in this cave all their lives. As objects pass, these prisoners see their shadows and call the names of the shadows in belief that they (the shadows they see) are actually the real objects they are calling and seeing, whereas it is only the shadows they can see.

Plato then supposes that one of the prisoners is able to escape and leave the cave and see the actual images, not the shadows. This man would be confused as he has grown accustomed to seeing and knowing only the shadows. But Plato further imagines that this escaped prisoner is able to adjust to the reality of things and gain knowledge of how this realm of reality works. This prisoner is then tasked with the moral duty of sharing his discovery with his less enlightened prisoners.

On his return to the cave, this escaped prisoner realises that he is no longer able to see clearly in the dark cave as he has become used to the sun's light. His fellow prisoners have no desire to leave the cave that they have lived in peacefully and refuse to follow him out of the cave to

> This would have been a good opportunity for the candidate to use the term 'dualist'. It would have been good if the candidate had indicated an intention to give an argument – will they be arguing that the Theory of Forms is useful, or not?

experience the transformation he has undergone. In fact, they are hostile to his suggestions to lead them out of the cave and are willing to go as far as killing him to remain in the cave.

Plato's analogy of the cave makes us understand that we are all like the prisoners; ignorant of the realm of Forms. We only see the shadows that the real objects (objects in the realm of Forms) cast before us. However, the escaped prisoner represents philosophers, who have been able to step out of the darkness and experience the realm of Forms (mentally) and see it as their duty to bring enlightenment to the rest of us.

In defending his Theory of Forms, Plato puts forward some arguments. He uses the abstract 'beauty' to explain his point. We only see beautiful things, like beautiful cars, beautiful houses, etc. but we never see 'beauty'. We can have beauty in different forms (as particulars), because more than one object can possess the quality of beauty. Plato further argues that what differentiates the particulars from the Form is that whereas the particulars may lose the qualities that make them beautiful (for example, a house can be razed, or a car wrecked), the Form can never lose the quality that makes it the Form (i.e. beauty can never lose its beauty). This therefore means that the Form can exist independent of the particular and is separate from the particular.

Plato's other argument for The Theory of Forms is that particular things are relative to various times or different people. For example, I may say a waterlily is a beautiful flower and someone else (say Bob), may feel a hibiscus is a beautiful flower and a nightshade is not a beautiful flower. Our perceptions of a 'beautiful flower' differ and so there is no knowledge of what a beautiful flower really is as both our opinions are uncertain. Plato believes that the Form of beauty is permanent and remains 'beautiful' to all who see it regardless of the time it is seen or by whom it is seen. Therefore, the Form of beauty has knowledge. The knowledge we have of this Form of beauty is intuitive and cannot be experienced through any of our senses; we just know it is what it is.

There have been lots of arguments against Plato's Theory of Forms. The most common being 'The Third Man' argument. The Third Man argument was propounded by Plato in one of his dialogues, 'Parmenides'. The Third Man argument is basically the idea that for a particular to resemble a Form, it has to resemble another Form. For example, birds; there are different breeds of birds but what these breeds have in common

This is clearly expressed and accurate, but the candidate has spent too long telling the story of the cave analogy, instead of concentrating on the Theory of Forms itself.

The essay is very descriptive; the examiner has no idea what the candidate thinks of Plato's views, as there is no critical evaluation of Plato yet.

is the bird-ness that makes it possible for us to identify each different breed as a bird. The Third Man argument believes that it is not possible for the Form of birds to be perfect and unchanging, and yet be present in the particular (each species of bird). Therefore, the Third Man argument believes that there must be more than one Form (a Form for sparrows, a Form for hummingbirds, a Form for eagles, a Form for larks, etc. and not just one Form of bird that is perfect). "If so," Parmenides concludes, "nothing can be like the form, nor can the form be like anything. Otherwise a second form will always make its appearance over and above the first form, and if that second form is like anything, yet a third. And there will be no end to this emergence of fresh forms, if the form is to be like the thing that partakes of it."

To conclude, I believe Plato believed in his Theory of Forms. His belief did not however stop him from welcoming the opinions of others, even those opinions that contradicted his theory. He understood that his theory is not perfect and must not be accepted without careful scrutiny. This may perhaps be why he openly criticised his views.

> The candidate says that criticisms have been made of Plato, but does not tell us whether these criticisms are strong ones, or whether this is the candidate's own view.

> The conclusion does not effectively tie up the arguments in the essay, because there is not much argument. We never find out whether the Theory of Forms is useful.

The examiner says:

This is a weak answer. It is clearly written and demonstrates knowledge, but it lacks a coherent argument that answers the question.

- For AO1 skills, the student has done quite well in some respects. They write clearly, making it easy for the examiner to follow what they are saying. Everything they say is accurate and they obviously have a good understanding of Plato's ideas. However, they spend too long telling us the story of the Analogy of the Cave, rather than focusing explicitly on the Theory of Forms. It would have been good to read more about the Forms in a hierarchy, with the Form of the Good at the top. It would also have been good to have some mention of how physical phenomena participate in the Forms.

- For AO2, the candidate has performed less well. They do not tell us whether they find the Theory of Forms useful or not, and that was the question. Although they have presented us with a criticism of Plato, they do not tell us whether they think it is a strong or a weak criticism. Their conclusion does not form a summing up of their argument, because the candidate does not have an argument.

To achieve a better mark, the candidate needs to:

» read the question more carefully and decide whether they think the Forms are useful or not from the start

» focus more explicitly on the question's emphasis on the Theory of Forms rather than Plato's thought more generally

» consider different points of view, explaining why some people might think Plato's ideas are useful while others might not, and show us which side they find more persuasive

» make clear whether they think the criticism presented of Plato is valid criticism, and whether they think Plato can be defended against these criticisms.

2. To what extent are criticisms of the ontological argument successful?

Many thinkers, both religious and not, have criticised the ontological argument. The most important were Gaunilo, Aquinas and Kant. Some of these are more successful than others, but if an overall judgment had to be made I would say that all in all these criticisms have been mostly successful. However, to understand why the arguments are successful or not, the strengths and weaknesses of each of them must be looked at.

Anselm argued that we just need to understand the nature of God in order to realise that he must exist. He said that God is that than which nothing greater can be thought, and therefore God must exist in reality because a God who exists only in thought is not as great as a real God.

Gaunilo, who was a French monk and a contemporary of Anselm's, disagreed with Anselm even though he was a Christian himself. He argued that the logic of Anselm's argument is flawed and if we look at the example of an island this can be seen clearly. In 'On behalf of the fool' Gaunilo writes that we can imagine a most excellent island in our minds, and if we use Anselm's logic this island must exist in reality. However such an island obviously does not exist. I see this to be a strong argument and one that springs to mind straight away when Anselm's ideas are looked at — I do not regard Anselm's counter-argument against it as strong (he stated that as God's existence is necessary and not contingent the example of an island does not apply) because I view it as a simple cop-out that has no logical basis to it at all. Gaunilo's argument, on the other hand, does — it is a completely logical idea that arises from Anselm's argument.

Aquinas also criticised Anselm's idea. He did not share Anselm's confidence that we all know what God is. He thought we could have a mental concept of the non-existence of God — people clearly manage to have such a concept, as does the fool who says in his heart 'There is no God'. I think this a strong argument because if we can imagine a state of godlessness (and we evidently can) the contradiction in terms that Anselm speaks of does not exist. Some may argue that we cannot really imagine a state of godlessness, but I believe these people to be wrong as it is up to the individual to decide what he can and what he cannot imagine.

Immanuel Kant also criticised Anselm. Many believe this to be the strongest criticism of the ontological argument to be put forward. Kant

A good introduction. Gets straight to the heart of the question immediately with a confident sense of direction and a clear intention to present an argument rather than just information.

A good idea to give a brief summary of the ontological argument without letting it take up most of the essay. Don't forget that Anselm was not the only thinker to present an ontological argument.

stated that 'existence is not a predicate' — it is not a characteristic that helps us describe an object, like colour or shape or size. Kant wrote that when we talk of God we talk of the concept of God and saying that this concept exists does not actually realise it. I agree with Kant's idea — for example we can have the concept of a fire-breathing dragon in our minds. We can state that this dragon exists, but this will not make it do so. Some have argued against Kant's point by stating that God's existence is different to that of a dragon, as it is necessary rather than contingent. However I think this is a particularly weak point as it is somewhat circular — we have to accept the premise that God's existence is necessary to come to the conclusion that his existence is necessary.

To sum up the above, I believe that the criticisms of the ontological argument are successful, and I especially agree with the views that Kant and Aquinas express on the matter as they made particularly strong points. In my opinion, no one has managed to come up with a persuasive counter-argument.

> Kant directed his criticisms at Descartes rather than Anselm, but otherwise the points made here are good. Counter-arguments are considered and could be developed further.

> A good clear conclusion, although the essay did not show that the candidate thought Gaunilo's criticism was weaker than the other two — better not to introduce new ideas in the conclusion.

The examiner says:

This is a stronger essay. It is clearly written, well-argued and coherent. It remains focused on the question throughout.

- For AO1 skills, the essay shows thorough knowledge and understanding. It would have been good if the candidate had shown recognition of other ontological arguments, such as that of Descartes.

  This essay is very well-structured. The candidate makes excellent use of paragraphs to separate the different points made. The structure gives the essay a strong sense of direction.

  The selection of material for this essay is very thoughtful. The candidate has selected three important criticisms of the ontological argument, without suggesting that these are the only three. The candidate has not wasted time telling us everything they know about this argument but has concentrated on the question and kept the focus on the criticisms.

  There is clear reference to 'sources of wisdom and authority', in this instance to the work of well-known thinkers. This is done accurately and confidently.

- For AO2 skills, the candidate has performed very well. There is a clear argument throughout the essay, which leads to a well-justified conclusion. They have looked at possible counter-arguments too, recognising that others might hold a different point of view. The material selected has been used in the formulation of an argument, rather than just being presented. Views of different thinkers are given critical analysis and evaluation.

To achieve a better mark, the candidate needs to:

» show knowledge and understanding of a wider range of thinkers, perhaps by referring to other ontological arguments as well as Anselm's and to critics in addition to Gaunilo and Kant.

» develop counter-arguments further, and comment on them. It is good to show recognition of counter-arguments but this should be followed by saying whether the counter-argument is successful or not. Simply pointing out that there are opposing views does not show which view is the stronger.

» spend a little more time planning the essay; the point made in the conclusion about Gaunilo having a weaker argument needed developing but the candidate did not think of this until the end. The conclusion should wrap the essay up rather than introduce new lines of argument.

Chapter 2.1 | Natural law

RECAP

Natural law in the Christian tradition is based around the thinking of Thomas Aquinas.

It is a system of ethics based on the principle that there is such a thing as **human nature** and that we should live in accordance with human nature – we should aim to fulfil our purpose.

Natural law is **deontological** – it has an absolute system of rules based on actions and duties.

Aquinas thought that human nature is fundamentally good and that all rational people seek goodness, which can be found in the vision of God.

The telos (ultimate end)

- Aquinas used the thinking of Aristotle to develop his own ideas about ethics.
- Aristotle argued that something was good if it fulfilled its purpose. He argued that people aim to achieve eudaimonia (happiness and flourishing).
- Aquinas thought that moral acts come from free, rational beings. We have to be genuinely free to make moral decisions and we have to make them using our reason, which was given to us by God.

- According to Aquinas, God should be the ultimate 'end' or purpose of human life. Being in the presence of God is the human 'telos', or ultimate reason for existing.
- Aquinas thought that people need help from God in order to direct their motives and their actions, making sure they do the right thing for the right reasons.

The four tiers of law

Aquinas thought morality was about following law. He identified four levels of law:

> 1. **Eternal law** – the unchanging reason of God, absolute for all people and all times. This is the highest form of law.

> 2. **Divine law** – the commandments given by God, usually found in the Bible, teaching people how to live.

> 3. **Natural law** – people can perceive eternal law by using their reason to reflect on the world and work out how they should behave and think. God uses natural law to make eternal law accessible to people. Natural law is universal.

> 4. **Human law** – the laws people come up with in response to the higher tiers of law, or in response to the needs of their society and the way it is organised. Human law is the lowest tier of law and can be broken if higher forms of law conflict with it.

The precepts

- The key precept (general rule for behaviour) of natural law is the rule of synderesis – do good and avoid evil.
- Aquinas claimed God gives us reason so that we can work out for ourselves what to do to fulfill our telos.
- Aquinas thought all human beings are inclined to do good because all species want to survive.
- He classified five primary precepts (or key rules to promote human flourishing):

  1. To worship God.
  2. To live in an orderly society.
  3. To reproduce.
  4. To learn and teach people about God.
  5. To defend the innocent and preserve life.

- Secondary precepts derive from the primary precepts – they illustrate the practical application of the primary precepts.

Real and apparent goods

- Aquinas made a distinction between real and apparent goods:

  Real goods are those which are in accordance with the primary precepts and God's wishes for humanity.

  Apparent goods are things which tempt us because they seem enjoyable but which do not further the aim of promoting human flourishing.

- We can use reason to distinguish real goods from apparent goods.

Natural or cardinal virtues

- Aquinas identified four 'natural' or 'cardinal' virtues that he thought were discovered by reason:

  prudence   temperance   fortitude   justice

- There are also other virtues identified in the Bible, for example:

  faith   hope   love

The doctrine of double effect

- Aquinas discusses situations where a single action has two effects, for example an act of self-defence resulting in the death of the attacker.
- He says that intention is important – if the intention was to do something good, then the action cannot be bad even if there was an unintentional bad result as one of the effects.
- This has become known as the doctrine of double effect.
- It might be used in cases of euthanasia, for example if the intention of giving powerful doses of a drug is to relieve pain, then that action is good even if an unintentional effect of the drug is to shorten life.

Possible strengths of natural law as a system of ethics

- The way natural law is applied can vary widely – this can be seen as a strength as it allows for consideration of different circumstances.
- Some see natural law as offering clarity and consistency in its answers to ethical problems.
- It offers a way of looking at the world which is absolute and applies to all times and cultures – the idea of universal moral law is appealing to many.
- It combines religious ideas with reason, allowing people to exercise some autonomy in decisions about right and wrong.
- Arguably, it is easy to work out what is right and wrong using natural law, making it a helpful system of ethics.

Key terms

Natural law: a deontological theory based on behaviour that accords with given laws or moral rules that exist independently of human societies and systems

Deontological: from the Latin for 'duty', ethics focused on the intrinsic rightness and wrongness of actions

Eudaimonia: living well, as an ultimate end in life which all other actions should lead towards

Telos: the end, or purpose, of something

Synderesis: to follow the good and avoid the evil, the rule which all precepts follow

Primary precepts: the most important rules in life: to protect life, to reproduce, to live in community, to teach the young and to believe in God

Secondary precepts: the laws which follow from the primary precepts

Possible weaknesses of natural law as a system of ethics

- The way natural law is applied can vary widely – this can be seen as a weakness as it is not always clear what to do in a moral dilemma.
- Aquinas' version of natural law presupposes a belief in God, which not everyone has.
- Our understanding of what is natural is not always accurate and not always unchanging. For example, homosexuality has been seen in the past as unnatural, but many people in the modern Western world now see homosexuality as natural.
- Sometimes natural law might seem overly legalistic and unsympathetic to particular circumstances.
- The world has changed since the time of Aquinas, so some applications of natural law might seem inappropriate today. For example, the use of artificial methods of contraception causes controversy – it might be seen to go against the precept of reproduction, but avoiding artificial contraception could lead to unwanted pregnancy or the spread of sexually-transmitted disease.

Change in perception of what is natural could be a weakness for natural law as a system of ethics

 APPLY

Test yourself on key knowledge (AO1)

1. What is missing from this list of primary precepts? To protect life, to reproduce, to teach the young and to worship God.
2. What is 'synderesis'?
3. What is 'eudaimonia'?
4. What are the four natural, or cardinal, virtues identified by Aquinas?
5. What is the second-highest tier of law, according to Aquinas?
6. What is the doctrine of double effect?
7. What does 'telos' mean?
8. What are 'apparent goods', according to Aquinas?
9. Did Aquinas think that people are fundamentally inclined to be good, or fundamentally inclined to be bad?
10. What does 'deontological' mean?
11. Aquinas thought that we could distinguish between real and apparent goods by using – what?
12. What did Aquinas think was the final, ultimate goal of human life?

> If you are unsure about any of the questions, look back over the key points on pages 70–73. You can check your answers on page 218.

Develop your skills in critical argument and evaluation (AO2)

For high marks in AO2, you need to think about the ideas in this chapter and develop your own perspective, so that you can produce critically evaluative arguments rather than just describing and presenting the views of others. At AS level, 50% of your marks are awarded for your skills in critical evaluation, and at A level, 60%.

Use the following questions to help you formulate your own views.

» Discuss them with friends, making sure you articulate your own view and listen to the views of others.

» Try writing your answers to these questions, to familiarise yourself with expressing your ideas in an academic style.

» Remember to give reasons for your views.

» Think about counter-arguments – what might someone say who held a different view from your own, and why do you think they are wrong?

1. **Is natural law helpful in decision-making? What makes an ethical system helpful or unhelpful? Is it easy to apply in different contexts, and does it lead to clear decisions? Do the 'answers' provided by natural law ethics seem to fit with your personal instincts about what 'feels' like a morally good decision?**

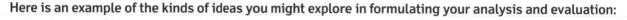

Here is an example of the kinds of ideas you might explore in formulating your analysis and evaluation:

You might argue that natural law is a helpful method of decision-making, especially as it has traditionally been supported by the Catholic Church so its application in different circumstances has already been considered. You might think that the combination of clear rules, coupled with the use of reason, provides straightforward answers to many moral dilemmas in all kinds of contexts, from morality within personal relationships to issues on a global scale. Alternatively you might argue that natural law is not always as straightforward as it seems, and there might be difficulties in deciding which actions might be best for doing good and avoiding evil. You might think that it is helpful for those who believe in God and seek an ultimate vision of God, but less helpful for those without religious belief. You might argue that views change about what is natural, highlighting a problem. You could use specific examples to illustrate times when natural law does not fit with ideas about what is good, for example when artificial contraception is considered wrong even in areas where AIDs and related illnesses are prevalent.

Now use your critical and evaluative skills to explore these questions on your own.

2. Contraception might be considered to contravene the primary precept to reproduce, so 'do not use contraception' would be a secondary precept. Can you think of any other examples of secondary precepts that might be derived from the primary precepts? Do you think secondary precepts are always clearly derived or might it sometimes be less straightforward to work out how to apply a primary precept?

3. Would you agree with Aquinas' claim that there is such a thing as 'human nature', or do you think that people are too different as individuals to have a distinct 'nature' as a species? Would you agree that people are fundamentally good and want to be moral, or do you think Aquinas is being overly optimistic, or perhaps his assessment is true of some people but not of others? Give reasons for your answers.

4. What do you think of the idea of 'telos'? Do you think that the universe as a whole has been designed with a specific purpose? Do you think that people are born for a reason, and if so, what do you think that reason is? Do you think that there is an ultimate purpose and goal for each human life? Are these questions that can be supported with reasoned argument or with evidence, or are they questions that depend solely on faith?

5. In ethics, how convincing is the idea that people are good if they are fulfilling their ultimate purpose? Do you think this is a helpful idea when deciding how to behave in a specific situation?

6. Aquinas identifies some 'natural' or 'cardinal' virtues. Do you agree with the virtues he chooses as being of prime importance? Are there any that you would add to the list or take away from the list? Give reasons for your answer.

Is there an ultimate purpose and goal for each human life?

 REVIEW

Practice Exam Questions

Try these practice questions. You could:

» write plans for each of them, to practise your skills in structuring an essay

» use them for practice in writing introductions and/or conclusions

» write the whole essay, perhaps against the clock.

1. Discuss critically the use of the concept of 'telos' in natural law ethics.

2. 'One of the greatest strengths of natural law is that it provides an absolute and universal standard for judging right and wrong.' Discuss.

Use page 9 to review your essay and make sure you have met the assessment objectives. See page 228–229 for a mark scheme.

Chapter 2.2 | Situation ethics

 RECAP

Situation ethics is a largely teleological ethical system based on the writings of Joseph Fletcher in his book *Situation Ethics*, published in 1966.

Fletcher's three approaches to moral thinking

- Fletcher divides moral thinking into three types:

  1. **legalistic** – based on fixed laws

  2. **antinomian** – having no laws at all

  3. **situational** – looking at the context of the moral problem and adopting the law of doing the most loving thing in that situation

- Fletcher thought that the third approach of situational provided the best middle path between legalism and antinomianism.
- Fletcher was influenced by other theologians such as Barth, Bonhoeffer and Bultmann, who thought that Christian ethics should not depend too heavily on trying to apply biblical laws directly to modern situations but should be flexible in expressing agapeic love.

Agape love

- Fletcher thought that agape love should be at the centre of ethics.
- Agape is understood as Christian love which is unconditional and reflects the love of God.
- Agape demands that people love their neighbours and also their enemies.
- Agape love is self-sacrificing, not self-interested.
- Fletcher thought that the 'law of love' should guide moral decision-making. People should aim to do the most loving thing, and if the consequences of their actions produce the most loving situation then they are doing the right thing.

Fletcher's six propositions

Fletcher suggested six propositions to consider when making a moral decision:

1. The only thing which is intrinsically good is agapeic love. Other things are good depending on whether they produce loving results, but agapeic love is good intrinsically, for its own sake.

2. Love is the ruling norm of Christian ethics. Fletcher gave examples of rules broken by Jesus when it was necessary for bringing about loving results.

3. Justice is love distributed. Justice is done when people act with love in a rational manner for the benefit of the community.

4. Love does not depend on emotional likes and dislikes but is an act of will, a deliberately chosen attitude.

5. Love should be the goal of a moral action, and if it is, then the means of getting to that goal are not important.

6. Love should be considered in the context of each situation as it arises, 'situationally not prescriptively'. Rules should not be made without the context of the moral situation being a serious consideration.

Fletcher thought that love should be the goal of a moral action

The four working principles

Fletcher used four working presuppositions, or 'rules of thumb', in helping to determine the right thing to do:

❶ **Pragmatism** – this is about practicality in the real world. Rather than following the abstract principles of a philosophy, the pragmatist looks for something which will work in the practical circumstances.

❷ **Relativism** – rules are not to be seen as fixed and absolute but can be changed according to the situation.

❸ **Personalism** – people matter more than laws. The needs of people should be considered when moral actions are taken.

❹ **Conscience** – conscience is not seen as a reliable set of internal rules but as activity, the use of reason in making loving moral judgements.

Fletcher's understanding of conscience

In the understanding of Fletcher, conscience:

- does not guide human action
- is not a store of reliable rules to which people can refer
- is not a kind of inner voice with access to divine truth
- is a verb, not a noun
- describes what people do when they are trying to make moral decisions and are weighing things up.

Possible strengths of situation ethics

- It is relativist, so allows for consideration of an individual's personal circumstances when making moral decisions.
- It does not have problems of being an outdated ethic as society moves on, because it is flexible.
- It could be considered quick and easy as a method of decision-making because instead of considering a range of duties, principles and outcomes, it simply recommends acting with agapeic love.
- It allows people autonomy by giving them the responsibility of choosing their own actions without having to obey the rules of others.
- It could be considered to fit well with a person's Christian faith and with the 'what would Jesus do' kind of approach to moral decision-making.

Fletcher believed that Jesus' actions demonstrated agapeic love

Key terms

Teleological ethics: moral goodness is determined by the end or result

Agape love: unconditional love, the only ethical norm in situationism

Pragmatism: acting, in moral situations, in a way that is practical, rather than purely ideological

Relativism: the rejection of absolute moral standards, such as laws or rights. Good and bad are relative to an individual or a community or, in Fletcher's case, to love

Personalism: ethics centred on people, rather than laws or objects

Possible weaknesses of situation ethics

- It is relativist, so does not give clear rules to help people know what to do in all circumstances.

- It can be difficult to apply because it is not always clear what is the most loving thing to do in a situation, just as it is not always clear what Jesus would do.

- It is also not always clear how to work out which people should be considered in the efforts to find a loving action, or what to do if an action would be loving for one person but at the same time the opposite of loving for another.

- It is relativist and so could be seen to allow people to justify any action they want to do, on the grounds that they thought it would bring about the most loving outcome. No action is ruled out as absolutely immoral and there are no moral rules that cannot be broken.

 APPLY

Test yourself on key knowledge (AO1)

1. In which year did Fletcher write his book *Situation Ethics*?

2. What does 'personalism' mean in Fletcher's four working principles?

3. What are teleological ethics?

4. What does 'pragmatism' mean in Fletcher's four working principles?

5. According to Fletcher, what is the only thing that is intrinsically good?

6. What does Fletcher say that justice consists of?

7. What is meant by 'antinomianism'?

8. Fletcher's four working principles involve relativism, pragmatism, personalism and what else?

9. In Fletcher's six propositions, he says that love's decisions are made situationally, not prescriptively. What does he mean?

10. What is the fifth of Fletcher's six propositions?

11. Does Fletcher agree that the morality of an action should be judged by its consequences?

12. What might a follower of situation ethics think about a law that completely banned euthanasia?

If you are unsure about any of the questions, look back over the key points on pages 76–79. You can check your answers on page 218.

Develop your skills in critical argument and evaluation (AO2)

For high marks in AO2, you need to think about the ideas in this chapter and develop your own perspective, so that you can produce critically evaluative arguments rather than just describing and presenting the views of others. At AS level, 50% of your marks are awarded for your skills in critical evaluation, and at A level, 60%.

Use the following questions to help you formulate your own views.

» Discuss them with friends, making sure you articulate your own view and listen to the views of others.

» Try writing your answers to these questions, to familiarise yourself with expressing your ideas in an academic style.

» Remember to give reasons for your views.

» Think about counter-arguments – what might someone say who held a different view from your own, and why do you think they are wrong?

1. **How easy do you think it might be to apply situation ethics in practice? Is it always clear what the most loving thing to do might be? How might situation ethics be applied if there are different people involved who have different needs and interests? Should an ethical system be easy to apply?**

Here is an example of the kinds of ideas you might explore in formulating your analysis and evaluation:

You might think that situation ethics could be easy to apply because all you have to do is think about which outcome would bring about the most loving consequences. You do not need to know a complicated system of rules, or work out how to interpret them. On the other hand you might think that it can be difficult to know what the most loving outcome might be, for example something that seemed loving in the short term might be less loving in the long term. You might be able to think of particular real or hypothetical situations where needs and interests could conflict, such as when two very ill patients both need expensive treatment but the available money can only stretch to treating one of them. You might think that morality is always difficult and that ease should not be a consideration when finding the right thing to do, or you might think that if a system does not give a clear answer then it is not of much use.

Now use your critical and evaluative skills to explore these questions on your own.

2. Do you agree with Fletcher that the only thing which is intrinsically good is agapeic love? Might other things also be intrinsically good, such as truth, or justice, or compassion? In natural law, Aquinas gave examples of cardinal virtues which could also be considered as intrinsically good. Are they just examples of agapeic love in practice or are they separate qualities and good in their own right?

3. Fletcher suggests that situation ethics is Christian, and uses examples of Jesus' teaching and actions as recorded in the New Testament to illustrate his view. Do you think that situation ethics presents a Christian approach to morality, or do you think that Christianity takes a more rule-based approach? Is it possible to know, or to work out, what Jesus might have done in a modern situation?

4. To what extent do you think people are capable of knowing which actions are likely to bring about the most loving circumstances for somebody else? Are people generally good at predicting what the outcomes of their actions will be? How often is it possible to know what will be the best for another person?

5. Some people might criticise situation ethics on the grounds that it leaves everyone free to make individual, subjective decisions and there is no solid, absolute grounding for moral rules to bind society together. Do you think a society needs a set of absolute, fixed rules? Give reasons to support your answer.

6. Situation ethics allows the circumstances of the individual to be taken into account when making a moral decision. How far do you think it is important to consider someone's personal situation before making a judgement about morality? Should the law of the land take more account of the circumstances of individuals when judging crimes, or should the same crime receive the same punishment regardless of the situation of the individual? How would you support your answer?

7. It could be argued that placing too much emphasis on the well-being of an individual is detrimental to the well-being of society as a whole. How far would you agree with this claim?

Situation ethics would consider the personal situation of a criminal defendant when assessing their guilt and punishment

 REVIEW

Practice Exam Questions

Try these practice questions. You could:

» write plans for each of them, to practise your skills in structuring an essay

» use them for practice in writing introductions and/or conclusions

» write the whole essay, perhaps against the clock.

1. How useful is situation ethics as a guide to moral decision-making?

2. 'An action is good if it produces the most loving result.' Discuss.

Use page 9 to review your essay and make sure you have met the assessment objectives. See page 229 for a mark scheme.

RECAP

Immanuel Kant was an important German philosopher of the eighteenth century.

Kant believed that there is a universal, objective moral law that we can access and know through our reason.

Kant believed in acting morally in accordance with the good regardless of the consequences.

Duty and good will

- Kantian ethics are deontological – they focus on the idea of duty.
- Kant thought there is objective and absolute moral law. Morality is not just personal preference or invented by society.
- Moral law can be known through reason.
- Kant thought the only thing that can be called good without any qualification is the good will. Purity of motive is important for Kant – an action is good if it is done for the right reasons, but the same action is not virtuous if it is done to impress others or for some other kind of personal gain.
- Morality should not be driven by emotion. We should do the right thing because it is the right thing, not because we feel sorry for someone or loyal to them, or for any other emotional reason.
- Kant gives examples of duties, such as:

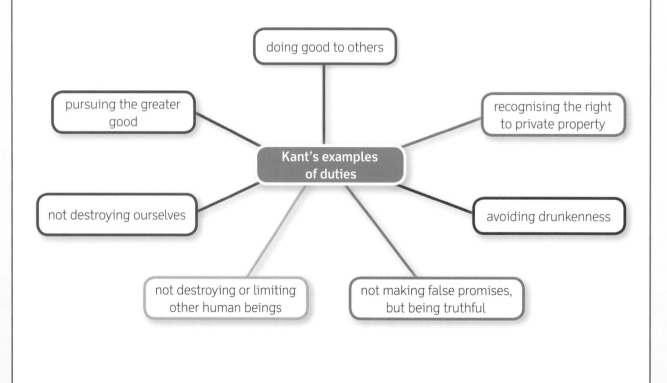

Kant's understanding of moral knowledge

Kant thought knowledge can be divided into two kinds:

> 1. Knowledge that comes from sense experience, 'a posteriori' knowledge.

> 2. Knowledge that we have at first hand, 'a priori' knowledge.

Kant thought moral knowledge is a priori:

- We do not need experience to know what is right and wrong.
- Moral knowledge comes from within.

He also thought knowledge is synthetic rather than analytic:

- We cannot tell whether something is right or wrong by looking at it. We bring additional information, from our knowledge of right and wrong.
- Because we bring additional knowledge when we are making judgements, Kant thought moral knowledge must be synthetic.

Imperatives

Kant understood moral law in terms of the hypothetical imperative and the categorical imperative.
He thought that moral law, which is good in itself, is categorical, not hypothetical.

The hypothetical imperative

'Hypothetical imperative' refers to rules we must follow if we want to achieve particular results. If I want to achieve X, then I must do Y. If I don't want to achieve X then it doesn't matter whether I do Y or not.

The categorical imperative

'Categorical imperative' refers to rules that must be followed with no 'ifs'. Moral rules are categorical imperatives. They must be followed, regardless of what we hope to achieve in the end results and regardless of our emotions or personal preferences.

Kant offers three principles or formulae in the categorical imperative:

1. **The universal law of nature** – our moral rules must be capable of being universal (they should be universalisable). They should be rules that apply to everyone at all times and in all cultures. We should not make rules where we expect to be allowed to break them when it suits us. Truth-telling is Kant's major example of this – we should always tell the truth.

2. **The end in itself** – people should not use others as a means to an end. They should treat others as people, not as tools to get what they want.

3. **The kingdom of ends** – people should act as if their behaviour is setting the laws in an ideal kingdom. Imagine we live in an ideal society of rational people. Which laws would we have to govern behaviour? Always behave as if you are following those rules.

Kant's three postulates

Kant makes three assumptions (postulates) which underpin his ethics:

1. **Freedom** – we are all free to make moral decisions. If we were not free to choose then we could not be praised or blamed for what we do as we would have no choice. We must assume we are free to do our duty.

2. **Immortality** – good people should be rewarded with ultimate happiness. This is the highest good (*summum bonum*). In this life we can see that it does not always happen that good people are rewarded with happiness. We must assume there is an afterlife in which justice is done in the end.

3. **God** – it seems that Kant assumes there must be a God to bring about the afterlife and to ensure that justice is done. Kant thought that human reason could not know God, but his ethics imply God.

Possible strengths of Kantian ethics

- Kant's ideas of moral absolutes can be appealing. Morality is not changeable depending on fashionable opinion; there are some things which are always absolutely right or wrong.

- Kant emphasises human moral reasoning, giving autonomy to people to act thoughtfully rather than blindly following commands.

- The categorical imperative as a quality of morality does not leave people wasting time wondering whether, in this circumstance, they still need to tell the truth. Rules are rules, which can make them easy to know and apply.

- Kant recognises the dignity and worth of other human beings, whatever their status in society.

Key terms

Maxims: another word for moral rules, determined by reason

Deontological: from the Latin for 'duty', ethics focused on the intrinsic rightness and wrongness of actions

Duty: duties are created by the moral law, to follow it is our duty. The word deontological means duty-based

Categorical imperative: an unconditional moral obligation that is always binding irrespective of a person's inclination or purpose

Hypothetical imperative: a moral obligation that applies only if one desires the implied goal

Kingdom of ends: an imagined future in which all people act in accordance to the moral law, the categorical imperative

Summum bonum: the highest, most supreme good

Possible weaknesses of Kantian ethics

- Kantian ethics can be seen as cold and lacking in compassion for people's individual circumstances.
- Some argue that Kant fails to recognise the importance of human emotion in moral decision-making.
- Sometimes Kant seems to be recommending sticking to rules even when it is clear that such actions will lead to terrible consequences.
- Kant does not tell us what to do when duties conflict. He does not give guidance about how to make a choice.
- Religious believers might think that Kant seems to give human reason a more important place in morality that he gives to God.

Kantian ethics can be difficult to follow in situations where there is a conflict of duty, or emotion

 APPLY

Test yourself on key knowledge (AO1)

1. Did Kant think that moral knowledge is a priori or a posteriori knowledge?

2. Which kind of knowledge did Kant think arises from sense perception?

3. What did Kant think is the only thing that can be called good without any qualification?

4. What name is given to a rule you must follow if you want to achieve particular results?

5. Why does Kant postulate (assume) human immortality?

6. Kant has three principles in the categorical imperative: the universal law of nature, the end in itself, and what else?

7. How does Kant think we can know moral laws?

8. What does Kant mean when he talks about a 'kingdom of ends'?

9. Under what circumstances did Kant think it is permissible not to tell the truth?

10. What is the name given to a system of ethics which is based on the idea of duty?

11. What does Kant mean by the term 'summum bonum'?

12. What does Kant mean when he says that a moral law must be universalisable?

> If you are unsure about any of the questions, look back over the key points on pages 82–85. You can check your answerson page 218.

Develop your skills in critical argument and evaluation (AO2)

For high marks in AO2, you need to think about the ideas in this chapter and develop your own perspective, so that you can produce critically evaluative arguments rather than just describing and presenting the views of others. At AS level, 50% of your marks are awarded for your skills in critical evaluation, and at A level, 60%.

Use the following questions to help you formulate your own views.

» Discuss them with friends, making sure you articulate your own view and listen to the views of others.

» Try writing your answers to these questions, to familiarise yourself with expressing your ideas in an academic style.

» Remember to give reasons for your views.

» Think about counter-arguments – what might someone say who held a different view from your own, and why do you think they are wrong?

1. **Supporters of Kant might say that his system of ethics is much better than more relativist systems because it gives a clear set of rules to follow, and these rules are the sort that any reasonable person could see were sensible for an ideal society. How far would you agree with this point of view? Are there counter-arguments that could be offered?**

Here is an example of the kinds of ideas you might explore in formulating your analysis and evaluation:

It could be argued that Kant's system is good because of its absolutism. People with moral dilemmas do not have to try to work out the likely consequences of their actions, or try to guess whether their actions will turn out to be loving or bring happiness. They know what to do straight away because there are rules. However, it could also be argued that sometimes human reason might object to the rules, leaving the person not sure what to do, for example truth-telling might not be at all rational in wartime if the person has a job as a spy and has been captured. It could be argued that in some cases sticking to the rules could be cruel, for example in cases where someone wants assistance to bring death more quickly. It could also be argued that sometimes duties conflict, for example a duty to turn up at work to do the job you are being paid for might conflict with a duty to care for a sick child.

Now use your critical and evaluative skills to explore these questions on your own.

2. Kant thought that the *summum bonum*, or highest good, is when people are both happy and virtuous – they are happy because they deserve to be, and their happiness is a direct result of their moral behaviour. Do you agree that this is the 'highest good'? If you were to define the best of all possible states of affairs, is this what you would also say or would you have a different vision of the *summum bonum*? Give reasons for your answer.

3. Kant thought that we have innate knowledge of morality, a priori. We know what is right and wrong. Do you agree? Do all people have the same fundamental basic rules of morality? If people 'just know' what is right and wrong, is it because human beings are made with a moral sense, or is it because the morality of society becomes imprinted on us from a young age? Give reasons for your answer.

4. For Kant, an action is only good if it is done from a good will and not for any ulterior motive. Do you think he is right? If you spend a day volunteering with vulnerable people and it makes you feel good to do this, is your volunteering less good than it would have been if you had done it only because it is the right thing to do? Does morality always depend on the motivation of the person, rather than on the action? Can you think of examples of when it does, and when it doesn't?

5. Kant thought that we should never use other people as the means to an end. Was he right? Are there times when it is acceptable to use people as a means to an end – can you give any examples? Give reasons for your answer.

6. Do you think Kant was right to say that we know what our duties are? Do we have duties? Do all people have the same duties, or do they depend on things like age, gender, wealth, culture and health? If there are absolute duties for all human beings, what do you think these duties are?

Do the motives of this volunteer matter when deciding whether his charitable acts are good?

7. Kant thought that morality should not be clouded by emotion. We should do the right thing because it is the right thing, not because of any other reason. Do you agree? Is emotion a help or a hindrance in moral decision-making? If two people need help and one of them is your own child, should you ignore your feelings of family love and loyalty, and instead obey universalisable laws? Give reasons for your answer.

REVIEW

Practice Exam Questions

Try these practice questions. You could:

» write plans for each of them, to practise your skills in structuring an essay

» use them for practice in writing introductions and/or conclusions

» write the whole essay, perhaps against the clock.

1. To what extent should ethical judgements about right and wrong be based on the extentto which duty is served?

2. 'Kantian ethics do not give enough importance to human emotions such as sympathy and compassion.' Discuss.

> Use page 9 to review your essay and make sure you have met the assessment objectives. See page 230 for a mark scheme.

Chapter 2.4 : Utilitarianism

Utilitarianism is an ethical theory that tries to create the greatest happiness for the greatest number.

It is **teleological**, focusing on the results of an action rather than the motivation of the individual.

The principle of utility

- Jeremy Bentham introduced the idea of utilitarianism. He wanted to find a way of doing ethics that did not rely on rules or the Church and that would help social reform.
- He thought that everyone desires pleasure and hopes to avoid pain.
- The principle of utility is otherwise known as the greatest happiness principle: it is a principle that says the best course of action to take is the one which maximises happiness for the greatest number of people, and minimises pain.

The hedonic calculus

- Bentham devised the hedonic calculus, or felicific calculus, as a way of measuring whether an action would bring about maximum pleasure and avoid pain.
- To calculate the pleasure or pain an action is likely to generate, there are several factors to consider:

1. **Intensity** – will it be intense pleasure, or just mild?

2. **Duration** – how long is the pleasure likely to last?

3. **Certainty or uncertainty** – will it definitely bring pleasure; how likely is it?

4. **Propinquity** – how far off (in the future) is the pleasure or pain?

5. **Fecundity** – is the pleasure likely to lead to other pleasures too?

6. **Purity** – will it bring pure pleasure or will there be some pain involved as well?

7. **Extent** – how far-reaching will the pleasure be; will it affect a lot of people?

- In his book *Utilitarianism* (1863), John Stuart Mill added to Bentham's ideas by making a distinction between 'higher pleasures' and 'base pleasures'.

- Mill says the quality of the pleasure should also be included – intellectual, aesthetic, social and spiritual pleasures.

- He said it is better to be a human being dissatisfied than a pig satisfied – we should not be content with just seeking sensual pleasure, like other animals.

- He thought that art and culture should be considered more important than pleasures such as getting drunk or gluttony.

- He thought that it could be right for an individual to sacrifice his or her own pleasure for the sake of other people.

John Stuart Mill classified cultural pleasures as higher than base pleasures such as eating cake

Act and rule utilitarianism

Utilitarianism is not a single system but has several different perspectives within it, including act and rule utilitarianism. There are also other kinds.

Act utilitarianism

- In act utilitarianism, each action is considered on its own.

- It looks at the balance of pleasure and pain that is likely to be produced by that particular action in those particular circumstances.

- There is no duty to adopt a particular approach because a different situation might involve different people with different interests.

- It avoids setting up rules. An act might bring about maximal pleasure in one set of circumstances, but the same act might bring more pain in another.

Rule utilitarianism

- In rule utilitarianism, the focus is on the 'common good' rather than on each individual action.

- It looks to create the greatest happiness for the greatest number in the long run.

- It considers what is best for society and what would happen if everyone behaved this way, as well as looking at the individual circumstances.

- Rule utilitarians recognise general rules that exist for the benefit of everyone, such as promise-keeping and truth-telling.

Possible strengths of utilitarianism

- It is flexible and allows for changes in public opinion as well as differences in individual circumstance.
- It involves reason and sensible consideration of different options.
- It does not depend on an external authority such as religion, but allows people to make their own decisions according to what they feel is best.
- It is based on practicality and on the observation that everyone wants to be happy.
- It is based on outcomes which are relatively straightforward to see and measure.
- Every individual is considered regardless of social status.

Those in the minority will always lose out to the majority following the principles of utilitarianism

Possible weaknesses of utilitarianism

- The hedonic calculus can be time-consuming and difficult to work out, and moral decisions often have to be made quickly.
- Some people argue that happiness is not a sufficient goal for ethics. Goodness and happiness are not the same.
- We are not always good at guessing what will make us happy, and it is even harder to work out what will make other people happy.
- Some people argue that the morality of an action should not be judged by its outcome but by its motivation.
- Some people criticise utilitarianism because it does not make any reference to God.
- If the greatest happiness for the greatest number is always the principle, then those who are in the minority, who are made happy by different things, lose out.

Utilitarian ethics are often used when making decisions about the best use of public money

Key terms

Principle of utility/greatest happiness: the idea that the choice that brings about the greatest happiness for the greatest number is the right choice

Hedonic calculus: the system for calculating the amount of pain or pleasure generated by an action

Consequentialism: ethical theories that see morality as driven by the consequences, rather than actions or character of those concerned

Quantitative: focused on quantity (how many, how big, etc.)

Qualitative: focused on quality (what kind of thing)

Act utilitarian: weighs up what to do at each individual occasion

Rule utilitarian: weighs up what to do in principle in all occasions of a certain kind

 APPLY

Test yourself on key knowledge (AO1)

1. What is the 'principle of utility'?

2. Who introduced utilitarianism first, Bentham or Mill?

3. What is the name given to systems of ethics that look at the outcomes of actions before deciding whether they are morally right or wrong?

4. What did Bentham think was the main motivation for human action?

5. In the hedonic calculus, what does 'propinquity' mean?

6. In the hedonic calculus, what does 'fecundity' mean?

7. What did Bentham mean when he talked about the purity of a moral action?

8. Mill added a qualitative dimension to the hedonic calculus – what does this mean?

9. What was the name of Mill's book about utilitarianism?

10. What kind of utilitarian would judge each action in its own individual circumstances?

11. How far does utilitarianism rely on taking into account the will of God?

12. Is utilitarianism relativist or absolutist as a system of ethics?

If you are unsure about any of the questions, look back over the key points on pages 88–90. You can check your answers on page 218.

Develop your skills in critical argument and evaluation (AO2)

For high marks in AO2, you need to think about the ideas in this chapter and develop your own perspective, so that you can produce critically evaluative arguments rather than just describing and presenting the views of others. At AS level, 50% of your marks are awarded for your skills in critical evaluation, and at A level, 60%.

Use the following questions to help you formulate your own views.

» Discuss them with friends, making sure you articulate your own view and listen to the views of others.

» Try writing your answers to these questions, to familiarise yourself with expressing your ideas in an academic style.

» Remember to give reasons for your views.

» Think about counter-arguments – what might someone say who held a different view from your own, and why do you think they are wrong?

1. In your view, is maximising happiness and minimising pain a suitable aim for a system of ethics? Do you think that there are other possible goals that are more important than pleasure – perhaps justice, or obedience to God, or doing right just because it is right? What do you think might be arguments for and against using happiness as a measure for morality?

Here is an example of the kinds of ideas you might explore in formulating your analysis and evaluation:

You might want to argue that happiness is a suitable goal for ethics, on the grounds that everyone wants to be happy, everyone wants their family and friends to be happy and everyone wants to live in a happy society. It could be seen as a readily achievable goal, as everyone recognises happiness when they see it, whereas people disagree about the nature of other possible goals such as justice or obedience to the will of God. On the other hand you could argue that there is a difference between goodness and happiness, and that some things which might make us happy are not necessarily good. You might think that Mill's qualification of Bentham's utilitarianism, where he considered 'higher and lower pleasures' was a useful contribution which helps to overcome this difficulty, or you might think that we need to look to some other moral goal instead. You could argue that looking at happiness as a moral goal ignores such things as developing virtues and learning to be self-controlled.

Now use your critical and evaluative skills to explore these questions on your own.

2. When deciding what to do using the greatest happiness principle, should you include only the people immediately involved in the situation, or should you also think about people who might be indirectly affected, or future generations, or other species? Give reasons for your answer.

3. How might a utilitarian go about deciding how to allocate limited funds donated to a charity, where there is more need than there is money? Do you think a utilitarian way of allocating the funds would be the right way, or is there a better way, and if so, what is it and why is it better?

4. Do you think that in general, people are good at judging what will make them happy and what will cause them pain? Are they good at it often enough for consequential happiness to be a reliable measure for judging what to do? Can you think of examples to support your point of view?

5. Do you think it is right to give everyone's wishes and interests equal consideration when making moral judgements? For example, should a criminal's future happiness be considered to be just as important as the happiness of a victim of the crime?

6. Is it always, sometimes, or never right to judge the morality of an action by its consequences, in your view? If someone meant to do something bad, but in the end the action surprisingly turned out well for everyone and caused happiness instead, does that make the action morally good? Can it be right to judge morality by outcomes in some circumstances but not others, and if so how might we know when teleological ethics are appropriate?

7. Some people argue that utilitarianism can be used to justify actions that are intrinsically immoral, such as putting pleasure-inducing drugs in public drinking water. Do you think there are any actions that are intrinsically immoral? If so, what is it that makes them immoral?

Critics of utilitarianism suggest that happiness does not always equal goodness

REVIEW

Practice Exam Questions

Try these practice questions. You could:

» write plans for each of them, to practise your skills in structuring an essay

» use them for practice in writing introductions and/or conclusions

» write the whole essay, perhaps against the clock.

1. How useful is utilitarianism as a guide to moral decision-making?

2. 'Utilitarianism fails because it is impossible to measure happiness and harm.' Discuss.

> Use page 9 to review your essay and make sure you have met the assessment objectives. See pages 230–231 for a mark scheme.

RECAP

Euthanasia comes from the Greek words for a 'good death'. It is a controversial issue raising questions of whether people should have the right to end their own lives or the lives of others at a time of their own choosing.

The sanctity of life

- People who believe in the sanctity of life believe that life is special, sacred and holy, and that it has an intrinsic worth.

- Often people who believe in the sanctity of life hold this belief for religious reasons. They might believe that life is sacred because it is a gift from God, and/or because people are made in the image of God.

- Non-religious people might believe that human life is sacred because people have reason and free will.

- Some people believe that all life is sacred, not only human life.

- The Bible can be used to support the view that human life has sanctity, for example: 'So God created mankind in his own image' (Genesis 1:27, New International Version).

- The Bible can also be used to question ideas about the sanctity of life, for example on different occasions when God commands war.

- The idea that life is sacred can be used as an argument against euthanasia, on the grounds that no one has the right to take away human life.

- The 'slippery slope' argument can be used in the context of the sanctity of life, saying that once life is considered to be less than sacred in some cases, it undermines all human dignity and allows people to be treated as disposable.

- It can be argued that the sanctity of life is not an unbreakable moral rule but that it can sometimes be moral to take life, for example killing someone who is murderously aggressive in order to save many others, or sacrificing one's own life in order to save others.

Some people argue the sanctity of life argument extends beyond humans to all animals

Quality of life

- Ideas about quality of life are often introduced into debates about euthanasia, sometimes as a counter-argument to 'sanctity of life' beliefs.

- The concept of quality of life involves considering how much enjoyment and fulfilment a person is getting given their state of physical and mental health. It includes looking to the future and the prognosis for their condition.

- Discussions about quality of life consider whether the life is worth living, or whether bringing about death would be preferable.

- Some people argue that if someone has a debilitating or painful terminal condition then they should not be compelled to live until they die naturally.

- Quality of life is commonly considered in cases of animal welfare, where it is considered by many to be cruel not to euthanise a suffering animal.

Personhood

- Issues of personhood involve the question of what makes a living thing a 'person'. The issue is important because if a living thing is not a person, perhaps it does not have the same rights, including the right to life, as persons do.

- Some argue that in order to be a person, there must be awareness of self and others, and ability to interact with the world.

- Others argue that in order to be a person, the only thing necessary is to be human.

- Others argue that other species as well as human beings should be considered as persons, or that personhood is a sliding scale rather than a strict either/or distinction.

- Personhood is usually linked to capacities and functions. This raises issues about whether a foetus is a person, whether someone with severe brain-damage or lack of brain development is a person, and whether higher-functioning animals such as primates might be persons.

- The question of potential is also an issue of personhood, raising discussion of whether a living thing should be accorded dignity and rights because of what it has the potential to become, or conversely, whether rights should be withdrawn if there is clearly no potential for higher-level function.

Voluntary euthanasia

- The ancient Greek Hippocratic oath, which still informs medical standards for today, obliges doctors to do good and avoid evil.

- Voluntary euthanasia is when a patient's life is ended at their own request. It is illegal in the UK but legal in some other countries.

- It is often the focus for legal challenges when people in very difficult circumstances challenge the law and ask that someone should be allowed to help them to die without fear of prosecution.

- Jonathan Glover discusses the issues in his book *Causing Death and Saving Lives* (1977).

- A key argument in favour of voluntary euthanasia is that people should have the right to avoid pain and should be able to choose a gentle, painless death as long as the decision is made rationally.

- Some people argue in favour of voluntary euthanasia because suicide is an option for able-bodied people and it is discriminatory not to allow it for disabled people.

- Some argue against voluntary euthanasia because the person might change their mind when they are no longer able to communicate.

The Hippocratic oath has informed the ethical responsibilities of doctors for centuries

- Some argue that allowing voluntary euthanasia will encourage unscrupulous people to put pressure on sick relatives to end their lives when this was not what they wanted.

- The 'slippery slope' argument is the view that if something is allowed in exceptional circumstances, it begins a process which becomes impossible to stop and the situation will get out of hand.

- Some also argue that it puts doctors and other health professionals in an impossible position.

Non-voluntary euthanasia

- This is when there is euthanasia without the request of the patient.
- It could happen in cases of severe brain-damage, or when a baby is born with multiple problems, or when someone is incapable of communication.
- Debates arise when there are cases of people who cannot communicate and who seem to be permanently incapable of functioning in ways that might give them an acceptable quality of life.
- Medical science has progressed to the extent that people with severe loss of brain function can be kept alive artificially for a long time.
- Some people write 'living wills' to clarify their wishes if they should become brain-damaged and incapable of communicating.
- Some argue that non-voluntary euthanasia is the most compassionate course of action when there is no prospect of the patient having an acceptable standard of brain function.
- Others argue that it is not for us to decide what is an acceptable standard of brain function; that is a decision that should be left to God.
- Some who oppose non-voluntary euthanasia argue that there is never a point where medical professionals can be totally certain that there is no hope of improvement.
- A distinction is often made between deliberate active euthanasia (doing something to bring about a death) and a non-treatment decision: i.e. the removal of 'extraordinary' treatment (such as performing a surgical operation that has very little chance of success). However, people do not agree about what kinds of treatment might be considered 'extraordinary'.

Applying ethical theories to euthanasia

Natural law

- In natural law ethics, an action is morally good if it accords with eternal law, divine law, natural law and human law.
- There is a primary precept to do good and avoid evil, and a primary precept to preserve life.
- Human life is considered to be a sacred gift from God. Divine law teaches in the Bible that God creates each individual person in his own image.
- Natural law ethics have been very influential on Catholic teaching, which says that euthanasia is wrong. It contravenes the precept of preserving life.
- Euthanasia is an apparent good – it seems to offer a good outcome, but it is not a real good.
- Natural law ethics are absolutist; they do not make exceptions for different circumstances or different likely outcomes.
- There is no obligation under natural law for people to go to great lengths to keep someone

Key terms

Sanctity of life: the idea that life is intrinsically sacred or has such worth that it is not considered within the power of a human being

Quality of life: a way of judging the extrinsic experience of life, that affects or justifies whether or not it is worth continuing life

Personhood: the quality of human life that makes it worthy – usually linked to certain |higher capacities

Voluntary euthanasia: when a person's life is ended painlessly by a third party at the person's own request

alive when the treatment offered is 'burdensome' and not meaningful.

- The doctrine of double effect could be used in end-of-life care, where the treatment offered to relieve someone's pain might have the double effect of shortening life. The intention would not be to kill, but to relieve pain, and therefore this would not be wrong.
- It could be argued that if the patient is so debilitated that they lack all the higher functions, such as reason, associated with personhood, then the rules about how persons should be treated might not apply.

Possible advantages and disadvantages of a natural law approach to euthanasia

- It gives clear guidance; there is no doubt about what to do and what not to do.
- It respects religious beliefs about the sanctity of life.
- It does not leave people vulnerable to unscrupulous relatives who might wish to benefit from their deaths.
- It avoids a 'slippery slope' where human dignity becomes less important over time.

- It could be seen as unsympathetic to people in great pain or with no quality of life.
- Medical advances make it difficult to judge whether some kinds of treatment should be regarded as burdensome or extraordinary. Life support, for example, is both common and extraordinary, as are many resuscitation techniques.

Key terms

Non-voluntary euthanasia: when a person is unable to express their wish to die but there are reasonable grounds for ending their life painlessly, for example if a person is in extreme pain

Involuntary euthanasia: where a person is killed against their wishes, for example when disabled people were killed by Nazi doctors

Active euthanasia: a deliberate action performed by a third party to kill a person, for example by lethal injection. Active euthanasia is illegal in the UK

Non-treatment decision: the decision medical professionals make to withhold or withdraw medical treatment or life support that is keeping the person alive because they are not going to get better, or because the person asks them to. Controversially it is also called passive euthanasia.

Situation ethics

- Fletcher, the leading advocate of situation ethics who wrote the book *Situation Ethics*, was in favour of legalised euthanasia. He became president of the Euthanasia Society of America.
- Situation ethics rejects absolute rules, and so it rejects an absolute ban on euthanasia.
- Fletcher thought that the ethical thing to do was to take account of each individual's personal situation.
- Situation ethics advocates applying the 'rule of love'. The ethical thing to do is whatever will bring about the most loving consequences. Euthanasia can be justified if it will bring about the most loving outcome for the patient and their friends and family.
- Fletcher thought the quality of life was more important than the sanctity of life. He thought life was not worth living if the patient did not have some basic functions, such as a minimal intelligence, self-awareness and ability to judge the passage of time.

Possible advantages and disadvantages of a situation ethics approach to euthanasia

- It could be seen as far more compassionate in individual situations than a blanket ban on euthanasia, recognising that many people would like to have this option available to them.
- It could be seen as less discriminatory towards disabled people.
- It places greater emphasis on human autonomy.
- It could be criticised as not giving recognition to the sacred nature of human life.
- The most loving course of action is not always easy to identify.
- Allowing euthanasia on a case-by-case basis makes legislation difficult.
- Legalising euthanasia might create a 'slippery slope' where people are euthanised when it might not be what they really wanted or they might have had a chance of recovery.

 **APPLY**

Test yourself on key knowledge (AO1)

1. What is the difference between non-voluntary euthanasia and involuntary euthanasia?

2. Why might some people think that it is acceptable to euthanise a dog but not a grandparent?

3. Who wrote the book *Causing Death and Saving Lives*?

4. How might followers of natural law apply the principle of double effect when making decisions about euthanasia?

5. What is a 'slippery slope' argument?

6. Why might some people think that making euthanasia illegal discriminates against disabled people?

7. Who wrote the book *Situation Ethics*?

8. What is the name for unconditional love that is at the centre of a situation ethics approach?

9. Which primary precepts of natural law are seen as inconsistent with allowing euthanasia?

10. What does the expression 'sanctity of life' mean?

11. Which medieval thinker was a profound influence on natural law ethics?

12. What does it mean to call euthanasia an 'apparent good'?

> If you are unsure about any of the questions, look back over the key points on pages 94–97. You can check your answers on page 218.

Develop your skills in critical argument and evaluation (AO2)

For high marks in AO2, you need to think about the ideas in this chapter and develop your own perspective, so that you can produce critically evaluative arguments rather than just describing and presenting the views of others. At AS level, 50% of your marks are awarded for your skills in critical evaluation, and at A level, 60%.

Use the following questions to help you formulate your own views.

» Discuss them with friends, making sure you articulate your own view and listen to the views of others.

» Try writing your answers to these questions, to familiarise yourself with expressing your ideas in an academic style.

» Remember to give reasons for your views.

» Think about counter-arguments – what might someone say who held a different view from your own, and why do you think they are wrong?

1. **Do you agree with the idea that human life has sanctity? Do you think there is something special and sacred about human life which makes it intrinsically worth preserving? If euthanasia is appropriate for an elderly dog with a terminal condition, should it also be appropriate for an elderly human, or are the two cases entirely different? Give reasons for your answer.**

Here is an example of the kinds of ideas you might explore in formulating your analysis and evaluation:

You might want to argue that there is something intrinsically precious about human life. Perhaps you hold a religious point of view and think that human life is a gift from God; you might believe that people are made in the image of God and that only God has the right to give and end life. You might believe that human beings are set apart from other species, or you might want to argue that all life is sacred, whether human or animal. Perhaps you think that human life has a special intrinsic worth without wanting to use the religious vocabulary of sanctity. Alternatively, you could argue that the autonomy to choose the time and manner of one's own death adds to human dignity rather than undermines it. You might want to argue that part of the respect that should be shown for people involves minimising suffering and allowing people to choose to avoid the indignity of total dependence on others or insufferable pain.

Now use your critical and evaluative skills to explore these questions on your own.

2. How convincing do you find the 'slippery slope' argum ent as a reason for not allowing euthanasia? Is it true that if euthanasia is allowed in extreme cases (perhaps where an individual who is clearly rational and has a terminal illness requests the right to die) then it will escalate uncontrollably so that euthanasia becomes the norm? Is the 'slippery slope' argument the best argument against euthanasia or are other arguments stronger?

3. Some people who are in favour of legalised voluntary euthanasia argue that personal autonomy and freedom to choose are more important than sanctity of life. What arguments might they present to support their point of view? What counter-arguments might be offered by their opponents? Which side of the debate do you find more convincing?

4. How persuasive do you find a natural law approach to issues of euthanasia? Is euthanasia an issue that requires absolute, rule-based ethics? Is it fair to say that a natural law approach to euthanasia lacks compassion for people in very difficult circumstances?

5. It could be argued that natural law ethics were devised for a time when medical practices were very different, and the options for saving or ending lives were very limited. Does the fact that natural law ethics date back a long way make them less relevant for the modern world? How easy is it to apply the thinking of Aquinas to twenty-first century decision-making?

6. How persuasive do you find a situation ethics approach to issues of euthanasia? Are questions of euthanasia best considered in terms of the outcome? How easy would it be to determine the most loving course of action in situations where the patients cannot speak for themselves? What should a situation ethicist do if the wishes of the patient are not the same as the wishes of the family?

7. On balance, do you think a deontological or a teleological approach is better for reaching moral decisions about euthanasia? Give reasons for your answer.

8. To what extent should a person have the right to decide when their life ends, in your view? If someone wishes to end their life with the aid of euthanasia, should other peoples' wishes be taken into account? If someone is in terrible pain, or faced with losing their ability to do anything for themselves, are they still capable of making a free rational decision, in your view?

9. Do you think there is a genuine difference between acting to end a life, and deciding not to act to save a life? Give reasons and examples to explain and support your point of view.

REVIEW

Practice Exam Questions

Try these practice questions. You could:

» write plans for each of them, to practise your skills in structuring an essay
» use them for practice in writing introductions and/or conclusions
» write the whole essay, perhaps against the clock.

1. 'Natural law provides excellent moral guidance for people making decisions about euthanasia.' Discuss.

2. How convincing is the claim that decisions about euthanasia should be made according to the principles of situation ethics?

> Use page 9 to review your essay and make sure you have met the assessment objectives. See pages 231–232 for a mark scheme.

Chapter 2.6 : Business ethics

Business ethics is an area of ethics that considers the duties and responsibilities a business has to its workers, its customers and other members of society.

Corporate social responsibility

- This is the concept that corporations (businesses) should be accountable for their actions and the impacts they have.

- Businesses have responsibilities to their shareholders. The shareholders are people who invest in the business and trust the managers of the business to use their money wisely and make a profit for them.

- Businesses also have responsibilities to their employees, for example providing them with safe working conditions and recruiting in a fair way.

- Milton Friedman argued that the only responsibility businesses have is to make a profit for the shareholders.

- Others argue that a business also has duties and responsibilities towards the community in which it operates, for example by trying to limit its negative effects on the environment. Anyone who is affected by the operation of a business is a stakeholder.

- Businesses risk damage to their reputations if they do things which have a negative effect on their stakeholders, such as being too noisy or creating litter.

- Many businesses find that the interests of their stakeholders and shareholders conflict. This causes problems.

- Businesses often try to enhance their ethical reputation by contributing to the community in a public way, such as giving surplus food to food banks or sponsoring local charity events.

For Kantians, an action is only truly good if it comes from a good will and not from anything else. So companies that sponsor charitable events or contribute to the community in other ways in order to promote their own reputations would not be considered particularly ethical. Similarly, if the reason for them caring about pollution or noise, or the safety of their workers, is primarily concern for their own reputation so that they make a profit, then a Kantian would not think this is good. A business should, according to Kant, act responsibly solely because this is the right thing to do.

The utilitarian would need to weigh up the potential pleasure and pain that corporate social responsibility might generate. Different people's interests would need to be considered in an attempt to calculate whether pleasure will outweigh pain. The utilitarian would probably decide that it was in a business' best interests to act responsibly, as in most cases it would be more likely to produce pleasure for the maximum number of people. However, if there were cases when acting irresponsibly would provide a greater amount of pleasure than pain, then the utilitarian should support acting irresponsibly.

After criticism about the amount of unsold food going to waste, Tesco began coordinating with FareShare, who redistribute in-date good quality food to charities and community groups who then turn it into nutritious meals for vulnerable people in need

Whistle-blowing

- This is when an employee of a business decides to make public their belief that the business is acting unethically.
- People tend to 'whistle-blow' when they think that the normal complaints procedure within the business will not remedy the situation or they will be punished for bringing up the problem.
- Whistle-blowers might go to some other authority such as the police, or might go to the press. They might express their concerns anonymously.
- Sometimes the whistle-blowers themselves are considered to be acting unethically, for example when they bring the business into disrepute and could have handled the problem more discreetly, or when they present only one side of the story.

For a follower of Kantian ethics, issues surrounding whistle-blowing could present difficulties. On the one hand, there is a duty to tell the truth, and to be honest and fair in dealing with customers, which could support whistle-blowing. On the other hand, there is a duty of loyalty and promise-keeping to shareholders and to the company itself as well as to colleagues. The Kantian would have to decide which duties outweighed which others; this could be difficult.

The utilitarian would have to weigh up whether whistle-blowing was likely to maximise pleasure or not. Perhaps in the long term, for the larger number of people, whistle-blowing would be a good idea, if the company needed a wake-up call about its ethics or its safety measures. Perhaps whistle-blowing might bring about the end of the company, causing job losses and financial losses for shareholders; although there are potential benefits if other companies learn a lesson from this. Act utilitarians would consider each situation on its own, whereas rule utilitarians would think about whether whistle-blowing in general, as a rule, was a good idea. The utilitarian would have to try to anticipate what long-term effects might be and which people might be affected; this could be difficult.

Good ethics is good business

- 'Good ethics is good business' is a slogan that claims doing the right thing will make a business more attractive and increase its profits because customers will like and trust it.

- It can also be interpreted to mean that doing the right thing is as appropriate in business as it is anywhere else.

- It can also be interpreted to mean that when businesses seem to be acting ethically, they are only doing it to increase their profits.

- Good ethics can be difficult for businesses, because sometimes an action that is beneficial for one group of people can have completely the opposite effect on others – for example, keeping milk prices low in the shops is beneficial for the customer but harmful for the dairy farmer.

- Sometimes good ethical practices make it difficult for a business to succeed alongside its competitors. For example, if it pays its factory workers a decent living wage, it might have to charge more for its products, but if the prices are too high then customers might shop with competitors instead.

Some companies such as The Co-operative have well-publicised ethical policies for how they operate their businesses

- It is often difficult to know how 'good ethics' will affect people in the long term.

- Some people think that a compromise position is the only practical one, where ethical expertise is brought in for the big, important decisions only.

A Kantian approach to 'good ethics is good business' would be to say that businesses, like individuals, should do the right thing just because it is the right thing, and concerns about profit or competition should be treated as irrelevant. However, this is difficult or even impossible for companies if they want to survive in a competitive, capitalist market. Trying not to treat people as a means to an end is a difficult principle to apply in business, because employees and suppliers and customers are all 'used' as part of the process of making a profit. However, some would argue that Kantian ethics might be attractive for business because there are clear rules that apply universally to everyone.

A utilitarian approach to 'good ethics is good business' might be easier to fit. Andrew Crane and Dirk Matten argue in *Business Ethics: A European Perspective* (2004) that there are close links between a utilitarian approach and the approach of economics, because decisions are based on whichever outcome is likely to produce the most beneficial results. However, it could be argued that the greatest happiness for a large group of people whose interests sometimes conflict can be impossible to judge.

Globalisation

- Globalisation is about the integration of business, economics, industry and culture between different countries across the world.

- With increased sophistication in communication and transport, people no longer need to do business entirely within their own geographical region. Companies might have producers in one country and customers in another. The range of people affected by what a business does is much wider than it used to be.

- Globalisation creates issues for business ethics because it is more profitable for businesses to hire workers in countries where wages are lower and health and safety requirements are fewer. Companies that employ workers in developing countries might help those people by providing employment and sometimes other benefits such as training, but they also might disadvantage them. For example, traditional occupations in developing countries might die out, or workers might be in unsafe conditions.

- Sometimes people in more developed countries put pressure on businesses to improve the conditions of workers in less developed countries.

- The collapse of the Rana Plaza factory building in Bangladesh is an example of when globalisation caused great harm to workers, but was also important in bringing about benefits once pressure was put on global companies.

Kantian ethics might help businesses to adopt some absolute guidelines for ensuring the well-being of workers around the world. In *Business Ethics: A Kantian Perspective* (1999), Norman Bowie suggests rules for business a Kantian might adopt, such as protecting the autonomy and rationality of every worker, providing a salary sufficient for independent living and operating according to the rules of justice. However, Kantian ethics might also be difficult to apply because businesses have to treat workers at least partially as a means to an end, and there are often situations in business where duties conflict.

Utilitarian ethics might argue that on a large scale, the good that is done to developing countries from globalisation greatly outweighs the harm. Everyone benefits when goods can be produced cheaply enough for most people to be able to buy them, and everyone benefits when people are employed and paid a wage. However, it could be argued that the rich gain a lot more than the poor through globalisation, and although the overall 'greatest happiness' might be achieved, the poorest people lose out and are exploited.

Key terms

Corporate social responsibility: a sense that businesses have wider responsibilities than simply to their shareholders, including the communities they live and work in and to the environment

Shareholder: a person who has invested money in a business in return for a share of the profits

Stakeholder: a person who is affected by or involved in some form of relationship with a business

Whistle-blowing: when an employee discloses wrongdoing to the employer or the public

Capitalism: an economic system based on the private ownership of how things are made and sold, in which businesses compete freely with each other to make profits

Globalisation: the integration of economies, industries, markets, cultures and policymaking around the world

Consumerism: a set of social beliefs that put a high value on acquiring material things

 **APPLY**

Test yourself on key knowledge (AO1)

1. What does it mean to be a 'shareholder' of a business?

2. What does the term 'stakeholder' mean in the context of business?

3. Which ethical system advocates doing your duty just because it is the right thing?

4. Give an example of an issue where an employee might resort to 'whistle-blowing'.

5. What is the name given to the idea that businesses should care about the impact they have on society?

6. How might 'consumerism' be defined?

7. Which ethical system advocates calculating the greatest happiness for the greatest number in each situation and making a decision based on that?

8. Which ethical system advocates having some general principles to use to enable achieving the greatest happiness for the greatest number?

9. Who wrote a book in 2004 called *Business Ethics: A European Perspective*?

10. Which economist claimed that the only duty a business has is to increase its profits for its shareholders?

11. What is the name of the economic system that allows free competition and private ownership of the means of production?

12. What is meant by the term 'corporate social responsibility'?

> If you are unsure about any of the questions, look back over the key points on pages 100–103. You can check your answers on page 218.

Develop your skills in critical argument and evaluation (AO2)

For high marks in AO2, you need to think about the ideas in this chapter and develop your own perspective, so that you can produce critically evaluative arguments rather than just describing and presenting the views of others. At AS level, 50% of your marks are awarded for your skills in critical evaluation, and at A level, 60%.

Use the following questions to help you formulate your own views.

» Discuss them with friends, making sure you articulate your own view and listen to the views of others.

» Try writing your answers to these questions, to familiarise yourself with expressing your ideas in an academic style.

» Remember to give reasons for your views.

» Think about counter-arguments – what might someone say who held a different view from your own, and why do you think they are wrong?

1. **Should a business be considered to be a 'moral agent', or do ethics only apply to individuals? What reasons and arguments might you give to support your answer?**

Here is an example of the kinds of ideas you might explore in formulating your analysis and evaluation:

You might want to argue that moral responsibility is something that is just for individuals, and that a business does not have a mind of its own with which to make moral decisions. You might also question whether a business has the same kind of freedom to make moral choices as private individuals do, given that businesses involve shareholders and have stakeholders to consider; they have little of the freedom of choice that is essential for moral

responsibility. On the other hand you could argue that a business is still made up of human minds working together, voting on decisions and making policies together and that it does have moral responsibility. You could argue that those in charge of a business are those who bear the burden of responsibility for ethical decisions, although you might want to argue that everyone who works for a company shares the responsibility for the decisions it makes.

Now use your critical and evaluative skills to explore these questions on your own.

2. Do you think that whistle-blowing is a practice that should be encouraged by businesses, or should it be discouraged? Should employees consider loyalty to their employers a moral duty? Are there ways in which an employee who wanted to act ethically could tell the truth and be loyal at the same time? Some people might argue that a Kantian approach to whistle-blowing is totally impractical – how far would you agree, and what reasons might you give to support your view?

3. Is Friedman right to argue that a business should concern itself only with making a profit? What reasoning might you present to support your argument?

Edward Snowden worked for the National Security Agency (NSA) in the USA and became a controversial whistle-blower in 2013

4. Which do you think would be better to use for ethical decision-making in the context of business: act utilitarianism, or rule utilitarianism? Or neither? Or do different ethics work better in different situations, for example does whistle-blowing require different ethics from corporate social responsibility? Give reasons for your answer.

5. Some people argue that Kantian ethics are impossible to apply in the context of business because businesses always treat their customers, producers and workers primarily as a means to an

end – that is just the nature of business. What do you think of this view? Do you think it could be possible and practical to adopt a Kantian method of moral decision-making in the workplace? Give reasons for your answer.

6. If a company offers financial support and sponsorship to a 'good cause' in order to raise its own profile and maximise its profits, does that financial support still count as a morally good action? Would it only be good if the company gave its support anonymously? Give reasons for your answer.

Practice Exam Questions

Try these practice questions. You could:

» write plans for each of them, to practise your skills in structuring an essay
» use them for practice in writing introductions and/or conclusions
» write the whole essay, perhaps against the clock.

1. 'Globalisation makes it impossible for businesses to act ethically.' Discuss.
2. 'Utilitarianism is the most practical way to deal with issues of business ethics.' Discuss.

> Use page 9 to review your essay and make sure you have met the assessment objectives. See pages 232–233 for a mark scheme.

Chapter 2.7 : Meta-ethical theories

 RECAP

Meta-ethics is not about how we should behave (that is normative ethics) but is about the **status** of ethical statements and claims.

Discussions about meta-ethics are discussions about what we mean when we call something good or bad, right or wrong. Meta-ethical debates are **debates about language**.

Absolutism and relativism

- Absolutists hold that there are fixed, unchanging truths about right and wrong.
- Relativists hold that morals are flexible and are not absolute. Right and wrong depend on what is right for the individual and society and the particular circumstances.

Naturalism

- Ethical naturalists are absolutists. They believe that right and wrong are fixed features of the universe.
- They believe that there are facts about right and wrong. Morals are not about different points of view, tastes and opinions, but are about facts of the natural world.
- Morals are not merely invented by human beings. If everyone in the world thinks that a particular course of action is morally good, they could all be wrong and in fact it could be bad.
- Ethical naturalism holds that we can tell what is right and wrong by looking at the world around us and using our reason. Morality is a feature of the universe that we can perceive.
- Aquinas was an ethical naturalist. He thought that we could use our reason and our powers of observation to access the facts about what is moral and immoral. Aquinas was a theological naturalist because he thought that goodness comes from the will of God.
- Many normative ethical systems (such as utilitarianism, situation ethics or Kantian ethics) have elements of naturalism in them. For example, they might claim as a fact that happiness is a good thing, or that agape love is an important goal.

Philippa Foot argues that we can observe virtue in people's behaviour

- F.H. Bradley and Philippa Foot are examples of more modern, leading ethical naturalists.
- Philippa Foot defended ethical naturalism by saying that we can observe morality when we see people's behaviour. We call someone a 'good person' or an 'honest person' because of our observations. Virtues can be recognised. Just as we can see in the natural world whether an animal is an excellent example of its kind or is defective, we can also see excellence or defectiveness in the moral character of people.

Possible criticisms of naturalism

- Empiricists (those who believe that truth can be found through observing through our senses) criticise naturalism on the grounds that right and wrong cannot be experienced with the senses. We can see that hitting someone makes them unhappy, but we cannot see that making someone unhappy is wrong. Morality is not observable empirically, they argue.

- In *A Treatise of Human Nature*, Hume argued that moral judgements are like judgements about heat or sound or colour or temperature. He said they come from perceptions and arise in the human mind, they are not facts that exist by themselves.

- Hume argued that we can see what there is, but we cannot see, as a result, what we ought to do. He argued there is no justification for moving from what is to what ought to be. This is often called 'Hume's Law' – 'you cannot derive an "ought" from an "is"'.

Intuitionism

- Intuitionism is usually associated with the philosopher G.E. Moore.

- Moore wrote about the naturalistic fallacy. He argued that it is a mistake to try to define good in terms of something else. So if we say something is good because it produces the greatest happiness for the greatest number, then we are defining good as something else: maximal happiness. Moore thought good cannot be equated with something else; it is not the same.

- For Moore, goodness is a 'simple notion'. Good is just good, and that's all.

- Moore compared good with 'yellow' – yellow can't be defined, or equated with something else, it just is yellow, and we know it when we see it.

- We know good when we see examples of it, by intuition, in the same way that we know beauty when we see it but have trouble defining it.

- H.A. Prichard argued that it is a mistake to try to find reasoned arguments to support what we feel our moral obligations to be. He thought that duty is not the same as the good thing to do, but goes beyond it – we might know by intuition what is the good thing to do, but the idea that we have a moral duty to do that good thing is adding something extra.

- Prichard thought that we know by intuition which of our moral obligations are more important than others.

- W.D. Ross was Prichard's student and also thought that goodness could not be defined by making reference to other things. He developed intuitionism by introducing the idea of prima facie duties – duties which seem the obvious course of action to take at first sight, when faced with a moral problem. These are followed unless there is an even more compelling duty which overrides it.

- Ross listed seven prima facie duties, but he did not think the list was complete:

1. Promise-keeping
2. Repairing harm done
3. Gratitude
4. Justice
5. Beneficence
6. Self-improvement
7. Non-maleficence

Possible criticisms of intuitionism

- If we know what goodness is just by intuition and it is impossible to define, then it becomes impossible to resolve disagreements about what is right and wrong or good and bad. People might have different intuitions about what is good.

- It can be argued that intuition is not a faculty in itself but is the same thing as human reason. Intuition might be the way reason works when it needs to take a shortcut. If intuition is just short-cut reasoning then we might be expected to support our intuitions with some reasoned justification.

- Many people challenge the idea that we 'just know' whether something is right or wrong, by pointing out the fact that people can 'just know' moral rules which differ widely. For example, some people 'just know' that abortion is always wrong, and others 'just know' that in some circumstances it would be wrong to expect a woman to carry a pregnancy to full term against her will.

Emotivism

- Emotivists hold that ethics arise as the result of our emotional responses.
- Emotivism is an ethical non-naturalist position, because unlike naturalism, emotivism holds that there are no facts about right and wrong.
- According to emotivism, when we say things like 'stealing is wrong' we mean that stealing evokes in us emotions of disapproval. When we say 'helping others is good' we mean that helping others gives us good feelings.
- Emotivism is sometimes known as the 'hurrah/boo' theory because our statements about what is good and bad, right and wrong are seen as expressions of our feelings, not as reference to any actual facts.
- A.J. Ayer was a leading emotivist. He held that statements such as 'stealing is wrong' cannot be about meaningful facts because they cannot be tested using the five senses. In Ayer's view, a statement is only meaningful if it can be empirically tested, and ethical statements cannot be. Therefore ethical statements must be about something other than facts. Ayer thought ethical statements were about emotion.
- C.L. Stevenson developed Ayer's thinking, saying that moral language has an emotive element and also a 'prescriptive' element. When I say 'stealing is wrong', I mean, 'I dislike stealing and I encourage you to dislike it too'.

Possible criticisms of emotivism

- Emotivism challenges the idea that there is any such thing as good and bad beyond our personal preferences and tastes. This seems counter-intuitive to many people when faced with terrible crimes or acts of great heroism or generosity. Statements such as 'genocide is evil' or 'the Gates family have done good things in helping to eradicate malaria' seem to many people to be far more than just 'I happen to dislike genocide' and 'my personal preference is for saving lives'.
- If emotivism is accepted then there is no compelling reason for people to act morally. If an ambulance driver happens not to have a preference for doing her job properly and responding to an emergency call, there is no 'bigger' reason why she should.

MacIntyre's criticisms of emotivism

Alasdair MacIntyre criticises emotivism for several reasons:

1. Emotivists confuse meaning with use – for MacIntyre, what is important about moral language is the significance it has for those who use it.

2. Stevenson presents the idea of an unpleasant world where people are trying to force their beliefs on each other – MacIntye does not think that moral language and behaviour works like this.

3. Emotivism is no help to us in making a distinction between morality and feelings about other things, such as our tastes in music or food.

Alasdair MacIntyre is a critic of emotivism

Key terms

Naturalism: ethical theories that hold that morals are part of the natural world and can be recognised or observed in some way

Hume's Law: you cannot go from an 'is' (a statement of fact) to an 'ought' (a moral)

Intuitionism: ethical theories that hold that moral knowledge is received in a different way from science and logic

Naturalistic fallacy: G.E. Moore's argument that it is a mistake to define moral terms with reference to other properties (a mistake to break Hume's law)

Emotivism: ethical theories that hold that moral statements are not statements of fact but are either beliefs or emotions

APPLY

Test yourself on key knowledge (AO1)

1. What is meant by the term 'naturalistic fallacy'?

2. Who developed Ayer's emotivism by saying that when we make moral statements, we are expressing our feelings and recommending them to others?

3. What is 'Hume's Law'?

4. What is the name of the book in which Hume explained his views about moral statements?

5. What is meant by moral 'absolutism'?

6. Was Aquinas a moral absolutist?

7. What is the name given to the belief that morality is flexible rather than fixed as a natural law?

8. What is an empiricist?

9. Why did Ayer think that ethical statements cannot be about facts?

10. Who criticised Stevenson, saying that moral statements are not just about people trying to force their beliefs on each other?

11. Who argued that we know by intuition which of our moral obligations are more important than others?

12. What is meant by a 'prima facie duty'?

> If you are unsure about any of the questions, look back over the key points on pages 106–109. You can check your answers on page 218.

Develop your skills in critical argument and evaluation (AO2)

For high marks in AO2, you need to think about the ideas in this chapter and develop your own perspective, so that you can produce critically evaluative arguments rather than just describing and presenting the views of others. At AS level, 50% of your marks are awarded for your skills in critical evaluation, and at A level, 60%.

Use the following questions to help you formulate your own views.

» Discuss them with friends, making sure you articulate your own view and listen to the views of others.

» Try writing your answers to these questions, to familiarise yourself with expressing your ideas in an academic style.

» Remember to give reasons for your views.

» Think about counter-arguments – what might someone say who held a different view from your own, and why do you think they are wrong?

1. Hume argued that we cannot derive an 'ought' from an 'is'. So for example, in the modern world we might see that children from a particular ethnic background perform worse in schools at GCSE than any other ethnic group. Some people then use these statistics to make a judgement: 'therefore we ought to put more money into helping children from this ethnic background' or 'therefore we ought not to waste money on trying to educate these children'. Do you think it is possible to work out what we ought to do, using the facts we can perceive and measure? If it is not possible, then how else might we work out what we ought to do?

Here is an example of the kinds of ideas you might explore in formulating your analysis and evaluation:

You might want to argue, along with naturalists, that it is possible to derive an ought from an is. Possibly you think that we can observe right and wrong in the world and recognise it when we see it, and that there is not a problem with seeing someone drowning and knowing that we ought to do something to help. You could make references to naturalist thinkers and give some examples to illustrate your points. On the other hand you might agree with Foot that there are qualities and characteristics in human behaviour which enable us to see and judge good and bad. You might, however, agree with Hume and argue that the natural world does not show us what we ought to do, it only shows us what there is. Possibly you think that there are absolute rights and wrongs but we have no way of knowing what they are, or possibly you think that there are no absolute rights and wrongs and that morality is flexible depending on the circumstances.

Now use your critical and evaluative skills to explore these questions on your own.

2. Do you think ethical statements are about facts? Is 'stealing is wrong' the same kind of statement as 'Canterbury is in Kent'? Or is it a statement about your own personal opinion, or about the rules society has invented for itself, or a statement about emotional responses to stealing, or something else? How would you justify your opinion, if this is even possible?

3. Moore and others claim that we know what goodness is by intuition, and that it cannot be defined. Do you think they are right? If you were trying to explain to someone what we mean by 'good' in a moral sense, would you be able to do it? Is it impossible, or just difficult, or perhaps even straightforward?

4. Do you think we all have the same intuitions about what is 'good'? When we recognise something as 'good', do we all agree? If there are differences in our opinions about what goodness is, how might we account for these differences, and is there any way of telling who (if anyone) has the right intuition?

5. Foot argued that we can observe morality. She thought we could see by observing someone's behaviour whether or not they are a good person. Do you agree? What arguments and examples could you use to defend your position?

6. Ayer thought that ethical statements sound as though they are about facts but really they are just expressions of our emotions about things; when we say something is right or wrong, we are just expressing our own likes and dislikes. Do you think he is right? What might be the implications of emotivism for practical ethical issues such as medical ethics or crime and punishment? What reasoning could you present to support your opinion?

7. Stevenson argued that when we make ethical judgements, we are both expressing our feelings and recommending that others do what we would do. MacIntyre, however, criticises Stevenson by saying that this misrepresents our use of moral language; MacIntyre does not think that we make moral statements in order to encourage others to think in the same way that we do. Which position do you find more convincing, and how would you support your opinion?

Intuitionism suggests we know by instinct or intuition what is the right and good thing to do, such as helping a drowning person

REVIEW

Practice Exam Questions

Try these practice questions. You could:

» write plans for each of them, to practise your skills in structuring an essay

» use them for practice in writing introductions and/or conclusions

» write the whole essay, perhaps against the clock.

1. 'Statements such as "stealing is wrong" are no more than expressions of emotion.' Discuss.

2. How convincing is the view that moral statements refer to facts that can be observed?

Use page 9 to review your essay and make sure you have met the assessment objectives. See pages 233–234 for a mark scheme.

Chapter 2.8 | Conscience

 RECAP

Conscience is the term people often give to their inner sense of right and wrong.

Discussions about the conscience consider what it is, where it comes from and whether the conscience can be a reliable source of moral knowledge.

Biblical passages that relate to conscience

- 'For I do not do the good I want to do, but the evil I do not want to do' (Romans 7:19, New International Version) – Paul struggles with the way his actions conflict with his inner sense of right and wrong.

- 'So God created mankind in his own image, in the image of God he created them; male and female he created them' (Genesis 1:27, New International Version) – some see the conscience as an aspect of humanity made in the image of God, created with the ability to discern right from wrong.

Aquinas' theological approach to the conscience

- Aquinas did not think that the conscience was an independent special faculty or power capable of telling people what is right and wrong. He thought that the conscience is an aspect of human reason.

- Aquinas thought reason is what separates us from other animals. He called the reason *ratio*.

- Aquinas believed reason is a gift from God, placed in every person because everyone is made in God's image and likeness (Genesis 1:27).

- *Ratio* enables us to work things out and make judgements about them. Aquinas made use of his understanding of reason in his ethical teaching about natural law, as well as his teaching about the conscience.

- Aquinas thought that within each person there is a principle called synderesis which encourages us to do good and avoid evil.

- He thought that we can cultivate synderesis in ourselves through effort, so that it becomes a habit. If we try to do good then our reason will help us.

- Aquinas thought that our consciences are binding because it is wrong to go against reason. He thought we should do what we think is right and that we also have a duty to make sure our reason is well-informed when we make moral decisions. He did not argue that conscience should be followed simply as a 'gut feeling'.

- People cannot be blamed if they follow their consciences when they make moral judgements based on the best of their knowledge, but they can sometimes do the wrong thing through ignorance.

- Ignorance can be divided into two kinds: vincible and invincible.

Vincible ignorance is a lack of knowledge which the person could have done something about. If people do the wrong thing through ignorance when they could have informed themselves better, then they are blameworthy.

Invincible ignorance is the opposite. Sometimes people act in good faith and follow their consciences but they get things wrong because of ignorance of facts they could not have been expected to know anything about. They cannot be blamed for this.

- Cardinal John Henry Newman, a leading Catholic of the nineteenth century, famously said 'to Conscience first, and to the Pope afterwards', showing his belief that conscience should take priority even over the teachings of the Catholic Church. Responsibility for moral actions falls on the individual.

Possible criticisms of Aquinas' ideas about conscience

- It could be argued that Aquinas does not take into account the extent to which our moral reasoning is influenced by our upbringing and our society. What seems to be conscience could be the values of society we have learned.

- Some disagree that the conscience is the human mind making moral decisions, and think that instead it comes more directly from God (Augustine, Joseph Butler and Cardinal Newman were more inclined to think this way).

Freud's psychological approach to the conscience

- Freud was one of the founders of psychoanalysis and wrote his major works in the first half of the twentieth century.

- Freud believed that the conscience is not rational decision-making but comes from an inner unconscious part of our minds that has been shaped by our upbringing.

- He thought that our minds have several layers, like layers of rock. We know what we are thinking about on the surface, but there are all kinds of deeper ideas, memories and habits that we are not always fully aware of, but that still influence the ways in which we think and behave.

- Freud thought that the way the mind works is closely linked to sexuality. He thought there are five stages of psychosexual development.

- Freud identified three aspects of the human personality: the id, the ego and the super-ego.

The ego manages and guides the id. The ego learns from parents and from society about behaviour that is considered appropriate in different social settings. The ego manages the id's feelings of frustration when immediate gratification is not possible. The ego acts in some ways as the conscience because it remembers which actions are appropriate and inappropriate.

The id is a powerful part of our personalities within us from birth. It leads us to seek pleasure and it wants immediate gratification.

The super-ego is where the mind 'stores' moral teaching and social rules received during upbringing. Religious and moral feelings as well as conscience are in Freud's view related to the super-ego.

- The three aspects of the mind are not totally separate but interrelate in dynamic ways.
- For Freud, the conscience arises from the interplay between the id, the ego and the super-ego. Our feelings about different actions arise because of the ways our minds have developed.
- Later thinkers such as Erich Fromm developed Freud's ideas. Fromm wrote of the immature and the mature conscience. The immature conscience is based on an unthinking response to feelings of guilt, whereas the mature conscience involves rational thinking and decision-making.

Possible criticisms of Freud's account of the conscience

- Freud does not consider the possibility of there being any relation between the conscience and God; he dismisses the idea of God without discussion.
- Many thinkers believe that Freud puts too great an emphasis on human sexuality as underpinning every aspect of psychology, rather than looking at a wider range of possible influences on the human mind.

Comparing the ideas of Aquinas and Freud on the conscience

- Both Aquinas and Freud understand the conscience as an individual making moral decisions.
- Both think the conscience can sometimes be in opposition to whatever the majority popular view held by society might be.
- Both think the conscience can be shaped or educated.
- Both see the conscience as something other than the direct voice of God.

- Both agree that guilt can be disruptive for humanity. Both see a link between guilt and human desires for sensual pleasure.
- Parallels can be drawn between Aquinas' understanding of the effective operation of reason in the cultivation of synderesis in a person of good character, and Freud's understanding of the mentally healthy state of a balance between the id, super-ego and ego. Both saw the importance of balance.

- **Aquinas** sees the conscience as the activity of a God-given reason.
- Aquinas sees wrongdoing in terms of sin, and right and wrong in terms of the will of God.
- Aquinas understands guilt in terms of feelings of being to blame for moral wrongdoing.
- Aquinas understands the conscience as the workings of the human reason when making moral decisions.
- Aquinas sees the conscience as morally binding.
- Aquinas was writing in the thirteenth century when people understood many puzzling aspects of the world in terms of theology.

- **Freud** does not include the idea of God at all in his account of the conscience.
- Freud does not have an idea of right and wrong as absolute values, and sees them in terms of the norms of society.
- Freud sees guilt in terms of internal conflict between different aspects of the personality.
- Freud understands the conscience to work on a more subconscious level.
- In Freud's view, the conscience does not relate to any kind of absolute right and wrong but reflects the operation of the id, super-ego and ego.
- Freud was writing in the early twentieth century when there had been significant advances in medicine and some development of the social sciences.

Freud believed the conscience works on an unconscious level but is influenced by social norms and teachings

Key terms

Conscientia: this is the name Aquinas gives to the process whereby a person's reason makes moral judgements

Ratio: the word used by Aquinas to describe reason, something which is placed in every person as a result of their being created in the image of God

Synderesis: for Aquinas, this means to follow the good and avoid the evil, the rule that all precepts follow

Id: for Freud, this is the part of the mind that has instinctive impulses that seek satisfaction in pleasure

Ego: Freud uses this word to describe the mediation between the id and the super-ego

Super-ego: Freud uses this word to describe the part of the mind that contradicts the id and uses internalised ideals from parents and society to make the ego behave morally

 APPLY

Test yourself on key knowledge (AO1)

1. What did Aquinas mean by synderesis?
2. What did Aquinas think was the role of reason in the working of the conscience?
3. Which system of normative ethics is usually associated with Aquinas?
4. What is the difference between vincible and invincible ignorance, according to Aquinas?
5. What are the three aspects of the mind that Freud identifies?
6. What did Freud mean by the super-ego?
7. Who said that he would drink to 'Conscience first, and to the Pope afterwards'?
8. What did Freud think was the role of God in the operation of the conscience?
9. What did Freud think was the role of the ego in the human personality?
10. Give an example of a thinker who believed, unlike Aquinas, that the conscience was the voice of God within us.
11. Who developed Freud's ideas and wrote about the immature and the mature conscience?
12. Why did Aquinas think it would be wrong to act against your conscience?

If you are unsure about any of the questions, look back over the key points on pages 112–115. You can check your answers on page 219.

Develop your skills in critical argument and evaluation (AO2)

For high marks in AO2, you need to think about the ideas in this chapter and develop your own perspective, so that you can produce critically evaluative arguments rather than just describing and presenting the views of others. At AS level, 50% of your marks are awarded for your skills in critical evaluation, and at A level, 60%.

Use the following questions to help you formulate your own views.

» Discuss them with friends, making sure you articulate your own view and listen to the views of others.

» Try writing your answers to these questions, to familiarise yourself with expressing your ideas in an academic style.

» Remember to give reasons for your views.

» Think about counter-arguments – what might someone say who held a different view from your own, and why do you think they are wrong?

1. **Do you think that the conscience should be regarded as the most reliable way of making a moral decision – should you go with your 'gut feeling' about whether something is right or wrong?**

Here is an example of the kinds of ideas you might explore in formulating your analysis and evaluation:

You might think that conscience is the most reliable way of making moral decisions, particularly if you agree with the idea that the conscience is like the 'voice of God' telling us what to do in particular circumstances. Perhaps we should always go with our own instincts, rather than letting other people influence what we know to be right and wrong. You could introduce thinkers such as Kant here to support your argument, with his view that we know where our duties lie and that there is absolute right and wrong. You could, however, argue that

conscience can be unreliable, because our gut instincts are so often influenced in ways we are not entirely aware of. We might have unacknowledged prejudices or we might have been brought up to believe that something is a matter of morals when really it is just a cultural practice. You might prefer Freud's analysis of conscience as arising from socialisation, which could make it only as reliable as society's moral views; or you might argue that moral views are no more than the voice of society anyway.

Now use your critical and evaluative skills to explore these questions on your own.

2. How convincing do you find Aquinas' understanding of the conscience? Are there aspects of his views that you find more convincing than others? Do you think that there are times when your conscience does not operate in accordance with reason?

3. Martin Luther King made a speech in 1968 in which he said that there are times when it is necessary to take a position that is dangerous and unpopular, if your conscience is telling you to do so. Was he right? Should you follow your conscience always, or just sometimes? If it is only sometimes, how should you decide whether a particular set of circumstances justify following

your conscience in the face of opposition? If you think you should always follow your conscience, how would you justify giving conscience a higher priority than, for example, the law of the land?

4. Some thinkers, such as Augustine, Butler and Newman, have suggested that the conscience is like the 'voice of God' within us. If they are right, would this mean that it could never be right to disobey your conscience? How might people who hold this view account for the fact that different people's consciences might lead them in opposite directions (such as holding different views on whether it is right to fight in a war)? What do you think might be the strengths and weaknesses of

the 'conscience as the voice of God' idea? Do you find it convincing? Give reasons to explain your answer.

5. Both Freud and Aquinas suggested that the conscience could be shaped. Do you think it is possible to train your own conscience to be better at identifying right and wrong courses of action? If so, what sorts of things might you do to train it?

6. Do you think it is true that some people lack a conscience? When some people commit terrible crimes, do you think they do it knowing that they are wrong, or do they not have a sense of right and wrong? How would you support your opinion?

7. Between Aquinas and Freud, which opinion do you find more convincing about the nature of the conscience? What reasons might you give to support your opinion?

Thomas Aquinas thought that within each person was synderesis, which directed them towards good and away from evil

REVIEW

Practice Exam Questions

Try these practice questions. You could:

» write plans for each of them, to practise your skills in structuring an essay

» use them for practice in writing introductions and/or conclusions

» write the whole essay, perhaps against the clock.

1. 'Aquinas' understanding of the conscience is convincing.' Discuss.

2. To what extent should the conscience be regarded as a reliable guide to moral decision-making?

Use page 9 to review your essay and make sure you have met the assessment objectives. See pages 234–235 for a mark scheme.

Chapter 2.9 | Sexual ethics

Discussions about sexual ethics are wide-ranging, including ideas about consent, homosexuality, premarital and extramarital sex and the effects of private relationships on wider society.

Ethical debates about sexual relationships often focus on the possibility that traditional views, such as Christian teaching, are no longer relevant for modern society.

Premarital and extramarital sex

Premarital sex

- Premarital sex refers to sex before marriage. It might mean sex between two people who are planning to marry each other, or it might mean having sexual relationships whilst being a single person.
- Premarital sex has become much more common since the introduction of reliable contraception.
- Having children without being married has become increasingly common in the UK and socially acceptable.
- Cohabitation used to refer to couples who lived together before getting married, but today many cohabiting couples have no intention of getting married. People bring up children together without feeling it necessary to get married.
- Traditional Christian teaching is that sex before marriage is a sin. Sex should be for a couple who are committed to each other in a marriage partnership. Sex before marriage can be seen as undermining Christian marriage and demonstrating a lack of moral discipline.
- Christians might refer to Genesis 2:24 to support their views: 'That is why a man leaves his father and mother and is united to his wife, and they become one flesh' (New International Version).
- The Catechism of the Catholic Church argues that premarital sex does not support Christian ideas about fidelity, exclusivity and commitment, and is seen as a sin.
- Some leaders of the Church of England accept that living together before marriage can be 'a step along the way' to marriage commitment, but others oppose it and insist on marriage as the proper context for a sexual relationship.
- Adrian Thatcher, in *Marriage after Modernity: Christian Marriage in Postmodern Times* (1999), points out the long tradition of 'betrothal' as the key point of commitment rather than the marriage ceremony. Traditionally sexual relationships were permitted after betrothal – but betrothal was considered seriously binding, unlike modern cohabitation.
- In Christianity there are different points of view, from those who think that cohabiting couples should be excluded from church to those who think that all forms of committed loving relationships should be encouraged.

Extramarital sex

- Extramarital sex refers to sexual relationships where one or both of the sexual partners is married to someone else.
- Christian teaching is firmly against extramarital sex (adultery). Adultery is forbidden in the Ten Commandments.
- The Catholic Church teaches that sex is exclusively for married couples. Because the Catholic Church does not recognise divorce, it considers anyone entering a new sexual relationship after separation or divorce as having extramarital sex.
- Christianity's stance against divorce probably developed as a way of protecting women against being used as bargaining tools.
- Consent is seen as a key issue in sexual relationships in the modern world.

Ethical approaches to premarital and extramarital sex

Natural law

- Followers of natural law take an absolutist view of ethics.
- Natural law ethics is linked to an understanding of human nature as having a purpose. People should do those things that allow them to flourish and reach their potential.
- Catholic teaching relies heavily on natural law.
- In natural law, reproduction is one of the primary precepts. This is interpreted to mean that reproduction should be considered the main aim of sexual activity.
- Premarital and extramarital sex are wrong, according to natural law, because they are not consistent with the flourishing of human society in bringing up children in stable families.
- The use of artificial methods of contraception is prohibited by the Catholic Church but not by most other denominations.
- Natural law could be seen as a good approach to issues of premarital and extramarital sex, as it gives clear rules rather than leaving people to make decisions in the heat of the moment.
- It emphasises the importance and sanctity of marriage and of reproduction, which could be seen as beneficial for the stability of society and in line with Christian principles.

Situation ethics

- Followers of situation ethics do not think that there should be rules guiding premarital or extramarital sex.
- Each situation should be considered in the context of its own circumstances, and the most loving course of action should be determined and followed.
- Situation ethics presents a relativist view of morality.
- Fletcher uses issues of sexual ethics to illustrate his view that there should not be absolute rules, with examples of a woman having sex with a prison guard in order to secure her freedom, or a spy having sex with an enemy in order to bring about the end to war.

Kantian ethics

- Followers of Kant take an absolutist view of ethics based around ideas of duty and the categorical imperative.
- People should not treat each other as a means to an end, which rules out exploitative and non-consensual sexual relations.
- In the kingdom of ends the commitment of marriage would be respected.
- Universalisability would prevent so much sexual freedom that society was undermined.
- Kant emphasised the importance of promise-keeping and truth-telling, which suggests secret extramarital sex would be unethical.

Utilitarianism

- John Stuart Mill argued that people should be protected from unnecessary legislation and should be free to behave how they wish unless it causes harm to others. This principle could be used by utilitarians to justify premarital sex, extramarital sex and homosexuality – although opponents might argue that these practices do cause harm because they undermine the seriousness of a heterosexual marriage commitment.
- In *The Subjugation of Women*, Mill argued that marriage can sometimes reduce women to the status of slaves. He was not against marriage but he was in favour of gender equality.
- Mill tried to make contraception available to the poor at a time when the Christian Church opposed artificial contraception.

Homosexuality

- Homosexuality is a term used to describe sexual attraction between people of the same sex.

- Attitudes towards homosexuality have changed dramatically over the last hundred years. In the first half of the twentieth century, homosexuality was a crime. It was decriminalised in England and Wales in 1967. The first same-sex marriages took place in England, Wales and Scotland in 2014.

- People disagree about homosexuality. There are still many instances of anti-homosexual attacks and discrimination, but also many instances of public acceptance and celebration of homosexual relationships.

- Christianity has traditionally opposed homosexuality as sinful.

- Some texts in the Bible condemn homosexual acts, such as 'Do not have sexual relations with a man as one does with a woman; that is detestable' (Leviticus 18:22, New International Version).

- There is disagreement about what these texts mean and whether they should be considered to be applicable and enforceable in the present day, especially as many other Old Testament rules are disregarded by Christians as no longer relevant.

- Homosexuality as an issue causes deep divisions between Christian Churches around the world and there are continuing debates. The Anglican Communion struggles to reach agreement about same-sex marriages in church and about the appointment of openly gay clergy. Some Churches such as the Methodists and the URC seek to welcome homosexual partners into Church life.

Ethical approaches to homosexuality

Natural law

- Natural law ethics see homosexual acts as wrong, because they cannot bring forth new life, and reproduction is seen as the telos of human sexuality.

- The Catholic Church has traditionally seen homosexuality as a sin, but in modern times some Catholics take a more liberal view of homosexuality.

- Pope Francis stated in 2016 that there are no grounds for considering a same-sex partnership to be similar to God's plan for marriage and family life.

- Some people criticise natural law approaches to homosexuality because plenty of sexual relationships do not and cannot bring forth new life, such as sex between an older married couple, between married people with fertility issues and between a husband and wife during pregnancy.

Situation ethics

- Situation ethics concentrates on finding the most loving outcome.

- It does not give rules about homosexuality in general, but would consider a homosexual relationship to be morally acceptable if it brought about agapeic love.

- Situation ethics might be difficult to apply to issues of homosexuality if the needs of other people as well as the needs of the couple are considered, but most would agree that it is unloving to forbid homosexual relationships and loving to support them.

Kantian ethics

- Kantian ethics is deontological, placing duty and autonomy at the heart of moral decision-making, and is used to formulate rules governing sexual behaviour.
- Applying Kantian principles to issues of homosexuality does not lead to one clear answer, but could be used to justify a range of attitudes.
- Kantians could argue that treating everyone with dignity must mean that homosexual relationships should be regarded as equal to heterosexual relationships.
- They could argue that the principle of universalisability means that everyone should have the right to express their sexuality in a relationship.
- Kantian ethics emphasises mutual consent and avoiding exploitation, and these principles should underpin relationships regardless of the sexuality of the partners.

Situation ethics, Kantian ethics and Utilitarianism could all be used to justify acceptance of homosexual relationships in different circumstances

Utilitarianism

- Utilitarians look for moral actions that will bring about the greatest happiness and cause the least harm.
- Many utilitarians would argue that homosexual relationships cause happiness to those in them and do not harm any one else.
- Some argue that homosexual relationships do harm the rest of society because they undermine marriage as a stable social institution.
- Most utilitarians reject the need for rules about private behaviour between consenting adults, if they cause no harm to others.

Key terms

Consent: freely agreeing to engage in sexual activity with another person

Homosexuality: sexual attraction between people of the same sex

Premarital sex: sex before marriage

Extramarital sex: sex beyond the confines of marriage, usually used to describe adulterous sex

Cohabitation: an unmarried couple living together in a sexually active relationship. Sometimes known pejoratively as 'living in sin'

Exclusive: a commitment to be in a sexual relationship with a person to the exclusion of all others. This is the opposite of an 'open marriage' or a 'casual relationship'

Betrothal: traditionally the exchange of promises to marry, which historically marked the point at which sex was permitted

Consummation: an act of sexual intercourse that indicates, in some traditions, the finalisation of the marriage

APPLY

Test yourself on key knowledge (AO1)

1. What is the word used for people living together, sometimes called 'living in sin'?

2. Who wrote a book called *The Subjugation of Women?*

3. Which Christian denomination relies heavily on the ethical system of natural law?

4. What is meant by the term 'premarital sex'?

5. In which year did same-sex marriage become legal in England, Wales and Scotland?

6. What does the Catholic Church teach about same-sex marriage?

7. What is meant by the term 'consummation'?

8. What does it mean to call an ethical system 'deontological'?

9. Are situation ethics relativist or absolutist?

10. What is Genesis 2:24 about?

11. What is Leviticus 18:22 about?

12. Which ethical system condemns homosexuality on the grounds that it cannot fulfill the telos of sexual relationships by bringing about new life?

> If you are unsure about any of the questions, look back over the key points on pages 118–121. You can check your answers on page 219.

Develop your skills in critical argument and evaluation (AO2)

For high marks in AO2, you need to think about the ideas in this chapter and develop your own perspective, so that you can produce critically evaluative arguments rather than just describing and presenting the views of others. At AS level, 50% of your marks are awarded for your skills in critical evaluation, and at A level, 60%.

Use the following questions to help you formulate your own views.

» Discuss them with friends, making sure you articulate your own view and listen to the views of others.

» Try writing your answers to these questions, to familiarise yourself with expressing your ideas in an academic style.

» Remember to give reasons for your views.

» Think about counter-arguments – what might someone say who held a different view from your own, and why do you think they are wrong?

1. **Some people (for example Mill) argue that sexual relationships do not need rules, as long as the relationship does not cause harm to anyone else: if they are both consenting adults and no one else will be hurt, there is no more need for ethical discussion than if they wanted to play tennis together. How far would you agree with this point of view? How would you justify your opinion?**

Here is an example of the kinds of ideas you might explore in formulating your analysis and evaluation:

You might agree with Mill and argue that rules are for social behaviour but do not need to be made for private individuals. You might agree that treating sex as something special and sacred is an outdated view, made to protect women and society against unwanted pregnancy, and that now there is reliable contraception there is no need to treat sex as anything other than enjoyable physical exercise.

On the other hand you might think that people need to have moral rules about sex because sexual instincts are so powerful that without rules, people forget to think rationally and behave in ways which are harmful to themselves or to others. You might agree with traditional Christian teaching and argue that sex is a gift from God, given to be used for reproduction.

Now use your critical and evaluative skills to explore these questions on your own.

2. Many (but not all) people's attitudes towards premarital sex have changed in the UK over the last hundred years. Do you think this means that once, people had the wrong attitude in condemning premarital sex, but now they have the right one in accepting it? Or once, people had the right attitude in condemning premarital sex, but now they have the wrong one in accepting it? Or do you think moral right and wrong is not absolute but is a reflection of the social opinions of the culture? Give reasons to support your answer; you could refer to your learning about meta-ethics.

3. Some people argue that same-sex marriages cause harm to the rest of society because they undermine the traditional idea of a marriage between two heterosexual people. How far would you agree with this view? How would you support your opinions and criticise those of others?

4. It could be argued that cohabiting before marriage is a much better idea than going into a lifelong commitment without much idea about whether you are compatible with your partner on a day-to-day domestic level. How far would you agree with this view? What arguments might be made against it?

5. If sexuality is not a personal choice but is part of the way each individual is made, does this make a difference to sexual ethics? Is it fair to prohibit someone from having a sexual relationship if they happen to be homosexual through no choice of their own? Do you think sexuality is a choice, or something we are born with, or something imposed on us as we develop? Give reasons for your answer.

6. Do you think that religious beliefs should have an influence on sexual ethics in society, or are they outdated? Should leaders of religion update their teaching on issues such as premarital sex and homosexuality now that we have more reliable contraception and know more about the prevention of sexually-transmitted diseases?

7. Which of the ethical systems you have studied do you think gives the most persuasive response to issues surrounding premarital and extramarital sex? Explain why you have chosen this system, what its strengths are and why other views are, in your opinion, weaker.

8. Do you think that there are some kinds of sexual relationships that should be forbidden, even if they are between consenting adults and take place in private (for example, incestuous relationships)? If so, why should they be forbidden?

REVIEW

Practice Exam Questions

Try these practice questions. You could:

» write plans for each of them, to practise your skills in structuring an essay

» use them for practice in writing introductions and/or conclusions

» write the whole essay, perhaps against the clock.

1. To what extent are natural law ethics helpful in guiding decisions about sexual behaviour?

2. How far might utilitarianism provide useful guidelines in discussions about the ethics of homosexuality?

> Use page 9 to review your essay and make sure you have met the assessment objectives. See page 235 for a mark scheme.

Sample student answers

1. 'A utilitarian approach is the best approach to take to resolve moral dilemmas that arise in the issues surrounding sexual ethics.' Discuss.

Whilst there are indeed a great number of issues surrounding sexual ethics, for the purpose of my essay I would like to discuss a utilitarian approach to dilemmas arising from extramarital sex and homosexuality. I myself believe that utilitarianism is far from the best approach to deal with such dilemmas, as sexual ethics is an extremely personal area and a theory that gives little value to the individual, instead concentrating on the larger picture, in my opinion is of little use.

Utilitarianism, broadly speaking, believes in the maximum amount of welfare for the greatest number of people. What exactly this welfare entails is subject of debate, with some such as Bentham equating it to the maximisation of pleasure and minimisation of pain, whilst others such as J. S. Mill believing in the importance of prioritisation of certain higher pleasures (mainly intellectual ones) over lower ones (mainly bodily ones). A clear distinction also exists between the three main types of utilitarianism: act, rule and preference. Whilst act utilitarians think that every situation should be considered on its individual merits, rule utilitarians believe a society with rules is better than a society without and thus try to pass rules which apply to various moral dilemmas. Preference utilitarians, on the other hand, believe the priority should be the fulfilment of every individual's self-preference, hence their name.

Some people will undoubtedly view utilitarianism as the best way to deal with issues arising in sexual ethics. On the surface the theory sounds brilliant: we apply the principle of utility, i.e that the right course of action brings about the greatest good for the greatest number, and we end up with a society where most are satisfied. For example, take the issue of extramarital sex; when faced with a moral dilemma involving this, let us consider what brings about more good: everyone cheating on their respective spouses, or everyone being faithful? The answer lies on the surface — a society in which everyone is faithful will seemingly be happier than a society full of infidelity, broken relationships and divorces. Indeed, it even seems like some forms of utilitarianism can provide for minorities, namely preference utilitarianism on the issues of homosexuality.

A good introduction. The writer makes clear the issues they will be considering, and also gives a firm sense of the direction the argument will take.

This is a good clear summary of utilitarianism. Further detail could have been given but the writer sensibly chose not to spend too much of the allotted time on background detail and description. The distinction between different kinds of utilitarianism is accurate and confident.

Whilst in many countries today the majority is strongly opposed to homosexuality, and in countries with Sharia law homosexuals face death as a consequence of being discovered, a preference utilitarian such as Peter Singer would argue that his theory protects them: it looks out for the preference of each individual in regard to themselves, and frankly what other people do privately is no business of yours. A strength of utilitarianism is that it is basically governed by the same principles as any modern democracy. It appears as if the fairest way to go about your business is to balance everyone's interests evenly and make decisions taking this balance into account. Utilitarianism virtually dictates our society — any modern democracy is built around these principles. Thus it seems logical to apply something that works for millions of people in other fields of our lives as well.

However, there are numerous problems to utilitarianism when facing moral dilemmas arising from issues surrounding sexual ethics. The primary one for me is the fact that the individual is given so little consideration if we apply utilitarianism; is it truly fair to dictate what should someone do with their private sexual lives on the basis of what would be best for everyone as a whole? I do not think so. For example, a woman wants to protect herself from having a child and thus uses contraception when having sex. Of course, if everyone uses contraception we will have a problem as then this current generation will be the last. So thus it follows that contraception must not be used — for the greater interest of society. Any rule utilitarian will attempt to follow this belief. However, is it fair to bring an unwanted child into an already overpopulated world? We cannot even theoretically calculate its future happiness and unhappiness as we simply do not know what the mother will do and it is too big an assumption to make. Thus the child's interests are completely overlooked and utilitarianism seems to be a problematic choice of theory to follow. Also, some forms such as preference utilitarianism can easily be used to justify taboo ideas, for instance incestuous adultery. Imagine a brother and sister, the latter of them being married. They have a passion for each other and, being adherents of preference utilitarianism, give in to it. Simply because the preferences of those committing the adultery are being carried out, does not suddenly make an intrinsically wrong act right. Another problem with applying utilitarianism to sexual ethics is the fact LGBT communities will be persecuted by adherents of act and rule utilitarianism in

Interesting use of preference utilitarianism which goes beyond the material required by the specification, showing evidence of further reading. However, it is taken for granted that the issues surrounding homosexuality are known to the reader. The candidate could have explained why homosexuality might be considered controversial.

societies where homosexuality is frowned upon. It seems to be that utilitarianism promotes ignoring the individual to such an extent which can (and, in the right circumstances, most likely will) lead to attracted being permitted.

Perhaps a better approach to issues arising from dilemmas of sexual ethics is situation ethics. After all, it is a teleological theory which looks at the individual circumstances of the person carrying out the action rather than using an arbitrary belief such as the maximisation of welfare. I think that sexual ethics are an extremely personal matter and dictating to someone what to do on the basis of what is good for others is a categorically incorrect approach, allowing potentially horrendous outcomes. However, if we aim to achieve a loving outcome I believe that a much lesser amount of harm can be done. Therefore, I think that a utilitarian approach is far from the best approach to take to resolve moral dilemmas that arise in the issues surrounding sexual ethics.

The writer has some good arguments here but they are rather jumbled together. The writer seems to have forgotten to concentrate on extramarital sex and homosexuality as outlined in the introduction and has strayed into other issues instead to make the points. Also, the candidate needs to justify why they think that sex between a brother and sister is 'intrinsically wrong'; this point of view is asserted and is a common view but it is not supported with reasoning.

The examiner says:

The structure is generally good, in dealing first with potential strengths of utilitarianism and then explaining why the weaknesses outweigh the strengths so that the argument is clear and leads to the conclusion. However there are times when the different points become jumbled and unclear.

- For AO1, the essay shows a good understanding of utilitarianism and recognises that there are different forms of it. Accurate reference is made to Bentham and Mill and to Singer, but there is little demonstration of knowledge of any other utilitarian thinkers or critics of utilitarianism. The candidate did not have much to say about the issues of extramarital sex and homosexuality outlined in the introduction.

- The AO2 skills are good, with a clear consistent line of argument supported with reasoning, although the points made are quite general rather than illustrated with specific examples or reference to specific issues. There is a sense of engagement with the topic and the candidate writes persuasively.

To achieve a better mark, the candidate needs to:

» make a brief plan before beginning to write, so that the issues outlined in the introduction are not forgotten about during the argument

» find a better balance between demonstrating knowledge and demonstrating skill in argument; this essay is stronger on argument than on knowledge.

2. Assess the view that Fletcher's situation ethics gives no useful guidance in moral decision-making.

Fletcher's situation ethics entails the idea of making moral decisions subjectively – and above all to achieve the most loving outcome (a rather teleological approach) – having criticised the legalistic approach of the Bible by Catholics. On the one hand, situation ethics offers us useful moral guidance in terms of not treating everything as black or white; however, multiple issues arise when actually applying the approach to complex issues, thus rendering the idea deficient and useless.

> This is a good introduction – it shows a confident grasp of situation ethics and also gives an indication of the argument that will be presented in answer to the question.

Coming up with six propositions, Fletcher tries to set some basic ideas about how to approach situation ethics. All hold both good and bad moral guidance for various reasons: the first proposition argues nothing is necessarily good or bad – except love which is always good. This is useful as we can take a subjective approach to issues that are controversial, such as abortion and euthanasia, and understand that to argue that they are intrinsically good or bad is wrong as there aspects of both. This allows an openness to these subjects that could result in perhaps fewer harsh decisions. However, what this proposition therefore leads to is a certain ambiguity as to what is right and wrong, therefore providing no useful guidance as we can never come to a decision of right and wrong, making moral laws almost impossible to create.

> Good use of examples to illustrate the point. An effective balance of knowledge of Fletcher's first proposition and assessment of its usefulness.

The second proposition argues that Jesus broke the rules of the Old Testament (Judaism), to do the most loving thing. Of course this is useful as it allows flexibility in terms of combating a legalistic approach to convicting someone of, for examples, killing in self-defence. A problem arises, however, as it is difficult to discern when to know the rules and why, leading to a weak legal system full of loopholes based around love, which is open to abuse.

The third proposition discusses that justice is simply the application of love – the two cannot be separated. Thus, doing the right, just thing is doing the most loving thing. So if a doctor must choose between the life of a mother of two and a family-less person, the just thing would be to save the mother. Although very logical and sensible, it could be very easily argued that nobody's life is worth more or less than anyone else's, so who are you to decide whom is more important? You can't, rendering the moral guidance flawed.

The fourth proposition talks about selfless love (agape) and that we should do the most loving thing whether we know someone or not. A stranger is just as deserving of agape love as a close family member. This provides good moral guidance as it encourages love for all, hopefully leading to a better society.

However, this contradicts slightly with the third proposition, which argues that calculated love is sometimes necessary — which the fourth criticises.

The fifth proposition is related to having the most loving outcomes, rather than the action itself. At first this may appear good, as it encourages considering the consequences of our actions, yet unfortunately it is also not without fault. This is because it essentially justifies doing bad things to achieve 'good' results. For example, it could be considered 'loving' to solve our population crisis by reducing our population to extend human existence and resources for future generations to benefit from. If the excess population were killed in a mass murder on a global scale, how can anyone argue that to be morally right?

The sixth proposition argues that love should be applied situationally, not prescriptively — therefore to subjective over legalistic approaches. Again, this provides good moral guidance through treating moral decisions wholly and not in such a way that would mean people suffer from simplistic right or wrong laws. But once again this simply isn't practical in any society as the list of situations for any decision is not exhaustive, so laws become almost defunct as they don't cover everything and will never be able to.

So, although the propositions have good, loving ideas that, in a perfect world, would ultimately lead as effective guidance in moral decisions making, at the end of the day we live in an imperfection-ridden world where the six propositions of situation ethics are either rendered impractical, contradictory or too ambiguous and open to abuse.

In terms of Fletcher's four presuppositions, moral guidance is once again offered but it isn't entirely useful and has similar, if not the same,

Good to use your own example, but there needs to be some justification of the claim that 'you can't' decide whom is more important. Some people would say that there are ways of deciding (such as applying utilitarianism) so this is a controversial claim which needs to be supported with reasoning.

Not entirely clear here.

issues as the six main propositions. Pragmatism focuses on what works rather than what is totally right – contradicting doing the most loving thing as it opens up 'settling for what isn't necessarily loving but what is practical'. Relativism argues there are no set rules to follow which is too ambiguous to follow without conflicting ideas. Positivism argues for religious judgement based on an experience or faith, but again this contradicts itself as it ultimately has the same result: belief in God – there's no alternative, which Fletcher himself argues against. Personalism argues thinking of loving people as people, not things, which of course is good but yet again raises ambiguity to what constitutes this.

Ultimately, situation ethics is a beautiful idea but just appears to have too many loopholes and issues that render it impractical for actual use in decision-making. Although some ideas can be taken away from situation ethics, it can be argued that the statement that situation ethics gives no useful guidance in moral decision-making is almost true. It doesn't guide moral decisions as such, but can support them as a potential approach. It is useful as moral inspiration but cannot guide us as there are no precise ways to apply it to moral dilemmas. In conclusion, the statement is somewhat true, but should not discourage the complete rejection or dismissal of situation ethics in its entirety.

> Good conclusion, successfully summarising the main argument of the essay and giving a direct answer to the question.

The examiner says:

This essay is strong in structure – taking situation ethics point by point by following the six propositions was a good choice for providing the essay with a sense of direction, although there are other structures which could also have worked well.

- For AO1, the essay shows a thorough understanding of situation ethics, but could have accessed higher marks if there had been reference to other thinkers, for example specific examples of critics of situation ethics, and/or thinkers with different approaches to ethics.

- The AO2 skills are mainly strong, with critical and evaluative comment made throughout the essay, often supported with well-chosen examples. The conclusion follows logically from the main body of the essay.

To achieve a better mark, the candidate needs to:

» make more use of a wider range of thinkers and other sources of wisdom and authority in support of the argument

» consider the idea that situation ethics might provide better moral guidance in some moral dilemmas than in others

» support all critical evaluation with reasons and examples, rather than simply making unsupported assertions.

Chapter 3.1 | Augustine's teaching on human nature

 RECAP

Augustine taught that human nature has been fatally damaged because of the Fall of Adam and Eve.

He taught that people are created by God, they are fallen in nature, and they can be redeemed.

He taught that only hope of salvation is through the grace of God, made available to the people God chooses through the sacrifice of Christ on the cross.

Augustine's life and influences

- Augustine lived in the fourth century. His mother Monica was a Christian.
- In his early life he followed the thinking of the Manichees, who taught that the universe was a battle between forces of good and evil, that human appetites trapped the body in the world of darkness, and that human reason could lead to enlightenment.
- Augustine was also very influenced by Plato and his follower Plotinus, who taught that human appetites were shameful and that study could lead people to the Form of the Good.
- The preaching of St Ambrose and the letters of Paul were instrumental in converting Augustine to Christianity.
- Augustine rejected Manichaeism because he came to believe that the grace of God through the sacrifice of Jesus was needed to bring people to wisdom and salvation, not just human reason. Augustine developed the belief that people could not be saved just through their own efforts.
- Augustine became a priest and then a bishop. He struggled with the demands of Christian life and wrote about them. His best-known writings are *The City of God* and *Confessions*.

Human nature as created by God

- Adam and Eve, the first people, are created in the image of God – for Augustine this meant they share some of the characteristics of God: rationality, freedom of choice and a moral nature.
- They have a special place in the universe.
- They are made from physical matter, like the rest of the natural world.
- They are given the responsibility of stewardship over the earth, told to be fruitful and multiply, and told not to eat the fruit of the tree in the middle of the Garden of Eden.

The Fall

- The Fall of Adam and Eve is described in Genesis 2–3.
- The serpent tempts Eve to eat the fruit and disobey God, and then Adam chooses to be disobedient too. This is called the 'Fall' of Adam and Eve because they fell away from their perfect nature through their own free choice and disobedience.
- Augustine taught that the Fall was catastrophic for humanity. They are banished from the Garden, made to work for a living, Eve is given pain in childbirth, the serpent has to crawl and is made the enemy of humanity, and people no longer have the same access to God that they had before they disobeyed.
- The Fall was the turning point for the whole of creation, in Augustine's view.

Adam and Eve, and therefore all humans, are made in the image of God

Human relationships before the Fall, according to Augustine

- In Genesis, before the Fall, Adam and Eve are depicted as having a close relationship with God. They can see God and walk and talk with God easily.
- Augustine thought people must have lived in a state of loving friendship before the Fall. He called
this state of easy, comfortable, supportive friendship 'concordia'.
- He thought they must have lived in a 'state of perfection', living without sin and in accordance with God's plans. They must have lived comfortably with their physical bodies and not worried about being naked.
- Augustine could not explain why Adam and Eve chose to disobey God, except that they had the freedom to do so.
- Before the Fall, people were able to live in peaceful society without the need for repressive political authority, but they would still have needed some kind of leadership.

Human relationships after the Fall, according to Augustine

- The human will could be pulled in different directions after the Fall, and flawed human nature makes it inevitable that people do wrong.
- There are different kinds of love which, after the Fall, flawed humans often confuse:

Cupiditas – this is love of worldly, impermanent material things and of selfish concerns. It can make people unhappy.

Caritas – this is generous love of others displayed through the virtues (prudence, fortitude, temperance and justice), which gives people spiritual happiness.

- Adam and Eve chose cupiditas after the Fall.
- The sin of Adam and Eve corrupted everything and passed on the tendency to sin to future generations so that everyone is now born with Original Sin.

- People are unable to live morally pure lives since the Fall. Original Sin has corrupted their ability to freely choose the good.
- People are beyond rescue by their own efforts and can be saved only by the grace of God through Christ.
- People are 'divided' – they are still made in the image of God and can still reason and have a moral nature, but the will is corrupted, so their inclinations are always to selfishness and lustfulness.
  They end up arguing with themselves, being pulled in different directions and doing things they disagree with.
- Augustine could relate to the spiritual struggles of Paul, described in Romans 7. Paul longs to be free from sin but he feels chained to it.

- Augustine thought sinful humanity is at the mercy of concupiscence. This refers primarily to sexual desire but also to other appetites for material things.
- He struggled with ideas about the extent to which people should refrain from sexual activity and lead lives of material simplicity.
- After the Fall, people need forceful political authority, otherwise their sinful natures will let society get out of hand.
- Augustine contrasted earthly peace with heavenly peace and thought that earthly peace was just a compromise between sinful individuals.

Augustine's teaching on grace

- Augustine taught that the only way people can be restored from the effects of Original Sin is through the grace of God – God's generous giving of love. Without this, people are doomed to eternal punishment.
- People will continue to sin even after they have been given God's grace and accepted it, but even though they continue to sin, God will accept some of them into heaven.
- For Augustine, God's grace is important in these ways:

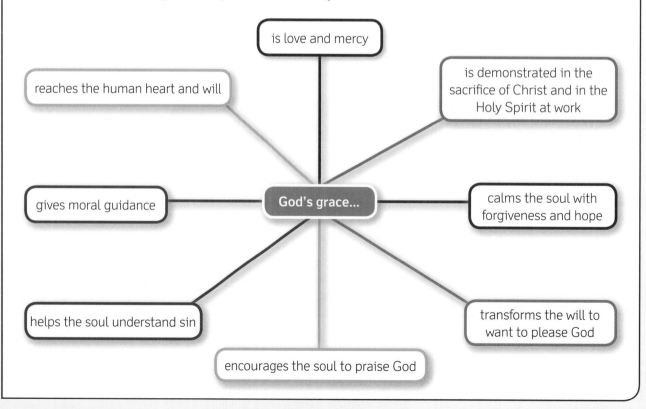

is love and mercy

reaches the human heart and will

is demonstrated in the sacrifice of Christ and in the Holy Spirit at work

gives moral guidance

God's grace...

calms the soul with forgiveness and hope

helps the soul understand sin

transforms the will to want to please God

encourages the soul to praise God

Possible strengths of Augustine's ideas about human nature

- Augustine encourages humanity to take responsibility for its own actions and recognise its failings.
- He understands and attempts to account for human emotions, especially contradictory ones.
- He makes valuable distinctions between love of material goods and love of others.
- He recognises his own weaknesses and is willing to engage with everyday human experience.
- He does not pretend that anything is possible for humanity as long as they try hard enough; instead he emphasises human dependence on the grace of God.
- Some thinkers agree that people are fundamentally selfish, such as Thomas Hobbes.

Possible weaknesses of Augustine's ideas about human nature

- The idea of Original Sin can seem unattractive in an era when we are used to thinking of ourselves as individuals, rather than as part of a whole species.
- The idea of a loving God punishing people for sins committed by others can seem hard to accept.
- Some people argue that Augustine is wrong to say human beings are fundamentally corrupt. Jean Jacques Rousseau argued that people are basically good; John Locke argued that people are born with a 'tabula rasa' (blank slate).
- The theory of evolution might make it difficult to accept that humanity is so very different in nature and purpose from other animals, and it calls into question the historical truth of the story of the Fall.
- Some argue that Augustine's focus on sin and corruption distorts the hopeful Christian message of the goodness and love of God and the promise of salvation.
- Some argue that Augustine assumes there is such a thing as 'human nature', whereas in fact we each have our own natures and cannot all be classified together. Jean-Paul Sartre held the view that we are each free to create our own natures.

Key terms

The Fall: the biblical event in which Adam and Eve disobeyed God's command and ate the fruit from the forbidden tree in the Garden of Eden; also used to refer to the imperfect state of humanity

Redeemed: in theological terms, 'saved' from sin by the sacrifice of Christ

Grace: in theological terms, God's free and undeserved love for humanity, epitomised in the sacrifice of Jesus on the cross

Concordia: human friendship

Sin: disobeying the will and commands of God

Will: the part of human nature that makes free choices

Cupiditas: 'selfish love', a love of worldly things and of selfish desires

Caritas: 'generous love', a love of others and of the virtues; the Latin equivalent of the Greek word 'agape'

Concupiscence: uncontrollable desire for physical pleasures and material things

Ecclesia: heavenly society, in contrast with earthly society

APPLY

Test yourself on key knowledge (AO1)

1. What was the name of the religious group Augustine joined before he became a Christian, who believed in opposing forces of good and evil?

2. What term did Augustine use for easy, comfortable friendship?

3. What term did Augustine use for unselfish love of others and of the virtues?

4. In the story of the Fall, what commandment of God did Adam and Eve disobey?

5. In which respects did Augustine think that humanity was 'in the image of God'?

6. In Augustine's understanding, what does concupiscence mean?

7. When Augustine argued that human nature is dominated by cupiditas, what did he mean?

8. Augustine sympathised with Paul when he wrote about his own internal struggles with sin – in which book of the Bible?

9. Give an example of a thinker who agreed with Augustine that human nature is fundamentally bad.

10. What does 'tabula rasa' mean?

11. Give an example of a thinker who argued that we create our own natures and do not come into the world with our natures already predetermined.

12. Give four examples of characteristics of God's grace, according to the thinking of Augustine.

> If you are unsure about any of the questions, look back over the key points on pages 130–133. You can check your answers on page 219.

Develop your skills in critical argument and evaluation (AO2)

For high marks in AO2, you need to think about the ideas in this chapter and develop your own perspective, so that you can produce critically evaluative arguments rather than just describing and presenting the views of others. At AS level, 50% of your marks are awarded for your skills in critical evaluation, and at A level, 60%.

Use the following questions to help you formulate your own views.

» Discuss them with friends, making sure you articulate your own view and listen to the views of others.

» Try writing your answers to these questions, to familiarise yourself with expressing your ideas in an academic style.

» Remember to give reasons for your views.

» Think about counter-arguments – what might someone say who held a different view from your own, and why do you think they are wrong?

1. **How far would you agree with the view that Augustine's understanding of human nature is pessimistic? Do you think that his ideas about Original Sin and the corruption of human nature are unnecessarily gloomy?**

Here is an example of the kinds of ideas you might explore in formulating your analysis and evaluation:

You might argue that Augustine paints an unnecessarily negative picture of human nature; perhaps you agree with thinkers like Rousseau who argue that human beings are fundamentally good, or with Aquinas who argued that people are naturally inclined towards doing the right thing. Alternatively, you might argue that people are born with a 'blank slate', neither good nor evil, or that they create their own natures, or you might take the view that there is no such thing as 'human nature'. You might be able to offer examples to support your point of view. You could argue that Augustine is not being pessimistic but merely realistic (or even optimistic), in pointing out the problems with human nature but also offering a solution to these problems by emphasising the grace of God.

Now use your critical and evaluative skills to explore these questions on your own.

2. Do you think that, in order to agree with Augustine, we have to accept a literal understanding of the story of the Fall of Adam and Eve? Are there lessons and insights that could be taken from Augustinian teaching on human nature, even for those who think that the story of the Fall is mythological rather than historically accurate?

3. Augustine makes a distinction between cupiditas and caritas. Do you think he is right to make this distinction? Is it a sharp and clear distinction or are there some kinds of love that have features of both? Are there other kinds of love he could also have included, or is he right that there are these two only? Give examples and reasons to support your opinion.

4. Augustine identifies four virtues as characteristics of caritas (unselfish love): prudence, fortitude, temperance and justice. Do you think he chose the right four? Do you think each of these is always a virtue, or are there times when too much prudence or too much fortitude could be a bad thing? If he has missed out any, in your opinion, which virtues would you add and for what reasons?

5. Augustine was a great believer in the value of friendship and wrote about his belief that Adam and Eve would have lived in a spirit of concordia, or loving friendship, before the Fall, because he saw this as the most perfect of human relationships. Do you think he was right to value friendship so highly? Are people always worse off if they have few friends, or is it a matter of personal preference? Might there be any disadvantages to friendly relationships?

6. Augustine developed the idea of 'Original Sin' in which humanity inherits the sinful nature of previous generations. How far do you agree with his view that a sinful nature can be passed from one generation to another? What arguments might be presented in support of the idea of Original Sin, and against it?

7. How far do you think Augustine is successful in presenting the idea of the Christian God as a God of love?

 REVIEW

Practice Exam Questions

Try these practice questions. You could:

» write plans for each of them, to practise your skills in structuring an essay

» use them for practice in writing introductions and/or conclusions

» write the whole essay, perhaps against the clock.

1. How fair is the claim that sin means humans can never be morally good?

2. 'It is impossible for modern people to believe Augustine's teachings about the historical Fall of humanity.' Discuss.

Use page 9 to review your essay and make sure you have met the assessment objectives. See page 236 for a mark scheme.

Chapter 3.2 | Death and the afterlife

Christianity teaches that people have souls that can survive the death of the body. There are divergent beliefs about life after death within Christianity, as different interpretations have been given to different ideas and teachings.

Resurrection

- Christians believe that after death, people will have a new life in a new kind of existence.

- They reject the idea that a human soul leaves one physical body and joins another in this same world (rebirth or reincarnation). They also reject Platonic ideas that the soul leaves the body and continues in a disembodied way.

- Instead they believe that the soul will be given a new spiritual, glorified physical body in which to continue to live after death (resurrection).

- They believe that the person who lives after death is still the same person but they will be incorruptible.

- They believe that resurrection is a miracle from God.

- Before Jesus, Pharisees believed in resurrection and it is mentioned in the Old Testament in the book of Daniel. Christians base their belief in resurrection on biblical accounts of Jesus' Resurrection.

- The gospels say that after Jesus was crucified and died, his body was placed in a tomb with a heavy stone over the entrance. On the third day the stone had been rolled away and the tomb was empty. Jesus was then seen and heard by his followers, as a man in a physical body.

- Christians believe that the Resurrection of Jesus demonstrates that they too will be resurrected after death.

- Paul writes about life after death in his two letters to the Corinthians – he uses metaphors to explain his beliefs:

In 1 Corinthians he uses the metaphor of a seed transforming into the new plant it will become, to show how the physical earthly body will be transformed to fulfill its potential.	In 2 Corinthians he uses the metaphor of a tent being replaced with a solid house, to show how life in this world is temporary and will be replaced by something long-lasting, and how life after death will provide a home.	In 2 Corinthians he also uses the metaphor of being naked in this world but clothed in the afterlife, to show that we will no longer need to be ashamed.

Key terms

Resurrection: living on after death in a glorified physical form in a new realm

Disembodied existence: existing without a physical body

Beatific vision: a face-to-face encounter with God

Parousia: used in Christianity to refer to the Second Coming of Christ

Universalism: the view that all people will be saved

Purgatory: a place where people go, temporarily, after death to be cleansed of sin before they are fit to live with God

Limited election: the view that God chooses only a small number of people for heaven

Original Sin: a state of wrongdoing in which people are born (according to some Christians) because of the sin of Adam and Eve

Heaven

- Traditionally Christians describe the afterlife in terms of 'going to heaven'.
- They use different symbols and analogies to describe heaven whilst also accepting that the nature of life after death remains a mystery yet to be revealed. Some of the symbols used are:

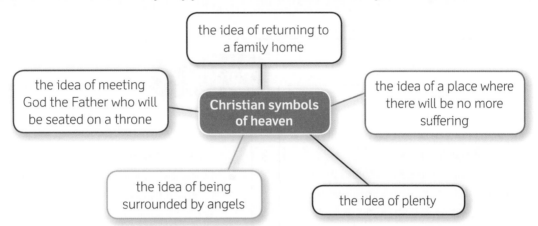

- These and other descriptions of heaven are not meant to be taken literally – most Christians do not believe that heaven is literally a 'place', but instead view it as a spiritual state. Heaven is the state in which a person recognises and accepts God's grace, and is forgiven and made whole (while hell is a state where a person rejects God and chooses sin).
- Some Christians understand heaven in terms of an eternity of endless days in which to praise God, whilst others understand it as timeless, often in terms of the beatific vision described by Aquinas.
- Heaven is sometimes understood as the transformation and perfection of the whole of creation, when Jesus will come to earth again (known as the Parousia or Second Coming).
- The Bible gives some ideas about heaven in symbolic language and in parables such as 'The parable of the Rich Man and Lazarus' in Luke 16:19–31.

- Some people argue against the idea of heaven after death, saying that it raises more questions than it answers, especially if people have resurrected physical bodies which take up space. If these bodies are physical then there are questions such as what and how people would eat and whether they would age.
- It is difficult to see how we could be 'the same person' in heaven if we have a different 'glorified' body and are eternal. Some people argue that this makes heaven nonsensical and others argue that it is a mystery we cannot expect to understand in this life.
- Bernard Williams criticised Christian ideas about heaven by saying that it would get boring after a while because people would run out of things to do and would not have the exciting challenge of making choices about how to use a limited lifespan. Some respond by saying that being in the presence of the wonders of God could never get boring, and that God would make sure we never felt boredom just as we would never feel pain.

Aquinas and the beatific vision

- Aquinas thought of the afterlife in terms of a beatific vision, in which people come face-to-face with God for all eternity.
- He thought that the beatific vision was not in time, so he rejected the view that Christians would see the face of God day after day, for ever.

- Instead he thought that it would be a timeless vision. There would be no more time, but the past, present and future would all be brought together. This might avoid the problems of the possibility of heaven getting boring or taking up room.

- The Catholic theologian Karl Rahner supported the view of a timeless afterlife, agreeing that the idea of endless days had too many problems.
- However, it raises philosophical issues of its own, such as how people might be resurrected into physical bodies for the beatific vision – given that physical bodies exist in time – and how people could continue to be the same person as they were before death, when so many human characteristics are directly related to living within time.

Hell

- Traditional Christian teaching presents the idea of hell as a place of eternal punishment, separated from God's presence.
- In the Bible it is sometimes described in terms of fire and torture, sometimes darkness and sometimes as a rubbish dump. It is often described as being in a downward direction from this world.
- The concept of hell raises difficult issues, with questions about whether hell is compatible with the idea of an omnipotent, loving and perfectly merciful God.
- Hume raised the question of whether there could be anything a human being could do that would justly deserve eternal punishment.
- Some people argue in response that wronging God deserves infinite punishment because God is infinitely good.
- The concept of hell also raises issues of whether hell would get boring after a while.
- Hick argued that a loving God would not allow his creatures to suffer for all eternity; he was a universalist, believing that there would eventually be salvation for all people and that the afterlife is an opportunity to continue a spiritual journey.
- Some people argue that there would be no point in having eternal punishment as it would achieve nothing (except perhaps as a deterrent from sin for those who have not yet died). This has led to the argument that notions of hell were invented as a form of social control.

Purgatory

- Purgatory does not appear explicitly in the Bible but was developed as a concept by early Christian thinkers such as Origen and Augustine.
- In the sixth century, Pope Gregory further explored the idea of a place or state where souls could be cleansed after death before they are fit to enter heaven. He understood a verse from Matthew's Gospel (12:32) to mean that there could be forgiveness after death.
- Purgatory is traditionally understood to be a place of pain and cleansing, often symbolised by fire, where the soul recognises its sin and is punished but not for ever.
- Catholic teaching includes the belief that the prayers of the living can help the souls of the dead to endure the experience.
- Rahner explored the doctrine of purgatory and argued that it should be understood not as a horrible place of pain, but as a metaphor for the soul's greater awareness of the consequences of sin and the holiness of God.
- Protestants usually do not believe in purgatory, on the grounds that it is not explicit biblical teaching and (in their view) the doctrine suggests that Christ's sacrifice on the cross did not bring about complete salvation. In the Middle Ages, the practice of charging people money to pay for a shortened time in purgatory (selling indulgences) was heavily criticised by Protestant reformers.

Election

- Election is sometimes called predestination. It is the belief that God chooses the eternal destiny of each human soul. God knows, before people are born, whether or not they will go to heaven.
- The idea is closely associated with sixteenth-century theologian John Calvin.

- Some Christians argue that because God is omniscient, he must know what will happen to each person before they are born. Because God is omnipotent, it must be in God's control to choose what happens to people.

- Augustine and others taught a doctrine of 'limited election', claiming that God would save some people through grace, but only a limited number. Augustine argued that no one could deserve salvation because of Original Sin. Augustine thought that election was a sign of God's grace and evidence of God's great love.

- Calvin taught that God chose some people for eternal life in heaven and some for eternal punishment.

- The idea of election is controversial and not accepted by all Christians. Karl Barth taught a doctrine of unlimited election, saying that Jesus brought salvation for the whole world and anyone who accepted the Christian message would be saved.

- The twentieth-century theologian Hick went further and taught that everyone will be saved eventually, whether Christian or not. Everyone will continue their spiritual journey after death and an all-loving God will ensure that everyone is saved.

- Hick's view has been criticised by, for example, Pope Benedict XVI, who said that if everyone is saved regardless of their faith then Christ's death seems pointless.

Judgement

- Christians share the view that after death there will be some kind of judgement from God.

- The question of whether each person is judged at the point of death, or whether there is a Judgement Day for everyone at the end of time, does not have a clear answer in Christianity. The Bible can be used to support a number of different possibilities:

Idea 1: Some people, such as prophets and saints, might have a kind of fast track to heaven while the rest have to wait until the time of God's choosing when the world ends.

Idea 2: Everyone has to wait until the end of time, for Judgement Day.

Idea 3: Each person goes to heaven or hell as soon as they die, and others join them as they die.

Matthew 25:31–46: The parable of the Sheep and the Goats

- This parable in Matthew's Gospel is told by Jesus.

- It describes what will happen when 'the Son of Man comes in his glory' (Matthew 25:31, New International Version). Christians interpret this to be a reference to Jesus himself.

- It describes a judgement when people are separated in the same way that a shepherd separates sheep from goats. Some people are sent to heaven and others are sent away to eternal punishment. There is no middle state.

- Those who go to heaven are chosen because of the way they have treated others when they are in need, and those who go to punishment are sent there because they have ignored those in need. Doing something for people in need is seen as doing something for Jesus himself.

- The parable says that God has 'prepared' a place for those who go to heaven, suggesting that God knew they would be coming.

APPLY

Test yourself on key knowledge (AO1)

1. What does the term 'disembodied existence' mean?

2. Which term does Augustine use for the idea that all human beings since the Fall are born into a state of wrongdoing?

3. What are the two metaphors that Paul uses in 2 Corinthians to illustrate his beliefs about life after death?

4. What is the name given to the view that everyone will eventually gain salvation after death, whatever their beliefs and behaviour in this world?

5. What does Aquinas mean when he writes about the 'beatific vision'?

6. Which sixth-century Pope helped to develop the Catholic idea of purgatory?

7. For what reasons do Protestant Christians usually reject the doctrine of purgatory?

8. 'Predestination' is another name for which belief?

9. What did Augustine believe about election?

10. How did Barth's views about election differ from those of Augustine?

11. On what grounds did Pope Benedict XVI criticise Hick's view of salvation?

12. According to the parable of the Sheep and the Goats, at what time would the sheep and goats be separated?

> If you are unsure about any of the questions, look back over the key points on pages 136–139. You can check your answers on page 219.

Develop your skills in critical argument and evaluation (AO2)

For high marks in AO2, you need to think about the ideas in this chapter and develop your own perspective, so that you can produce critically evaluative arguments rather than just describing and presenting the views of others. At AS level, 50% of your marks are awarded for your skills in critical evaluation, and at A level, 60%.

Use the following questions to help you formulate your own views.

» Discuss them with friends, making sure you articulate your own view and listen to the views of others.

» Try writing your answers to these questions, to familiarise yourself with expressing your ideas in an academic style.

» Remember to give reasons for your views.

» Think about counter-arguments – what might someone say who held a different view from your own, and why do you think they are wrong?

1. **How convincing do you find the idea of hell as a place of eternal punishment for those who are not sorry for their sins and who reject God?**

Here is an example of the kinds of ideas you might explore in formulating your analysis and evaluation:

You might want to argue that the concept of hell is convincing on the grounds that there are references to it in the Bible, including teaching from Jesus about it. If you regard the Bible as a source of wisdom and authority then this would support a belief in the existence of hell. You might argue that the idea of hell is symbolic rather than literal, but that the symbols do refer to something real – perhaps a permanent separation from God.

You might want to argue in favour of the view of hell as a 'second death' where the death of the body is followed by the death of the soul, so that there is a permanent separation from God but not the eternal punishment traditionally taught by Christianity; you could support this view with the argument that eternal punishment would serve no purpose or that it is incompatible with the idea of a loving God.

Now use your critical and evaluative skills to explore these questions on your own.

2. Williams suggests that heaven would become boring after a while because much of the excitement of earthly life comes from having a range of choices and a limited lifespan in which to make decisions. Do you think he is right? Is the idea of living in eternity appealing? Some people respond by saying that God would ensure that we would never get bored, or that coming face-to-face with an infinite God would be infinitely enthralling. Are these counter-arguments successful? Can you think of other points that could be made on either side of this debate?

3. The problem of evil is addressed by different thinkers with different theodicies. How far, in your view, do these theodicies depend on ideas about life after death? Could there be a satisfactory response to the problem of evil without any reference to life after death? Give reasons for your answer.

4. Which do you find more convincing, if either: Aquinas' understanding of the beatific vision after death, or the idea of heaven as a place of everlasting happiness and endless days in which to praise God? Give reasons for your answer.

5. Some people argue that doctrines of election suggest a God who is unfair, who chooses some people and not others so that they cannot do anything about their own destiny. Do you think this is a fair criticism of this doctrine? Would it be possible for an omniscient God not to know which people would go to heaven or hell?

6. Think about the ethical issues related to life after death. Some people object to the idea of heaven on the grounds that it suggests people only behave kindly to others out of self-interest. Kant, on the other hand, argued that an action was only genuinely good if done out of goodwill and for no other reason. Do you think belief in heaven and hell might encourage Christians to act morally only out of self-interest? Is it fair to call a desire to go to heaven 'selfish'? Give reasons for your answer.

7. Think about the religious language issues raised by discussion of life after death. Why do you think Paul uses analogies in an attempt to describe life after death? Do you think they are effective in explaining what life after death might be like? In what ways do they help and in what ways are they unclear? Have the analogies he has chosen, of the seed, the tent and clothing, stood the test of time – do they still carry the same connotations today? Would it have been better if Paul had used the *via negativa*? Are Paul's assertions about life after death susceptible to the criticisms made by logical positivists? Are the claims he makes falsifiable, and if not, does it matter? Think of other analogies and symbols used by Christians when talking about the afterlife and compare their success to Paul's.

REVIEW

Practice Exam Questions

Try these practice questions. You could:

» write plans for each of them, to practise your skills in structuring an essay

» use them for practice in writing introductions and/or conclusions

» write the whole essay, perhaps against the clock.

1. How persuasive is the view that God's judgement takes place immediately after death?

2. 'Purgatory is a state through which everyone goes.' Discuss.

> Use page 9 to review your essay and make sure you have met the assessment objectives. See page 237 for a mark scheme.

Chapter 3.3 | Knowledge of God's existence

In religion, the question is raised of how limited human beings who live in a physical world bound by time and space can have knowledge of an infinite God.

Christians have different views about whether knowledge of God can be reached through human reason and observation, or whether knowledge of God can only be obtained when God chooses to reveal himself to us.

Christians believe that human beings have finite, sinful and imperfect minds and cannot reach a true and comprehensive understanding of God.

Many Christians and other religious believers claim that sense experience and reason are not the only ways in which knowledge can be gained.

They argue that we can not only have knowledge that there is a God, but can have knowledge of God personally and form a relationship with God.

Christians make a distinction between natural theology and revealed theology.

Bonaventure's ways of seeing

- Bonaventure was a Franciscan monk of the thirteenth century.
- He thought the mind has different ways of knowing, and used the analogy of an eye that has different ways of seeing.
- Bonaventure wrote about three 'eyes':

The eye of the flesh: this is a way of seeing using the senses (empiricism). Using this 'eye' we gain knowledge of the physical world.

The eye of reason: this is a way of seeing using reason. Using this 'eye' we gain knowledge of mathematics and philosophical truth.

The eye of contemplation: this is a way of seeing using faith. Using this 'eye' we gain knowledge of God.

Natural theology

Discovering truth through natural theology

- Natural theology is about gaining knowledge of God through observation and reason.

- It contrasts with revealed theology, which is knowledge of God that can be gained through religious experience and scripture.

- Many Christians think that God can be known both through natural theology and revealed theology, but some reject natural theology.

- Paley's design argument relied on natural theology: he thought that observing the natural world showed clear evidence of the existence of a loving God.

- In the Bible some writers claim that something of God can be known through experience of the natural world, for example Psalm 8 and Romans 1.

- Aquinas used natural theology to show that Christian belief is reasonable and does not have to contrast with logical philosophy or common sense.

- Calvin argued that we are all born with a sense of the divine so knowledge of God should be easy to gain for everyone, not just the educated or intelligent. He thought the natural world is a 'mirror' of God or a 'theatre' for God, so no one can pretend to be unaware of the existence of God.

- Calvin argued that any 'epistemic distance' (distance in knowledge) between humanity and God arises because of humanity's own fault when we misuse our free will.

- Swinburne argued that the world displays characteristics of order, design and purpose, and we can use these observations to conclude the probability that God exists.

The sense of the divine

- Some people argue that human beings are born with a sense for God, an 'innate sense of the divine'.

- Cicero and many others argue that in all times and cultures, people have had a sense that there is an infinite being in control of the universe, even when these cultures have never met. They often develop religious beliefs that are remarkably similar. This could be considered evidence that we are all born with a recognition of God.

- The idea that we are born with a sense of the divine could be supported by biblical passages such as Genesis 2:7, where God breathes into Adam with his own breath.

- In the sixteenth century, Calvin wrote 'There is within the human mind, and indeed by natural instinct, an awareness of the divine'. Calvin thought this was universal to all human beings, not just Christians, so there is no excuse for people who fail to worship God.

- Some thinkers extend the idea to argue that we all have an innate sense of morality which comes from our sense of the divine. Thinkers such as Butler, Newman and C.S. Lewis argued that we instinctively feel guilt when we have done something wrong, and this 'inner voice' is evidence of the sense of God within us.

The order of creation

- Some argue that God can be clearly seen in the order, beauty and purpose of creation (teleological arguments).

- This is not an alternative to the idea of the sense of the divine, but goes with it as another way in which natural theology might work.

- It is argued that we can naturally recognise that there must be a God behind the beauty, purpose and order of creation. When we look at the natural world, it must be obvious to us that this could not have happened by chance. We can tell, using our observation, that there must be an infinite power in control of the universe and of creation.

- Aquinas, Calvin, Paley, Tennant and many others argue that the natural world reveals the existence of God.

Revelation

Revealed knowledge of God

- Revealed theology is the name Christians give to knowledge which they believe God has chosen to show people. These are not ideas people could have observed or worked out for themselves. They might include ideas such as life after death, the doctrine of the Trinity or the nature of salvation.

- The distinction between natural and revealed theology began to be made in the Middle Ages, to distinguish what people could work out for themselves from truths that could come only from God.

- Revealed theology is said to be available to everyone through faith.

- Revelation means 'unveiling' or 'uncovering'. God uncovers truths that were previously hidden.

- Immediate revelation is the name given to direct encounters with God through religious experience, such as in the story of Moses and the Burning Bush (Exodus 3).

- Mediate revelation is the name given to knowledge gained about God less directly, for example through reading about someone else's religious experience or hearing religious ideas explained during a sermon in church.

- The twentieth-century theologian Barth argued that God can only be known through revealed theology and not through natural theology. Barth argued that God reveals himself to us when he chooses, and we should not claim to be able to gain knowledge of God through our own efforts.

- Revealed knowledge of God is said to be the result of God's grace in choosing to show himself to people. It has to be accepted through faith as it cannot be supported by reason or by evidence available to the senses.

The grace of God

- In Christianity the grace of God is understood to be God's unconditional love and undeserved gifts to humanity.

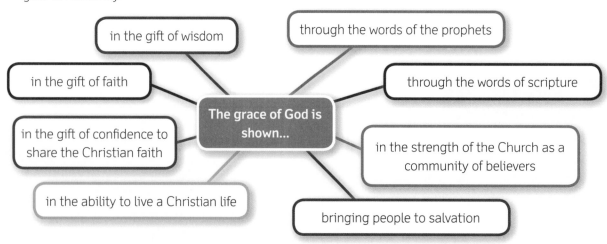

- Christians believe that none of these things would be possible without the grace of God.

The Bible and knowledge of God

- The Bible does not make a distinction between natural and revealed theology. It teaches that knowledge of God can be gained in a variety of ways:

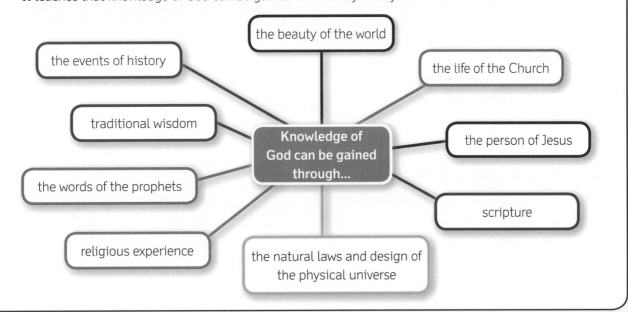

the events of history

the beauty of the world

the life of the Church

traditional wisdom

Knowledge of God can be gained through...

the person of Jesus

the words of the prophets

scripture

religious experience

the natural laws and design of the physical universe

A study of Acts 17:16–34

- In Acts 17:16–34, the first followers of Jesus are working as missionaries, trying to spread the Christian message to non-believers after Jesus' death. The passage describes the difficulties the first missionaries encountered and the ways in which they overcame problems with the help of the Holy Spirit.
- The apostle Paul speaks in the marketplace to the people of Athens. In Athens there were many idols to different gods.
- Paul uses natural theology by demonstrating reason and logic in his debate with the Jewish leaders as he tries to show them similarities between the Messiah they are expecting and the figure of Jesus.
- He talks to them about looking for the one cause of the universe rather than being superstitious about little gods. He seems to be referring to the kind of thinking used by Aristotle.
- Paul tells them that reason should lead his listeners to knowledge of an almighty God.
- Calvin uses this passage in his own writings to argue that everyone has the capacity to have knowledge of God.

Key terms

Natural theology: drawing conclusions about the nature and activity of God by using reason and observation of the world

Empiricism: a way of knowing that depends on the five senses

Faith: voluntary commitment to a belief without the need for complete evidence to support it

Revelation: 'uncovering'. In theological terms, this is when God chooses to let himself be known

Immediate revelation: where someone is given direct knowledge of God

Mediate revelation: where someone gains knowledge of God in a secondary, non-direct way

Grace of God: God's unconditional and undeserved gifts

 **APPLY**

Test yourself on key knowledge (AO1)

1. Bonaventure described three different 'eyes' through which we might gain knowledge – the eye of reason, the eye of contemplation, and which other?

2. Who wrote: 'There is within the human mind, and indeed by natural instinct, an awareness of the divine'?

3. Calvin argued that the natural world is a mirror of the divine. Which other analogy did he use to show that God can be seen in nature?

4. Which arguments for the existence of God claim that beauty, order and purpose in the natural world reveal the existence of God?

5. What is the term used in theology for a distance in knowledge and understanding?

6. Was Paley in favour of or against the use of natural theology to gain knowledge of God?

7. What do theologians mean when they make a distinction between immediate and mediate revelation?

8. What does the word 'revelation' literally mean?

9. What do Christians understand by 'the grace of God'?

10. What did Barth think about natural theology?

11. In which city did Paul speak to people about knowledge of the one almighty God who is the cause of the universe?

12. Who used Paul's speech in his own writings to demonstrate that everyone is capable of gaining knowledge of God?

> If you are unsure about any of the questions, look back over the key points on pages 142–145. You can check your answers on page 219.

Develop your skills in critical argument and evaluation (AO2)

For high marks in AO2, you need to think about the ideas in this chapter and develop your own perspective, so that you can produce critically evaluative arguments rather than just describing and presenting the views of others. At AS level, 50% of your marks are awarded for your skills in critical evaluation, and at A level, 60%.

Use the following questions to help you formulate your own views.

» Discuss them with friends, making sure you articulate your own view and listen to the views of others.

» Try writing your answers to these questions, to familiarise yourself with expressing your ideas in an academic style.

» Remember to give reasons for your views.

» Think about counter-arguments – what might someone say who held a different view from your own, and why do you think they are wrong?

1. **Some people argue that faith is not a sound basis for knowledge. Dawkins, for example, thinks that faith is an enemy of knowledge, because it encourages people to make a blind commitment to something without any kind of supporting evidence, and so obscures the search for the truth that science offers. How far would you agree with Dawkins? Do you think that faith is an obstacle to true knowledge?**

Here is an example of the kinds of ideas you might explore in formulating your analysis and evaluation:

You might want to argue that faith is a barrier to knowledge and agree with Dawkins. Perhaps you think that where there is insufficient knowledge, the right thing to do is to suspend judgement and continue to make enquiries until evidence is found. You could argue that 'blind faith' can lead people to refuse to be open-minded to different points of view because they are not using evidence or reason and so do not want to hear any. On the other hand, you might think that

faith is an important part of religious belief and of life in general. We make 'leaps of faith' when we choose life partners or decide to follow a career path or have children; perhaps many important life decisions involve an element of risk. You could argue that anyone can hold a belief when firm evidence is placed in front of them but that it is an act of will to have faith, and this could be commendable as long as faith is placed in the right thing.

Now use your critical and evaluative skills to explore these questions on your own.

2. What do you think of Bonaventure's idea that we can use the 'eye of faith' to gain knowledge of God? Do you think that we can gain knowledge of God through faith, just as we can gain knowledge of the physical world through our senses and of logical processes through reason? Can faith be a reliable guide to knowledge? Give reasons to support your answer.

3. Many people argue that we can use observation and reason to gain knowledge of God (natural theology). What do you think 'evidence for the existence of God' might look like? What might 'evidence of the absence of God' look like? Do we need to know about what a God 'usually does' in order to be able to draw conclusions through natural theology? Give reasons for your answer.

4. Some people, most notably Barth, argue that revealed theology gives knowledge but natural theology can only give a very flawed, impartial picture or perhaps no picture at all. Barth argued that knowledge of God is gained through Christ. Everyone can observe the world and use reason, whether Christian or not, so if knowledge of God can be gained only through Christ then natural theology cannot be very productive. What do you think of Barth's view? How might you support or disagree with him?

5. In the Catholic tradition, knowledge of God can be communicated through the life of the Church; the Church acts as a witness to God and a mediator of God's presence in the world. It is argued that the Church can reveal God through teaching the Bible, through celebrating the Eucharist and through demonstrating the love of God in its actions. How effective do you think the Church is at communicating knowledge of God? What do you think might be obstacles for the Church in communicating knowledge of God? Give reasons and examples to support your views.

6. Do you agree with the view of Calvin that everyone is born with a sense of the divine? Do you think that everyone has the same degree of 'religious sense', or that some people have more than others, or that the whole idea is nonsense? Give reasons for your view.

7. How far, if at all, do you think people should adopt religious beliefs based on faith? Should they insist on evidence before making up their minds to commit themselves to a religious affiliation? Are there some contexts in which a leap of faith is justifiable, and others where it is not? How might religion be distinguished from superstition, if at all? Try to support your responses with reasons and examples.

REVIEW

Practice Exam Questions

Try these practice questions. You could:

» write plans for each of them, to practise your skills in structuring an essay

» use them for practice in writing introductions and/or conclusions

» write the whole essay, perhaps against the clock.

1. 'Because of the Fall, people can have no natural knowledge of God.' Discuss.

2. Discuss critically the idea that the existence of God can be known through reason alone.

> Use page 9 to review your essay and make sure you have met the assessment objectives. See page 238 for a mark scheme.

Chapter 3.4 : The person of Jesus Christ

 RECAP

The question of who Jesus was is a key question in Christian theology.

There is well-documented evidence that a man named Jesus really lived at the time the Bible says he did. He is mentioned not only by people who were keen to spread the message of Christianity but also by several Roman historians (Suetonius, Tacitus and Pliny the Younger) as well as by the Jewish historian Josephus.

Theologians discuss the nature of Jesus and debate what it means to call Jesus 'Son of God'. They discuss whether he was a teacher of wisdom in the traditions of Judaism, whether he was an independent revolutionary and whether he had sympathies with political groups of the time.

Jesus the Son of God

The title 'Son of God'

- Jesus is often referred to as Son of God in Christian teaching. The doctrine of the Trinity, where God is understood as Father, Son and Holy Spirit, places Jesus as the Son of God.
- The idea of Jesus as Son of God is central to Jesus' authority.

- In the gospels, Jesus is referred to as God's Son in the stories of his baptism and Transfiguration.
- Paul speaks of Jesus as God's own Son in his letter to the Romans.
- Jesus did not refer to himself in terms of the Son of God.

Jesus' knowledge of God and of his own nature

- The idea of Jesus as God's Son is linked to discussions about Jesus' knowledge. It could be that Jesus was the Son of God in the sense that he had a unique knowledge of God.
- Biblical writers speak of Jesus as 'the word' of God, suggesting that the words spoken by Jesus were the very words of God, giving Jesus' teaching divine authority. The idea of Jesus as God's word also suggests a relationship with

the creation, where God created the universe by saying 'Let there be…' (Genesis 1, New International Version); Jesus as God's word suggests Jesus was present at the time of the creation.

- The idea that Jesus had full knowledge or special knowledge of God creates a puzzle because it implies that Jesus and God are separate beings who know each other.

- The early Church developed the doctrine of 'hypostatic union' between Jesus and God, where two natures are united in one person, but this does not completely clarify the issue.

- Questions of Jesus' knowledge raise a large number of issues – did Jesus have freedom to act in any way other than the way he acted (and if not, can he be praised for his actions if he could not have done anything else)? Did Jesus have omniscience – did he know he would be crucified, and did he know what his place was in God's plan for the universe? Were his expressions of emotion genuine or did he secretly know how things were going to turn out? Did Jesus gain knowledge through his experience of the world, like every other human being?

- The Catholic theologian Rahner suggested that Jesus had layers of consciousness, with human self-consciousness nearer to the surface and God-consciousness deeper within him.

Jesus as God and man

- Christians believe that only God has the power to save humanity from sin – so if Jesus saved people from sin, then he had to be (in some sense) God.

- Christians also believe that Jesus had to be human in order to live on the earth as we do, suffer pain for the sake of humanity and submit to human death.

- The idea that Jesus was both fully human and fully divine creates issues, because God and humanity are very different so it is difficult to see how anyone could be both at the same time. Christians rejected the demi-god idea found in ancient Greek and Roman mythology.

- According to Christian teaching, Jesus did not have the sinful nature that other human beings have. He was capable of being tempted by evil, but he rejected that temptation (unlike Adam and Eve) and so was able to bring humanity to reconciliation with God.

- Medieval Christian theologians thought that Jesus might have knowledge of God in three ways:

1. Face-to-face knowledge of God and of all eternal and created things (scientia visionis).

2. An 'infused' knowledge, which is knowledge that is not learned but is given by God (scientia infusa).

3. Knowledge of life in the normal human way, gained through experience (scientia experientiae).

- Most Christians today accept the agreed teaching on Jesus' human and divine nature as confirmed at the First Council of Nicea in AD325 and then at the Council of Chalcedon in AD451. They agreed that Jesus was 'of the same substance' as God, as one being – a doctrine known as homoousios. They rejected the idea that Jesus was some kind of mix or blend of two natures.

- The question of what Jesus might or might not have known about his own nature is a difficult one to answer. Gerald O'Collins writes about the problem in *Interpreting Jesus* (1993), saying that we cannot draw conclusive answers about the inner life of anyone; knowledge and how it is gained is an extremely complex subject; but we can conclude that Jesus knew he had a unique relationship with God and had a mission.

The miracles of Jesus

- In the New Testament, Jesus is shown as being a miracle worker. Miracles include healing the sick, feeding the hungry, driving out demons, calming the storm, walking on water and turning water into wine.
- In the eighteenth century, Hume argued that when presented with an account that
  says a miracle has taken place, we should always treat it with scepticism and believe a more likely explanation of the event (such as that the witnesses were mistaken or deliberately deceiving).
- Other writers, such as Edward Schillebeeckx, argue that miracles should be interpreted as having a spiritual, metaphorical meaning rather than a literal meaning.
- N.T. Wright suggests that the miracle stories should be understood in terms of the intentions of the writers as showing that Jesus had the power and authority to unite people and restore communities. The miracle stories are included in the Bible as exemplars to illustrate Jesus as, for example, having the authority to forgive sins; they are not just accounts of what Jesus did.

The Resurrection of Jesus

- In Christian belief the Resurrection of Jesus is an essential part of the Christian message.
- Paul writes in his letters that there could be no Christian faith without the Resurrection: if God had not raised Jesus from the dead then the sins of humanity would not have been washed clean and Jesus would have died for nothing. Preaching the gospel would be pointless without the Resurrection.
- Theologians such as N.T. Wright and E.P. Sanders write that it is the belief in the Resurrection of Jesus that has maintained the strength of Christianity as a belief system.
- The Resurrection of Jesus has many implications for Christianity:

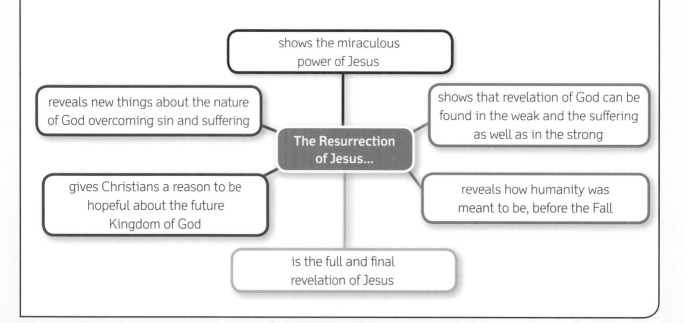

Jesus the teacher of wisdom

Is Jesus best understood as a teacher of wisdom? Some people cannot accept ideas such as that Jesus was the Son of God, but they still admire the wisdom of his teachings.

Jesus as rabbi

- In Judaism the term 'rabbi' is used for a teacher and leader – someone who studied the scriptures and could interpret and teach them.

- Some of Jesus' followers used the title 'Rabbi' when they addressed him. It is clear that Jesus could read and that he was familiar with the Jewish scriptures.

- He taught in synagogues and in the open; gospel accounts suggest that people who heard him were surprised at his level of education. Scribes and Pharisees asked him questions, perhaps because they genuinely wanted to know or perhaps to test his level of knowledge.

- Jesus spoke about the interpretation of scripture, about moral issues (especially morality related to the poor and oppressed), and about the importance of love even in the face of hatred. His moral teaching includes: the forgiveness of sins; love of enemies; love for God and love for each other; inclusion for outcasts; self-giving sacrifice; and choosing moral purity over worldly wealth.

- Lewis argued in 1952 that it does not make sense to accept Jesus' moral teaching but not accept that he was the Son of God, because of the claims Jesus made about himself. Lewis said that when Jesus made claims about himself (such as 'I am the bread of life') he was either telling the truth or not. If he was telling the truth, then he was the Son of God, and if he was not telling the truth then he was deceitful or delusional – not the kind of person whose moral messages should be followed.

- Bonhoeffer linked the idea of the incarnation with the idea that we meet God in other human beings; the incarnation of Christ allows us to encounter God in human life in a special and unique way.

The challenge of *The Myth of God Incarnate* (1977)

- Hick and others contributed to a book called *The Myth of God Incarnate* (1977) in which they argued that the idea of Jesus as God incarnate is best understood mythologically.

- Hick argued that the kind of moral example and teaching given by Jesus could also be found in others, including leading figures from other world religions such as Moses, Jeremiah, Ramakrishna, Guru Nanak and Muhammad.

- Linking with his ideas about religious pluralism and inclusivism, as well as ideas about religious language, Hick and his fellow authors argued that the idea of a transformation from self-centredness to love-centredness in many world religions show that there are many different paths to salvation.

- The idea of God coming to earth as a human should be understood as a metaphor, rather than as literal truth. Jesus was human, with special insights and gifts inspired by God.

- Jesus remains an exemplar of a wise and holy man who gave important moral teaching and who makes an excellent role model.

- Christians who reject Hick's point of view argue that Jesus' moral nature cannot be separated from his divine nature. They argue that God in Christ sacrificed himself to save the world from sin, in a single act of universal significance that goes beyond a personal decision to be less selfish and more loving.

Jesus the liberator

Jesus' challenges to social injustice

- Christians often present Jesus as a liberator who challenged social conventions, as well as in a more theological sense liberating humanity from the imprisonment of sin and death.

- Jesus spoke out against the domination of the rich over the poor. He included social outcasts such as tax collectors and Samaritans in his mission.

- Many later Christians have become involved in social change as a result of Jesus' teaching, such as the Salvation Army and followers of Liberation Theology.

- Luke's Gospel in particular emphasises Jesus' inclusion of women in his mission, even though women at the time of Jesus were not considered to be the equals of men.

Jesus challenged the authority of the Jewish leaders when he drove the money-changers out of the Temple

Jesus' challenges to political authority

- At the time of Jesus, Palestine was under the control of the Romans. The Jews were allowed to continue in their traditions as long as they did not cause trouble.

- The situation was uneasy and ended with the burning down of the Temple in Jerusalem in AD73 (after Jesus' lifetime).

- During Jesus' lifetime many Jews hoped for a Messiah who would come and lead them to victory over the Romans, as a warrior king rather like King David of the Old Testament.

- One group of militant Jews at the time of Jesus was the Zealots, who called for violent revolution. Some biblical scholars, such as Reza Aslan, argued that Jesus may have been more closely linked with the Zealots than the way he is presented in the gospels:

> Jesus did say 'I did not come to bring peace, but a sword' (Matthew 10:34, New International Version). His followers drew weapons in the Garden of Gethsemane, suggesting they carried daggers with them most of the time, and some of Jesus' followers seem to have been Zealots.

> Jesus rode into Jerusalem on a donkey to welcoming crowds, suggesting that this was a deliberately organised event meant to show that Jesus was the new leader and King of the Jews, in fulfilment of the messages of the prophets.

> The Romans put the name 'King of the Jews' on Jesus' cross (according to John's Gospel), perhaps because Jesus was seen as a leader of a political revolutionary group.

- However, not all scholars agree that Jesus was a political revolutionary. They point to examples such as:

> He stopped his disciples from using violence at his arrest.

> He did not accept or use political titles for himself.

> Judas might have betrayed Jesus because Jesus was not being radical or militant enough for the Zealots.

> Jesus was careful with his answers to questions about Roman rule and taxes and did not suggest openly defying them.

> Jesus emphasised peace.

> Jesus spoke of a spiritual rather than a worldly Kingdom of God.

Jesus' challenges to religious authority

- Jesus seems to have been on good terms with people in religious authority.
- However, he does challenge some of the rules about religious rituals, for example by healing on the Sabbath when it was meant to be a day of rest. Jesus speaks in a way that suggests he has authority to say when a rule should be strictly obeyed and when it needs to be broken.
- Jesus associated with people who were traditionally 'unclean' such as Samaritans and a woman with a haemorrhage.
- Jesus suggests that the Temple will be replaced by something better, and is critical of some of its practices, especially the practice of money-changing for profit.
- Jesus came into conflict with religious leaders and was called to the Sanhedrin (the Jewish court) to answer accusations.
- Some biblical scholars, such as Sanders, think that the gospel writers may have exaggerated Jesus' conflicts with Judaism in order to fit their own Christian agenda, and that Jesus was more Jewish in his outlook than the New Testament presents.

Key terms

Son of God: a term for Jesus that emphasises that he is God incarnate, one of the three persons of the Trinity

Hypostatic union: the belief that Christ is both fully God and fully human, indivisible, two natures united in one person

Homoousios: of the same substance or of the same being

Incarnation: God born as a human being, in Jesus Christ

Liberator: a general term for someone who frees a people or group

Messiah: in Christianity, the word is associated with Jesus Christ, who is believed to be the Son of God and the Saviour

Zealot: a member of the Jewish political/military movement that fought against Rome in the first century AD

Redemption: the action of saving or being saved from sin, error, or evil

 **APPLY**

Test yourself on key knowledge (AO1)

1. Who edited a book called *The Myth of God Incarnate* in which the writers suggested that the idea of Jesus as the Son of God was a metaphor?

2. Which biblical scholar suggested that Jesus' conflicts with the Jewish authorities might have been exaggerated by the gospel writers?

3. Who were the Zealots?

4. Give an example of a Roman or Jewish historian whose writings provide evidence of the historical existence of Jesus.

5. Who suggested that Jesus was either telling the truth in the claims he made about himself, or else he was a deceiver or delusional?

6. Which philosopher argued that we should always take a sceptical attitude towards stories of miracles?

7. What did medieval theologians mean when they said Jesus would have had 'scientia infusa'?

8. Give an example of a socially outcast group that Jesus deliberately included in his mission.

9. Who argued that the incarnation of Christ allows us to meet God in other human beings in a special and unique way?

10. Which biblical scholar argued that Jesus might have had closer links with the Zealots than people usually imagine?

11. What do theologians mean by the term 'homoousios'?

12. Did Jesus refer to himself as the Son of God?

> If you are unsure about any of the questions, look back over the key points on pages 148–153. You can check your answers on page 219.

Develop your skills in critical argument and evaluation (AO2)

For high marks in AO2, you need to think about the ideas in this chapter and develop your own perspective, so that you can produce critically evaluative arguments rather than just describing and presenting the views of others. At AS level, 50% of your marks are awarded for your skills in critical evaluation, and at A level, 60%.

Use the following questions to help you formulate your own views.

» Discuss them with friends, making sure you articulate your own view and listen to the views of others.

» Try writing your answers to these questions, to familiarise yourself with expressing your ideas in an academic style.

» Remember to give reasons for your views.

» Think about counter-arguments – what might someone say who held a different view from your own, and why do you think they are wrong?

1. **Many people today argue that Jesus' moral teachings are valuable but do not accept he was the Son of God. Some scholars, however, argue that Jesus' moral teachings cannot be separated from his nature as God in human form. Which point of view do you find more persuasive? Give reasons for your answer.**

Here is an example of the kinds of ideas you might explore in formulating your analysis and evaluation:

You might want to argue that Jesus' moral teachings are valuable, giving examples, and you might want to show that these teachings can also be found elsewhere (perhaps in the teachings of other religious leaders). Perhaps the teachings are valuable regardless of who said them. Conversely,

you might think that Jesus' moral teaching is not as good as some other kinds of ethics; you might have studied Nietzsche and prefer his way of looking at morality, or you might prefer a secular ethic such as utilitarianism. You could explore the reasoning of Lewis or Bonhoeffer; perhaps you

> think that Jesus' teachings cannot be separated from his nature and that it was only because of Jesus' relationship with God that he was able to have such moral insights and speak with authority.
>
> In your response, try to support your views with reasoning and examples, rather than just relying on your own religious faith or non-belief to support your view.

Now use your critical and evaluative skills to explore these questions on your own.

2. In the gospels, Jesus is often shown expressing emotion. For example, he becomes angry when he sees money-changers in the Temple, he is sad when Lazarus dies, he is concerned when the five thousand are hungry. Can you find other examples? Do you think that these examples are compatible with the view that Jesus had the same kind of knowledge that God is believed to have, or do they show that Jesus' knowledge was the same as other human beings, or are they inconclusive? Give reasons for your answer.

3. Do stories in which Jesus performs miracles serve to illustrate that he was the Son of God? Do you think the writers of the stories meant readers to take them literally, or are they meant to be poetic, mythological ways of describing some kind of spiritual changes? Some people (including Hume) argue that it is unreasonable to believe stories of miracles, whilst others might argue that of course a God who created the world can perform miracles. How would you interpret stories of Jesus performing miracles, and what reasons would you give for this interpretation?

4. Consider the different interpretations you have studied of the idea that Jesus was the Son of God.

What do you understand this term to mean? Do you think it can be seen as a 'divine mystery', beyond human comprehension, or is that just a way of disguising that the concept makes no sense? Give reasons for your answer.

5. Scholars disagree about the extent to which Jesus can be considered to have been a political revolutionary. Of the points of view you have studied, which do you find the most convincing and for what reasons? Do you think it would be possible for someone to be a 'spiritual liberator' but at the same time not become involved with human issues of oppression?

6. The Resurrection of Jesus is seen as central to the Christian message. However, some thinkers believe that it should be understood as a metaphor rather than as literal truth, as a poetic way of talking about the importance of Jesus' example and teaching living on after his death. Do you think the Resurrection stories were meant to be taken literally? If people choose to interpret them as symbolic rather than literal, do you think their views are still 'Christian' views? Give reasons to support your answer.

REVIEW

Practice Exam Questions

Try these practice questions. You could:

» write plans for each of them, to practice your skills in structuring an essay

» use them for practise in writing introductions and/or conclusions

» write the whole essay, perhaps against the clock.

1. 'Jesus was more than a political liberator.' Discuss.

2. How convincing is the claim that Jesus' relationship with God was unique?

> Use page 9 to review your essay and make sure you have met the assessment objectives. See pages 238–239 for a mark scheme.

Chapter 3.5 | Christian moral principles

 RECAP

Christian moral principles are based on the teachings of the Bible, especially Jesus' moral teachings, in combination with the traditional teaching of the Church, using reason and conscience, and trying to apply principles of agapeic love. Catholic Christians also use the principles of natural law.

These different but related sources of moral guidance can give rise to issues for Christians if they appear to be giving different advice.

There are different views about which sources of moral authority for Christians should take precedence.

Using the Bible as a source of moral guidance

- In *Biblical Imperatives* (1994), the theologian Richard Mouw argues that Christians need to be aware of the different commandments and stories in the Bible, and not just take something like the rule of love and try to apply it without studying different passages.

- In *SCM Study Guide to Christian Ethics* (2006), the theologian Neil Messer argues that moral guidance in the Bible can be found not just in the commandments, but also in other passages. Figures could be seen as role models, and stories of history could have a moral implication for modern political life.

- The Bible can be approached in either a propositional or a non-propositional way:

> A **propositional** approach to the Bible accepts that the words of the Bible are true messages from God.

> A **non-propositional** approach to the Bible looks at biblical stories, especially the life, death and Resurrection of Jesus, as speaking to a Christian's own life and experience.

The Bible as the direct word of God

- For some Christians the Bible reveals God's word directly, making it the only source for Christian ethics.

- The Bible is understood as the literal, inspired 'breathed in' word of God.

- It is believed that the human authors simply wrote down the words as God told them, without adding any interpretation of their own.

- In this view the Bible is an infallible guide to life and its commandments apply at all times. Christians who have this understanding of the Bible might use verses to support their opinions on homosexuality or divorce or other moral issues.

- The view that the Bible should be understood literally tends to be more popular amongst evangelical Protestant Christians.

Criticisms of this view

- The Bible appears to contain some contradictions of fact, such as different accounts of Jesus' last words on the cross.

- If the Bible is the direct word of God, it is difficult to understand why it contains so many different styles of writing and interests; this suggests some degree of human authorship.

- Some parts of the Bible's moral teaching seem to be in direct contradiction with other parts, for example in the Sermon on the Mount in Matthew's Gospel, Jesus contradicts some of the laws given in the Old Testament.

- Some of the facts in the Bible do not match modern scientific knowledge.

The Bible as the interpreted word of God

- For other Christians, the Bible is a source of moral guidance but does not necessarily have to be understood literally.

- Those Christians believe that it was written by authors inspired by God, but using their own words, rather than the exact words of God.

- It is believed that the Bible was written in particular times and cultures and that some parts of it are more appropriate for the past, but a lot of it is appropriate for the present day.

- In *The Moral Vision of the New Testament* (1996), Richard B. Hays points out a number of factors that can affect a Christian's reading of the Bible. For example, a Christian might use only a narrow range of texts or favourite images and stories, so that even Christians who claim to take the Bible literally are probably being selective and bringing their own judgements and biases to it.

Criticisms of this view

- It can lead to disagreements and disunity, for example on verses relating to women in leadership or on homosexuality, where some argue that biblical teaching needs reinterpretation for the modern world and others say that it holds a truth which should be upheld.

- It can be seen to be 'cherry-picking', where Christians ignore the parts of the Bible they find too challenging to adopt in their own lives.

- It is not always easy to tell which parts of the Bible are meant to be for all time and which can be understood as cultural or as myth.

Church tradition and the Bible

- Catholic Christians believe that the Bible grew out of the teaching of the Church, because the Church made the decisions about which pieces of writing would form scripture.

- Protestants often hold that the Church grew out of the Bible and that the Bible is the principal source of moral and religious authority.

- Many theologians note the closely intertwined relationship between the Church and the Bible in Christian thinking:
  - Hays notes that interpretation of the Bible does not happen in a vacuum but is shaped by the teaching of the Church.
  - William Spohn points out that scripture cannot be examined in isolation from the Christian communities and traditions in which it functions.

Church tradition in Anglican understanding

- The common understanding of the Anglican Church is that Church tradition relates both to the practices and beliefs of the first Christians and also to current traditions in the Church.

- The Bible comes first but it is not the only source of understanding.

- Influences from the Bible and Church tradition are combined when making moral decisions or decisions about practices within the Church.

- Anglicans see Church tradition as a shared understanding of the kind of community the Church is, including where it has come from, its prayer life, its organisation and its teachings. It should be seen as a vital, living part of the Anglican community today and not just a fixed backward-looking insistence on doing things the way they have always been done.

Church tradition in the Catholic understanding

- Catholics have a different understanding of Church tradition than Anglicans, and refer to it as Sacred Tradition.

- They see tradition as having a precedent over the Bible, because it was the Church community that decided which texts should be considered sacred and form the Bible. The authority of the Church gave the Bible its authority.

- Sacred Tradition is a means of coming to know the revelation of Jesus. It follows the oral tradition handed down by Jesus to the first Christian leaders in an unbroken chain of Apostolic Succession, which is the line of bishops and priests ever since the first apostles.

- Tradition is seen as the way in which the Holy Spirit works in the world.

- The task of interpreting the Bible is given to the Church, and the Church is the only authority which is able to give authentic interpretation of scripture.

- The council of Vatican II formally declared that Sacred Tradition and the Bible are linked in such a way that one cannot stand without the other.

- Sacred Tradition is seen as a binding authority on moral life, although the importance of the individual conscience is not ignored.

- Catholic Sacred Tradition is summarised in the Catechism of the Catholic Church, which gives summaries of Catholic teaching on a wide range of issues such as abortion, nuclear weapons and employment rights. This teaching is reached through a process of integrating tradition and scripture with reasoning.

- The Catholic Church draws on natural law as a method of ethical decision-making.

Issues raised by the idea of Church tradition

- Protestants have problems with the view that Church tradition is equal to the Bible.

- The concern comes from the Reformation, which was critical of practices of the Catholic Church, saying that many of them were not in accordance with the teachings of the Bible but had been invented to enable the Church to keep hold of its power. Protestant reformers argued that the Bible should have precedence and should be the judge of Church traditions.

- In his teachings as described in the gospels, Jesus sometimes criticises traditional teachings because people have become too entrapped in their own rigid interpretations of law and forgotten about caring for others. However, there are also positive things said about the traditions handed down.

- Some feminist thinkers, such as Rosemary Radford Reuther, have criticised Church traditions for ignoring women's perspectives.

Key terms

Bible/Scripture: a collection or canon of books in the Bible which contain the revelation of God

Agape love: unconditional love, the only ethical norm in situationism

Church tradition: the traditions of how Christian life in community works, in worship, practical moral life and prayer, and the teaching and reflection of the Church handed down across time

Sacred Tradition: the idea that the revelation of Jesus Christ is communicated in two ways. In addition to scripture, it is communicated through the apostolic and authoritative teaching of the Church councils and the Pope

Reason

- Reason is used for logical decision-making, to process and reflect on experiences and to apply theory to practice.

- Modern philosophers such as Alasdair MacIntyre and Hays argue that reason is not objective or neutral, as Enlightenment thinkers seemed to agree, but operates according to our culture and biases.

- Reason can present different interpretations of the Bible and different responses to ethical dilemmas, for example reason might lead some people to a 'just war' approach to the ethics of conflict and might lead others to a pacifist approach.

- In moral decision-making, Christians need to find a route that uses their reason alongside biblical principles and Church traditions.

- Catholics use reason alongside the Bible and Sacred Tradition in natural law ethics. Using the revelation of God through tradition and the Bible, and using their observation of the natural world, Catholics use their reason to determine the right course of action. Reason is understood as a gift from God, given to enable humanity to access God's revelation.

- Protestants see the Bible and reason as the primary sources of moral decision-making, with the teachings and traditions of the Church providing useful and helpful commentaries. When making moral decisions they will use prayer and Bible study to help them work out what to do.

- Some Christians have concerns about reason being set in opposition to faith. Debates about the relationship between science and religion sometimes suggest that religious faith works in opposition to reason, where there is seen a choice between 'common-sense' reason and 'blind' faith. Christians would argue that their faith is not blind and that it is both reasoned and reasonable.

Love (agape) as the only Christian ethical principle

- The principle of unconditional love (agape) is central for Christian morality.

- It is at the heart of Jesus' teachings and actions and is a prominent theme in the New Testament.

- Jesus' summary of the law was that people should love God and love their neighbours as much as they love themselves.

- Christians are told to love their enemies and do good to them.

- In 1 Corinthians 13, Paul spells out the nature of Christian love.

- 1 John 4:8 says that people who do not love cannot know God, because God is love.

- Bultmann pointed out that Christians are challenged not only to be kind to others but to forgive wrongs. Christian moral behaviour should not be about laws and being judgemental, but should focus on God's forgiveness.

- Tillich, the Protestant theologian, suggested that Christians should use three ethical principles: justice, love and wisdom, of which love is the most important. He criticised 'moral Puritanism' for being too closely tied to fixed rules, and argued instead for love guided by wisdom as a person-centred approach to ethics. He thought people should not feel compelled to follow traditional laws unconditionally. He argued that the ultimate authority should be the Christian's own decision, and traditions should be considered but need to be interpreted with love for the actual people involved in the moral situation.

- Tillich's thinking was very influential on Fletcher who advocated using agape as the guiding moral law in his situation ethics.

- Pope Francis has been revisiting some of the rules and traditions of the Catholic Church to remind people of the emphasis on love. He criticises approaches which take an authoritarian, rigid attitude and aims to show compassion and openness to the grace of God.

 **APPLY**

Test yourself on key knowledge (AO1)

1. In which letter in the New Testament does Paul spell out the nature and characteristics of Christian love?
2. Give an example of where the Bible might be considered to have some errors of fact.
3. What is meant by the term 'Apostolic Succession'?
4. Which normative method of ethical decision-making is most widely practised by Catholics?
5. Give an example of a modern philosopher who has argued that reason is not objective and can be affected by culture.
6. Which theologian emphasised that a morality based on love has to be a morality based on forgiveness?
7. Which theologian was a particular influence on Fletcher when Fletcher worked out his system of situation ethics?
8. For what reason has Reuther criticised the idea of prioritising Church tradition in moral decision-making?

9. Which three ethical principles did Tillich choose as important for Christians to employ in moral decision-making?
10. Why did some Protestants of the Reformation object to Church tradition having prominence in Christian morality
11. What did Jesus say when he gave a summary of the Old Testament law?
12. Which Christian denomination argues that Church tradition was responsible for the formation of the Bible and therefore should be considered to have precedence over the Bible?

If you are unsure about any of the questions, look back over the key points on pages 156–159. You can check your answers on page 219.

Develop your skills in critical argument and evaluation (AO2)

For high marks in AO2, you need to think about the ideas in this chapter and develop your own perspective, so that you can produce critically evaluative arguments rather than just describing and presenting the views of others. At AS level, 50% of your marks are awarded for your skills in critical evaluation, and at A level, 60%.

Use the following questions to help you formulate your own views.

» Discuss them with friends, making sure you articulate your own view and listen to the views of others.
» Try writing your answers to these questions, to familiarise yourself with expressing your ideas in an academic style.

» Remember to give reasons for your views.
» Think about counter-arguments – what might someone say who held a different view from your own, and why do you think they are wrong?

1. **Do you think that Christians can use the Bible as a guide to moral life in the twenty-first century? Can rules and guidance from a different time and culture be applied to modern life? Are there moral dilemmas today which did not exist in biblical times, and if so, can the Bible be of any help in guiding Christians to deal with them?**

Here is an example of the kinds of ideas you might explore in formulating your analysis and evaluation:

You might want to argue that the Bible continues to be a practical source of guidance for Christians today. You could argue that if modern society has moved away from biblical practices, then modern society should change because the Bible is the unerring word of God. You might want to argue that the Bible might not be able to be directly applied to modern society because we no longer have concerns about our oxen or our wheat, but instead are concerned about climate change and globalisation. You might argue

that biblical principles can be applied, such as love and forgiveness, or that biblical figures can be used as role models even though society has changed. Perhaps you would argue that biblical teaching, reason and Church tradition need to be combined in order to reach a moral decision, or you might consider that this method of combining sources of authority leads to such a wide range of possible outcomes that there is very little authoritative guidance. Give reasons to support your point of view, and examples to illustrate it.

Now use your critical and evaluative skills to explore these questions on your own.

2. It could be argued that agape love with an emphasis on forgiveness is an impossible ideal for Christians to follow, because it demands too much of people. Do you agree with this criticism? In your view, are there some actions that can never be forgiven? Are there some actions that it would be morally wrong to forgive? Give reasons and examples to support your answer.

3. Reuther argued that following Church tradition means that people are following a patriarchal system of morality because women had a lower status in the past than they have today. How far would you agree with this point of view? Do you think Church tradition should be abandoned, if she is right?

4. How fair is the claim that following Sacred Tradition keeps Christianity backward-looking, doing things simply because they have always been done that way and not allowing room for fresh insights?

5. Tillich advocates using love, justice and wisdom for moral decision-making. How practical do you think this might be in ethical dilemmas? Are there reliable ways of knowing what is a just thing to do? How can we judge whether the decision we are thinking of making is wise?

6. Do you think there is anything distinctive about Christian ethics, or are they just the same as the ethics of non-Christians except with the word 'God' in the rationale? Do Christian ethics make demands of people that non-Christian ethics avoid? Is the goal of Christian ethics the same as the goal of other systems, such as utilitarianism? Give reasons and examples to support your answer.

7. In your view, are Christian ethics primarily about the individual who wants to follow God's commands and develop their own character, or are they primarily about the good of society? Can it be possible to live a Christian life in isolation from other people? Are there times when Christians should follow the will of the rest of a Christian community rather than following their own consciences? Give reasons for your answer.

REVIEW

Practice Exam Questions

Try these practice questions. You could:

» write plans for each of them, to practise your skills in structuring an essay

» use them for practice in writing introductions and/or conclusions

» write the whole essay, perhaps against the clock.

1. How fair is the claim that the principle of love is all that is necessary for Christian ethics?

2. 'In order to lead a moral Christian life, Christians need more than just the Bible for guidance.' Discuss.

> Use page 9 to review your essay and make sure you have met the assessment objectives. See pages 239–240 for a mark scheme.

Chapter 3.6 | Christian moral action

RECAP

Christian moral principles can lead Christians into conflict with authorities.

Dietrich Bonhoeffer was a German Lutheran pastor whose Christian faith led him to oppose Nazism.

He developed a theology of discipleship and an ethic that has been highly influential and thought-provoking.

His best-known writings are *The Cost of Discipleship* (1948) and *Letters and Papers from Prison* (1953).

The German Church at the time of Hitler

- Bonhoeffer was ordained as a Christian minister in 1931. In the 1930s, when Hitler and Nazism were rising in popularity in Germany, the German Protestant Churches were divided.

- Some German Christians joined the Nazi party, believing that Hitler was an embodiment of Christian values. They prohibited ministers with Jewish ancestry from working for the Church and some tried to remove the Old Testament from the Bible because it is the holy scripture of Judaism. Nazi ideology gained a strong hold over the German Church.

- Other Christians, including Bonhoeffer, disagreed with Nazism and saw it as contrary to the Christian message.

- A new Church was formed called the Confessing Church, which rejected Nazi ideology. It called Christians to confess their faith, be true to their calling to discipleship and keep the commands of God.

- Bonhoeffer's criticism of the Nazis brought him into conflict with them as soon as they came to power. He saw enthusiasm for Hitler 'the Fuhrer' as cult-like. He criticised their distortion of the Christian call to discipleship and their persecution of the Jews.

Bonhoeffer's call to obedience and discipleship

- Basing his teaching on the gospels, Bonhoeffer believed that all Christians are called to discipleship – they are all called to be followers of Jesus.

- He pointed out that Jesus' first followers did not accept a set of doctrines but responded to Jesus' authority immediately with obedience to Jesus' call. For Bonhoeffer this is an example to all Christians, who have to choose which leader to obey.

- The call to discipleship is a call to leave an old life behind and move into the unknown. All responsibilities to other forms of authority are abandoned. Christians should not try to fit their faith around their previous existence in a way that is convenient for them, but should leave all of that behind and instead be obedient to Christ.

- This caused controversy for Bonhoeffer because he was saying that Christians do not need to feel they have to obey other laws, such as the laws of the land. It opened the possibility of civil disobedience.

- Bonhoeffer stressed the urgency of Christianity, where there is no time to deliberate over whether or not to treat someone as a neighbour. Christianity demands immediate and single-minded obedience to Jesus.

- Bonhoeffer thought that obedience is learned and understood by practising it.

Civil disobedience

- Civil disobedience is an active and open refusal to obey certain laws set down by the government.

- Bonhoeffer thought that civil disobedience was sometimes necessary as, in his view, duty to God was far more important than duty to the State.

- He wrote to his friend, the theologian Reinhold Niebuhr, that German Christians had to make a choice between wanting their nation to be defeated so that Christianity could survive, or wanting their nation to win but losing Christian civilisation as a result. He did not think there was a third option.

- He argued that it was not enough for Christians to keep out of doing what the Nazis were doing, and then feel as though at least they, personally, were not to blame. Christians needed to make active challenges against injustice.

In his own life, Bonhoeffer challenged Nazism openly. He spoke against Nazism in the university where he was employed, and lost his job. He went to public lectures and raised objections to Nazism, and was banned from going to them. He criticised the Confessing Church when it did not stand up to Hitler with the strength Bonhoeffer was looking for. He openly prayed for the defeat of his country and called Hitler the anti-Christ.

Bonhoeffer became a double agent, working for German military intelligence but actually linking with the Resistance and with the Allies. He used Church meetings to smuggle information. He disguised Jews as members of military intelligence and smuggled them across the border to safety in Switzerland.

Bonhoeffer's own acts of civil disobedience

There are rumours that Bonhoeffer was part of a plot to assassinate Hitler, but it is unclear whether this was true because there was so much secrecy around such efforts, and a lot of people were unjustly accused of trying to do this.

The role of the Church

- Bonhoeffer saw the role of the Church in terms of a community of believers and as a source of spiritual discipline.

- He used the Sermon on the Mount in Matthew 5–7 as inspiration for the idea that followers of Jesus must be like 'salt' and 'light'. The metaphor of salt shows that Christians need to add 'flavour' to a community, even if they are small in number, by leading exemplary Christian lives, and the metaphor of 'light' is used to show that Christians must be a leading example for others and not try to keep their beliefs hidden. They must be a visible community.

- Bonhoeffer notes that the Bible says Christians do not have the salt, but are the salt. They are not called just to share Christian teaching with others, but are to do it themselves.

- Bonhoeffer lists some of the 'good works' that Christians are asked to do and to suffer, including poverty, peaceableness, persecution and rejection.

- He wrote of 'religionless Christianity', looking forward to a time after the war when Christians would focus on their call to discipleship rather than on being 'religious'.

Bonhoeffer's role in the Confessing Church and at Finkenwalde

- The Confessing Church was formed in 1934 as a breakaway from the national Reich Church in Germany. The Reich Church would not allow ministers who had Jewish or other 'non-Aryan' ancestry, and they merged their Church youth groups with the Hitler Youth.

- The leaders of the Confessing Church came under increased pressure from Hitler as he grew in power.

- Bonhoeffer opposed taking a civil oath in support of Hitler.

- Bonhoeffer was asked in 1935 to run a secret training school, or seminary, for new pastors. This school was secret and illegal because it was not applying 'Aryan restrictions'.

- The school for pastors met in a disused private school in a town called Finkenwalde.

- Bonhoeffer advocated a life at the seminary which was monastic (monk-like). The trainees were encouraged to spend their time in prayer, Bible study and reflection, as well as singing 'spirituals', the religious songs of the black community in America.

- The training at the Finkenwalde seminary was controversial – some people said that in Nazi Germany, there was not time for such an emphasis on quiet reflection. Bonhoeffer, however, thought it was essential for the next generation to be trained to listen to God.

- At Finkenwalde, Bonhoeffer experimented with ideas about Christian community, which he thought should be a source of spiritual renewal and a refuge for those who were persecuted. It should train Christians to be a caring service under the word of God.

- The Gestapo under Himmler discovered the Finkenwalde seminary in 1937 and closed it down, arresting many former students.

- Bonhoeffer became disappointed with the Confessing Church because he thought the leaders were weak for not criticising Nazi policies.

The cost of discipleship

Bonhoeffer drew a distinction between 'cheap grace' and 'costly grace':

Cheap grace

- Bonhoeffer called 'cheap grace' the 'deadly enemy of the Church'.

- He used the term to describe what he saw as the habit amongst Christians of accepting the freely given gifts of God, but not bothering to do anything uncomfortable or risky in their Christian lives.

- Bonhoeffer thought that people were imagining that, because Jesus had paid the price for sin, they were off the hook and did not need to make any changes or be sorry for their wrong actions or even notice God at all.

- The reliance on cheap grace made the Church secular, willing to take on the beliefs and values of the modern world.

- Bonhoeffer wrote of 'millions of spiritual corpses'.

Costly grace

- Bonhoeffer thought that people should be prepared for 'costly grace'. The grace of God is something worth sacrificing everything for.

- Grace is costly because it calls Christians to follow Jesus and make changes to their lives and their decisions.

- Bonhoeffer said that Christians should reflect on how God sacrificed his only Son to save people from sin, and people should respond by being ready to sacrifice everything to God in absolute obedience.

Sacrifice, suffering and the cross

- For Bonhoeffer, the call to Christian discipleship is closely linked to the passion of Jesus – his rejection, suffering and death.
- Anyone who follows Jesus must pick up the cross and follow Jesus' path of rejection, suffering and death.
- Discipleship and costly grace involve self-denial and endurance. Rejection for the sake of Christ is a central part of Christian life.
- Being Christian is not just 'being normal' but is a life of suffering for Christ.

Dietrich Bonhoeffer (1906–1945)

Solidarity

- 'Existing for others' or 'solidarity' was a central part of Bonhoeffer's theology. He thought it was closely linked to the idea of discipleship.
- Bonhoeffer was offered the opportunity to stay in London and learn from Gandhi about the principles of non-violence, but he chose instead to run the Finkenwalde seminary.
- Bonhoeffer could have escaped to safety in the USA, but he stayed only three weeks before returning to Germany to share in the suffering of other German people.
- He argued that the purpose of Christian life is not to be 'religious' but to be in a relationship with God through living for others. This life for others allows the Christian to participate in the being of Jesus.
- For Bonhoeffer, solidarity led him into the Resistance movement in Germany against the Nazis. He was accused of conspiring to assassinate Hitler and was sent to a concentration camp to await execution. Bonhoeffer was hanged on 9 April 1945 without a trial, just two weeks before American soldiers liberated the concentration camp.

Key terms

Discipleship: following the life, example and teaching of Jesus

Cheap grace: grace that is offered freely, but is received without any change in the recipient, and ultimately is false as it does not save

Costly grace: grace followed by obedience to God's command and discipleship

Passion: Jesus' sufferings at the end of his life

Solidarity: an altruistic commitment to stand alongside and be with those less fortunate, the oppressed, those who suffer

 **APPLY**

Test yourself on key knowledge (AO1)

1. What was the name of the new Church formed in Germany in opposition to the teaching of the Nazis?

2. What is 'civil disobedience'?

3. From where in the Bible does Bonhoeffer get his metaphors of 'salt' and 'light' to describe the role of a Christian community?

4. What 'Aryan restrictions' were in place in the Reich Church in Nazi Germany?

5. Why was Bonhoeffer sacked from his job as a university teacher?

6. What did Bonhoeffer mean by 'solidarity'?

7. What did Bonhoeffer mean by 'cheap grace'?

8. What was the name of the seminary where Bonhoeffer trained new pastors for the Christian ministry?

9. What happened to the seminary in 1937?

10. How did Bonhoeffer help Jews to escape to safety?

11. Why did Bonhoeffer think that Christians needed to suffer?

12. Who did Bonhoeffer refer to as the 'anti-Christ'?

> If you are unsure about any of the questions, look back over the key points on pages 162–165. You can check your answers on page 219.

Develop your skills in critical argument and evaluation (AO2)

For high marks in AO2, you need to think about the ideas in this chapter and develop your own perspective, so that you can produce critically evaluative arguments rather than just describing and presenting the views of others. At AS level, 50% of your marks are awarded for your skills in critical evaluation, and at A level, 60%.

Use the following questions to help you formulate your own views.

» Discuss them with friends, making sure you articulate your own view and listen to the views of others.

» Try writing your answers to these questions, to familiarise yourself with expressing your ideas in an academic style.

» Remember to give reasons for your views.

» Think about counter-arguments – what might someone say who held a different view from your own, and why do you think they are wrong?

1. **Bonhoeffer talked about 'costly discipleship' and the need for Christians to respond to the grace of God by being prepared to suffer the rejection, physical pain and death that Christ suffered. Some people might criticise this view as being unnecessarily gloomy. Do you think this is a fair criticism? Give reasons to support your answer.**

Here is an example of the kinds of ideas you might explore in formulating your analysis and evaluation:

You might want to argue that Bonhoeffer's emphasis on costly discipleship fails to recognise the joy, peace and comfort that many people experience through their Christian faith. You could give examples to support this view, such as the joy felt by the first Christians at Pentecost (the coming of the Holy Spirit). You could argue that Bonhoeffer emphasised suffering in his theology because of the culture in which he was writing, where he felt some of his fellow Christians needed reminding that they had to be prepared to take risks for others and not just keep quiet; perhaps if he had been writing during a time of peace, he would have focused on something different. Alternatively, you might want to argue that Bonhoeffer was not just writing about physical danger during wartime, but meant to include ideas such as self-denial and giving up a comfortable life in order to follow God's commands, which could be seen to be applicable in all times. You could argue that Bonhoeffer was not ignoring the joyful side of Christianity because he saw suffering as something that enabled people to get closer to God, so it has a worthwhile outcome and is not tragic.

Now use your critical and evaluative skills to explore these questions on your own.

2. Bonhoeffer placed great emphasis on obedience to the will of God, even when it brings people into conflict with the authorities. What factors might have contributed to Bonhoeffer's conviction that opposing Nazism was the will of God? How reliable are guides to Christian morality such as the Bible, the traditions of the Church, the conscience and human reason? Is it possible to be certain of the will of God? Give reasons and examples to support your answer.

3. Bonhoeffer lived at a time and in a culture when there was extreme oppression of minority groups, and when the world was at war. Do you think that his thinking was applicable only to his own unusual circumstances, or might it be equally relevant to Christians today? Give reasons for your answer.

4. Although Bonhoeffer emphasised solidarity and being there for others, it could be argued that some people do not deserve such solidarity. For example, those people who were fanatical supporters of Hitler and who carried out atrocities on behalf of the Nazi party might be considered not to deserve the solidarity of Christians. How far would you agree with this point of view?

5. Bonhoeffer argued that duty to God was far more important than duty to the State. Critics of this point of view might argue that 'the State' is something we are all part of, and that it is selfish to give personal beliefs more weight than the rules society has agreed. How far would you agree with this criticism? Are there times when personal beliefs should be suppressed in favour of conformity to the State, and times when it should not? If so, how might we judge when civil disobedience is appropriate? Give reasons and examples to support your answer.

 REVIEW

Practice Exam Questions

Try these practice questions. You could:

» write plans for each of them, to practise your skills in structuring an essay

» use them for practice in writing introductions and/or conclusions

» write the whole essay, perhaps against the clock.

1. Discuss critically the claim that Bonhoeffer's theology puts too much emphasis on suffering.

2. 'Civil disobedience is never necessary for Christians who live in Christian countries.' Discuss.

Use page 9 to review your essay and make sure you have met the assessment objectives. See pages 240–241 for a mark scheme.

Chapter 3.7 : Religious pluralism and theology

 RECAP

This topic deals with questions of the relationship between Christianity and other world religions. If Christianity is true, does this mean other faiths must be wrong? Is salvation a possibility for people who are not Christian?

Theology of religion

- The term 'theology of religion' refers to Christian thinking about its relationship with people who belong to other religions or who have no affiliation to a particular religious tradition. Christianity has needed to consider its relationship to other faiths since it began.

- Theology of religion deals with issues such as salvation, truth, belief and practice, and dialogue between Christians and those with other beliefs.

- The writer Alan Race identifies three broad perspectives within the theology of religion. He calls them 'exclusivism', 'inclusivism' and 'pluralism' (*Christians and Religious Pluralism*, 1982).

- These classifications have subdivisions within them. They might be best understood as positions on a spectrum of theology rather than as three distinct views.

- Other models in the theology of religion have also been suggested, for example by Paul Knitter.

Exclusivism

- In Christianity, exclusivism is the view that people must have explicit faith in Jesus as the Son of God, and have to believe that salvation is found in Jesus, otherwise they cannot be saved.

- Exclusivists argue that Jesus' sacrificial death on the cross and Resurrection were real events of cosmic significance for all humanity. They reject the idea that there might be other ways to salvation without belief in the saving act of Christ.

- Some exclusivists believe that truth can be found in other religious traditions, but not enough for salvation.

- Some people prefer the term 'particularist', finding it less negative in tone than 'exclusivist', to describe the view that there is one particular way to salvation.

- Hendrik Kraemer was an exclusivist who argued that salvation is only for Christians, although God's revelation can be seen by people outside the Christian faith. He argued that religions have to be understood as a whole and it does not make sense to say that some aspects of a religion are true. Either a religion accepts the salvation offered by Christ, or it does not.

- Barth is usually classified as an exclusivist. He emphasised a 'theology of the Word' and asserted that knowledge of God can be found only when God chooses to reveal it through his Word. In Barth's view Jesus was the living Word of God, and the Bible is the word of God as a witness to the truth of God in Christ.

168

- Within exclusivism there are different shades of opinion:

'Narrow' exclusivists argue that salvation is only for some, not all Christians. Augustine taught that God will choose which Christians go to heaven and that people cannot consider themselves entitled to salvation but are subject to the grace of God. Some who take the Bible literally believe that more liberal Christians are not going to be saved. The Catholic Church before Vatican II taught that there was no salvation outside the Catholic Church: *'extra ecclesiam nulla salus'*.

'Broad' exclusivists argue that all who accept Christ through faith are saved, whatever their denomination or style of worship.

- Gavin D'Costa divides exclusivists into two kinds:

'Universal-access' exclusivists – Christ's salvation is offered to all and the will of God is that everyone should come to him through faith in Christ.

'Restrictive-access' exclusivists – following a similar view to that of Augustine and John Calvin, where God saves only those whom he has chosen.

Possible criticisms of exclusivism

- Exclusivism is not compatible with the idea of an all-loving and forgiving God. It suggests that God loves some people more than others, because some people have much more opportunities to become Christian than others.

- Exclusivism causes social division and conflict.
- Exclusivism fails to recognise the richness and wisdom of different world religions.
- Exclusivism is arrogant in its assumptions that Christians know best.

Inclusivism

- The term inclusivism is used for a range of views between exclusivism and pluralism. Inclusivists tend to argue that Christianity is the best route to salvation but that there is the possibility of salvation for those outside the Christian tradition.
- Inclusivists agree that Jesus' death and Resurrection were unique events of cosmic significance for salvation, but they are uncomfortable with the idea that a God of love would always reject someone who was sincerely trying to follow God through the context of a different religious faith.
- Some inclusivists argue that there might be the possibility after death for non-Christians to accept the truth of the Christian message.

- Some inclusivists argue that when truth is found in other religions, it is Christian truth even though it has not been recognised as such. Other religions sometimes have 'rays of truth' or 'rays of light' where they agree with the teachings of Christianity.
- Some argue that people from non-Christian faiths call Christ by other names without realising that it is Christ at work. For example, when Sikhs share free food at their place of worship with everyone, especially the poor, they could be doing the work of Christ in feeding the hungry without recognising it.
- Rahner, the Catholic theologian, was very influential in developing a Catholic position on theology of religion.

Christianity is the 'absolute' religion with a unique offering of salvation through the grace of God in Christ.

Karl Rahner argued that...

Some people, through no fault of their own, are not exposed to the message of Christianity, for example if they lived before Jesus or in a country the gospel has not reached.

People could be 'anonymous Christians', following Christian ideals without realising that they are actually following Christ.

There could be a partial truth in other non-Christian religions, especially if they are structured in a similar way to Christianity.

People may achieve eternal salvation if they seek God with a sincere heart in contexts other than Christianity.

Possible criticisms of inclusivism

- The Christian message is diluted if there is the suggestion that Christ need not be necessary for salvation.
- Inclusivism is still arrogant, stating that Christian belief is the best and putting itself as the judge and measure of other faiths.

- People who have made free choices to have beliefs that are not Christian should not be labelled as 'anonymous Christians'; if they wanted to be Christians, they would say so.

Pluralism

- The term 'pluralism' is used for a range of positions that argue many different religions have the potential to lead their followers to salvation and that truth is not exclusive to one particular religious tradition.
- Pluralists often argue that different religions share the same goals, even if they disagree on details of doctrine and practice. Doctrines and practices are human constructs, attempting to find ways to respond to God or the divine or the 'Real'.
- They argue that there is no need for members of one religion to try to convert others to share their beliefs; instead people from different religious traditions can communicate with each other and share different perspectives and styles of worship.
- Hick argued for a pluralist understanding of religion because of his belief that a God of love would not deny salvation to people just because

they happened to be born in a non-Christian culture or happened to have chosen a religious tradition other than Christianity through which to seek God.

- Hick thought that God wills universal salvation and that eventually everyone will be saved, continuing their spiritual journeys towards God after death.
- Hick argued for a 'Copernican revolution' in theology, removing Christianity from the centre of the universe and replacing it with 'God' or 'the Real'. All religions, he thought, revolve around the Real.
- Hick used Kant's distinction between the noumenal and the phenomenal to make his point. The noumenal is the world of things as they really are, and the phenomenal is the world as we see it through the filter of our limited human understanding. Religions are a human, phenomenal attempt to uncover the noumenal.

- All religions are therefore flawed and limited, because humans are flawed and limited. No religion can claim to have got everything right. Hick thought that truth-claims of religion such as that Jesus was God incarnate need to be interpreted as myth rather than as literal truth.
- Raimon Panikkar was a pluralist thinker from Hindu and Catholic traditions. He emphasised the mystery of the divine and the need for humility and openness to truth wherever it may be found. He thought that God makes himself known in a variety of ways and cultural contexts, and that there is a need for people to understand that God can reveal himself in whatever way he chooses. Panikkar saw pluralism as a spiritual attitude rather than a reasoned philosophical perspective.

Possible criticisms of pluralism

- A pluralist approach to the theology of religion is not a Christian approach. A pluralist message rejects the idea that Christ came to the world to save humanity once and for all from sin; this is the central message of Christianity.
- A pluralist approach can take human ideas of fairness and imagine what God ought to do to make salvation fair, which is no less arrogant than exclusivism or inclusivism. God is free to save whomever he wants and is not confined to behaving in the way people think they would behave if they were God.
- Pluralism can be seen as self-contradictory because it imposes a pluralist view as 'the right view', suggesting exclusivism and inclusivism are wrong. In claiming a relativist view as the right view, it is being absolutist.

Key terms

Exclusivism: the view that only one religion offers the complete means of salvation

Inclusivism: the view that although one's own religion is the normative (setting the standard of normality) means of salvation, those who accept its central principles may also receive salvation

Pluralism: the view that there are many ways to salvation through different religious traditions

Biblical texts to use in support of different perspectives

Exclusivists might support their beliefs by using texts such as:

John 14:6: 'Jesus answered, "I am the way and the truth and the life. No one comes to the Father except through me"' (New International Version).

1 Timothy 2:3-6: 'For there is one God and one mediator between God and mankind, the man Christ Jesus' (New International Version).

Inclusivists might support their beliefs by using texts such as:

Matthew 25:40: 'whatever you did for one of the least of these brothers and sisters of mine, you did for me' (New International Version).

Job 19:25 *(Job lived before Jesus and yet seemed to have Christian-like beliefs)*: 'I know that my redeemer lives, and that in the end he will stand on the earth' (New International Version).

Pluralists are less likely to use the Bible to support their beliefs but might use texts such as:

Micah 6:8: 'And what does the Lord require of you? To act justly and to love mercy and to walk humbly with your God' (New International Version).

 **APPLY**

Test yourself on key knowledge (AO1)

1. What does the term 'theology of religion' mean?

2. What does D'Costa mean by the term 'restrictive-access exclusivist'?

3. Give an example of a thinker who might be described as a restrictive-access exclusivist.

4. What does D'Costa mean by the term 'universal-access exclusivist'?

5. Which twentieth-century thinker emphasised the 'theology of the Word' in his answer to issues relating to non-Christian religions?

6. What does the expression *'extra ecclesiam nulla salus'* mean?

7. Which Catholic theologian wrote about the possibility of 'anonymous Christianity'?

8. Why did Kraemer think that it was wrong to pick out 'true aspects' of religions other than Christianity?

9. What did Kant mean when he talked about noumena and phenomena?

10. What did Hick mean when he talked about a Copernican revolution in theology?

11. Who wrote about the need for a pluralist approach as a spiritual attitude rather than a philosophically reasoned perspective?

12. Give an example of a biblical text that might be used to support an exclusivist position in Christian theology of religion.

> If you are unsure about any of the questions, look back over the key points on pages 168–171. You can check your answers on page 219.

Develop your skills in critical argument and evaluation (AO2)

For high marks in AO2, you need to think about the ideas in this chapter and develop your own perspective, so that you can produce critically evaluative arguments rather than just describing and presenting the views of others. At AS level, 50% of your marks are awarded for your skills in critical evaluation, and at A level, 60%.

Use the following questions to help you formulate your own views.

» Discuss them with friends, making sure you articulate your own view and listen to the views of others.

» Try writing your answers to these questions, to familiarise yourself with expressing your ideas in an academic style.

» Remember to give reasons for your views.

» Think about counter-arguments – what might someone say who held a different view from your own, and why do you think they are wrong?

1. **Many religions support their truth-claims by making reference to scripture. How effective do you think this is in an argument about differences between religion? What are the issues arising from claims religious believers make to special revelation from God?**

Here is an example of the kinds of ideas you might explore in formulating your analysis and evaluation:

You might be able to give some examples to illustrate ways in which some religions use scripture to evidence their truth-claims, for example Christians might quote Jesus saying 'No one comes to the Father except through me'. Jews might quote passages from Exodus about being especially chosen as a holy nation, and

Muslims might refer to the revelation of the Qur'an to the Prophet Muhammad. You could argue that claims to special revelation make progress difficult because each religion teaches that its scripture is true and yet the scriptures sometimes make conflicting claims. You could argue that only believers in that tradition are likely to be impressed by reference to scripture. You could explore the nature of revelation, especially through religious experience, and argue that individuals interpret their religious experiences in different ways through their own cultural lenses, so scripture needs to be understood as a human response to God rather than as absolute; or you could argue that Barth was right in his 'theology of the Word' in arguing that God makes himself known through the Christian faith only.

Now use your critical and evaluative skills to explore these questions on your own.

2. Do you think there is an ultimate truth, an absolute right and wrong, about religious truth-claims? For example, if a Christian says that Jesus was God incarnate come to earth to save humanity from sin, and a Jew says that Jesus was not God incarnate, must one be right and the other wrong? Is there any possibility that they could both be right in different ways? Give reasons to support your answer.

3. Are different religions just different cultural responses to the same ultimate truth? Pluralists claim that they are, but do you agree that (as far as you know) different religions are seeking the same goal and giving essentially the same message? Give reasons for your answer and try to support it with examples from different religious traditions.

4. Kraemer argued that religions should be judged as whole systems. We should not take them to pieces and say we agree with this piece of teaching and this practice but not those other ones. Do you think he was right? Does a religion have to be considered as a whole, or is there something to be gained from looking at particular aspects of doctrine and practice on their own?

5. Do you think it is important for people to have a particular, specific religious identity, rather than just being generally theist? What might be the advantages of having a specific religious affiliation? Some people criticise what they call a 'pick and mix' approach to religion, where people choose the ethics of Christianity but not the belief in Jesus as the Son of God, and perhaps combine this with Buddhist meditation practices and Muslim self-discipline in charitable giving. Is there anything wrong with 'pick and mix' religion?

REVIEW

Practice Exam Questions

Try these practice questions. You could:

» write plans for each of them, to practise your skills in structuring an essay

» use them for practice in writing introductions and/or conclusions

» write the whole essay, perhaps against the clock.

1. 'If different world religions offer different paths to salvation, then Jesus died on the cross for nothing.' Discuss.

2. 'The best response Christians can make to living in a multi-faith society is to take an inclusivist approach.' Discuss.

Use page 9 to review your essay and make sure you have met the assessment objectives. See pages 241–242 for a mark scheme.

Chapter 3.8 | Religious pluralism and society

 RECAP

Multi-faith societies raise issues of the extent to which Christians should respect, tolerate or try to change the beliefs of non-Christians.

Questions are raised about how people of different religious persuasions should communicate with each other.

The development of multi-faith societies

- The UK became a predominantly Christian country around the seventh century as the result of missionary work by Christians. Before the Romans came to Britain, there were local religious practices centred around fertility and ancestor worship.

- The UK has changed from being dominated by Christianity to being a multi-faith society, although there have been small groups of people from other faiths living in the UK for hundreds of years. For centuries most people never encountered anyone from a religion other than Christianity.

- In the 2011 UK census, 59.3% of people responded to the question 'what is your religion?' with 'Christian'.

- Multi-faith societies develop as travel and communications become easier and less expensive. People move to different countries for work, or as refugees, to seek a better quality of life for their children and for many other reasons. People convert to a different religion more readily as information is more easily available and more people can read, giving people insights into the beliefs and practices of others.

- Atheism and agnosticism have become socially acceptable, with many people openly rejecting religious beliefs and practices.

The challenges of a multi-faith society for Christianity

- Christianity originated in a multi-faith context amongst Jews and those who followed Greek and Roman religion. It has had to face the challenges presented by other religions from the outset.

- Living in a multi-faith society can present positive opportunities for Christians:
  - It can provide opportunities for demonstrating co-operative living together in peace.
  - It can encourage Christians to think more deeply about the reasons for holding their own beliefs rather than just accepting Christianity because everyone else does.
  - It can provide everyday opportunities for missionary work in talking to non-Christians about Christian faith.

- Living in a multi-faith society can also present Christians with challenges:
  - It could be seen to undermine the uniqueness of the Christian message by providing ready alternatives to Christian faith.
  - Some Christians worry that living in a multi-faith society might lead their children to be attracted by false beliefs.
  - Some Christians are uneasy about the popular insistence on tolerance of beliefs they think are wrong and damaging.

Inter-faith dialogue and Christian responses to it

- Inter-faith dialogue is about communication between people who have different beliefs about religion. It is sometimes called inter-religious dialogue or inter-belief dialogue.

- Inter-faith dialogue is not new but has been given more attention as multi-faith societies have developed.

- It is about exchanging ideas and perspectives with the aim of promoting better understanding between people of different faiths and of no faith.

- The Church of England's document 'Sharing the Gospel of Salvation' (2009) identifies four strands of inter-faith dialogue:

1 'The dialogue of daily life' – informal conversations that strike up naturally where people talk about their beliefs.

2 'The dialogue of the common good' where different religious groups work together to benefit others.

3 'The dialogue of mutual understanding' where people get together for formal discussions.

4 'The dialogue of spiritual life' where people of different religious faiths get together for prayer and worship.

- The theologian David Ford drew attention to two strands in recent history which called attention to inter-faith dialogue:

The Holocaust of the Second World War caused many Christians to rethink their relationship with Judaism. They had to come to terms with old ideas of Judaism as a 'failed religion' that had not recognised Jesus as Messiah, and acknowledge the part Christianity had played in anti-Semitism. The Jewish community of rabbis and scholars from around the world invited Christians to engage in inter-faith dialogue initiated by a document called *Dabru Emet* ('Speak the Truth').

Leading Muslim scholars sent a letter in 2007 to Christian Churches. The letter was called 'A Common Word Between Us and You'. It was an invitation for Christians and Muslims to consider what they had in common as well as their differences and to engage in inter-faith dialogue.

Redemptoris Missio

- *Redemptoris Missio* is a papal encyclical issued by Pope John Paul II in 1990. It was intended to revisit some issues that had arisen during the Council gathering of Vatican II and update them.
- The title translates as 'The Mission of the Redeemer' and the aim of the document was to clarify Catholic teaching on the role of missionary work in a multi-faith world.
- Pope John Paul II reaffirmed that missionary work is essential for Christians.
- He said that there is only one saviour, Jesus Christ, and that Christ is the only way in which God is revealed to the world.
- Christians should be empowered by the Holy Spirit to bring other people to Christian faith.
- The Pope recognised that missionary work can be seen in a negative way in a multi-faith world, as arrogant and intolerant. He wanted to give guidance to help Catholic Christians continue to be missionaries for their faith whilst still respecting other people in their diversity.
- He said that inter-faith dialogue should be seen as part of Christian mission rather than in opposition to it.
- God wishes to share his revelation with people of all faiths even though other religions could contain 'gaps, insufficiencies and errors'.
- John Paul II said that the Catholic Church gladly acknowledges all that is true in Buddhism, Hinduism and Islam.
- However, Christians still have a duty to emphasise that the way to salvation is through Jesus Christ. Christianity is unique in offering the means to salvation.
- He underlined the need for respect in inter-faith dialogue and said that Christians should use it with the aim of uncovering universal truths.
- He said that Christian mission can take place in many forms, such as in interactions with neighbours.

'Sharing the Gospel of Salvation'

- 'Sharing the Gospel of Salvation' is a document issued by the Church of England Synod in response to a question raised by one of its members, Paul Eddy, in 2006. He asked where the Church of England stood on the question of whether Christians should claim publicly that salvation could be found only in Christ. The document was published in 2010.
- 'Sharing the Gospel of Salvation' reaffirms that God's plan for the salvation of the world is uniquely achieved in Jesus Christ and that the Church has a mission to be a witness to this.

Confirms that all Christians are called to discipleship, which always involves sharing faith with others.

Reminds Christians that their own faith and traditions are a result of the missionary work of others.

Calls Christians to go beyond tolerance of other faiths and find ways of actively engaging with people. They are to be sensitive to the feelings of others and to the potential difficulties faced by people who want to convert from a different religion to Christianity.

'Sharing the Gospel of Salvation'

Reminds Christians that their history and their mission has not always lived up to the teachings of the Bible.

Warns against treating Christian mission as a kind of marketing exercise of salesmanship; people are converted because of the work of God, not because someone has made a successful sale.

Reaffirms Christian beliefs about the oneness of God and beliefs about Jesus as the incarnation of God. Christianity offers salvation to everyone and Christians are called to bring others to explicit faith in Christianity and baptism into the Christian Church.

The Scriptural Reasoning Movement

- Scriptural Reasoning began amongst Jewish scholars in the USA with meetings to discuss Jewish sacred texts.
- Christians from the UK asked if they could join in as listeners and the Scriptural Reasoning Movement developed into an inter-faith forum, part of the Cambridge Inter-faith Programme.
- Participants from Islam, Judaism and Christianity meet together to read passages from their sacred texts on different subjects, and talk about how they understand the texts and how the texts influence their thinking.
- The goal is not to achieve agreement but to look deeply at beliefs in different contexts, to foster a spirit of openness and respect.
- They recognise that there are differences of belief and try not to over-emphasise points of similarity in a superficial way.
- There is an agreement not to use meetings as an opportunity for missionary work, although participants can talk about their own commitment to their faith.

Key terms

Multi-faith societies: societies where there are significant populations of people with different religious beliefs

Missionary work: activity that aims to convert people to a particular faith or set of beliefs, or works for social justice in areas of poverty or deprivation

Inter-faith dialogue: sharing and discussing religious beliefs between members of different religious traditions, with an aim of reaching better understanding

Encyclical: an open letter sent to more than one recipient

Synod: the legislative body of the Church of England

Social cohesion: when a group is united by bonds that help them to live together peacefully

 **APPLY**

Test yourself on key knowledge (AO1)

1. What does the Church of England mean when it refers to 'the dialogue of spiritual life'?

2. Ford highlights two recent events that encouraged inter-faith dialogue – what were they?

3. What does Ford call the kind of dialogue where people meet together for formal discussions?

4. What was the title of the letter from the Muslim community to which Ford refers?

5. The Jewish scholarly community wrote a document called *Dabru Emet* to encourage discussion – what does this title mean in English?

6. What is an 'encyclical'?

7. What does the title *Redemptoris Missio* mean in English?

8. Which Pope issued the encyclical *Redemptoris Missio*?

9. When was the Church of England statement 'Sharing the Gospel of Salvation' published?

10. The Church of England asks its members to go beyond mere tolerance of other faiths, and asks them to do – what?

11. Is Christian missionary work still necessary in a multi-faith society, according to Catholic teaching?

12. Is Christian missionary work still necessary in a multi-faith society, according to Church of England teaching?

> If you are unsure about any of the questions, look back over the key points on pages 174–177. You can check your answers on page 220.

Develop your skills in critical argument and evaluation (AO2)

For high marks in AO2, you need to think about the ideas in this chapter and develop your own perspective, so that you can produce critically evaluative arguments rather than just describing and presenting the views of others. At AS level, 50% of your marks are awarded for your skills in critical evaluation, and at A level, 60%.

Use the following questions to help you formulate your own views.

» Discuss them with friends, making sure you articulate your own view and listen to the views of others.

» Try writing your answers to these questions, to familiarise yourself with expressing your ideas in an academic style.

» Remember to give reasons for your views.

» Think about counter-arguments – what might someone say who held a different view from your own, and why do you think they are wrong?

1. **If some religious believers are completely convinced that their faith is right and that believers in other religions have got things wrong, is there any point in them trying to talk to each other? Is it necessary for participants in inter-faith dialogue to admit the possibility that they could be wrong?**

> **Here is an example of the kinds of ideas you might explore in formulating your analysis and evaluation:**
>
> You might want to argue that inter-faith dialogue is only going to work when everyone is willing to listen to each other with an open mind and accept that the other person's point of view might be right. Perhaps a firm conviction that Christianity is right and the only way to salvation makes meaningful dialogue impossible because it will just lead to arguments and increase rather than decrease tension. You could argue, however, that even if all the participants are not going to change their minds, it is still useful to develop a greater understanding of different perspectives in order for people to be more sensitive to each other's beliefs, even if they think they are wrong.

Now use your critical and evaluative skills to explore these questions on your own.

2. Some people prefer to send their children to 'faith schools' rather than sending them to schools where there are children from all kinds of religious backgrounds and from no religious background. In Christianity, schools sometimes have a religious foundation for historical reasons because they were started charitably, but sometimes they have a religious foundation because people want their children to be educated in their Christian religious tradition with a Christian ethos positively promoted. What do you think of the idea of having faith schools? What are their advantages and disadvantages, in your view?

3. *Redemptoris Missio* emphasised that there is still a need for Christians to tell others that Christianity offers the only means of salvation, even if this is a difficult task. What reasons might a Christian give for claiming that their faith is the only one to offer salvation? How far would you agree that Christians should make efforts to tell others about their faith?

4. The Church of England document 'Sharing the Gospel of Salvation' warns people to be sensitive when trying to convert members of other faiths to Christianity. What do you think might be some of the difficulties for someone from a different faith who wanted to convert to Christianity?

Do you think it would be more loving for a Christian to leave people to worship God in the traditions of whatever religion and culture they belong to? Give reasons to support your answer.

5. The Scriptural Reasoning Movement could be accused of being relativist in its outlook, by suggesting that all religions have something to learn from each other's scriptures. A Christian might argue that God is fully and finally revealed in Jesus Christ through the witness of the Bible and therefore there is nothing that a Christian can learn from other scriptures. How far would you agree with this point of view? Do you think Scriptural Reasoning is relativist? Is there anything wrong with a relativist approach to study of sacred texts?

6. Some people might argue that Christians should not attempt to convert others to Christianity, because it can make people feel uncomfortable if they are not interested, it sounds arrogant to suggest that you know the truth and other people are wrong, and it is intolerant of other religious faiths. Do you think these criticisms of missionary work are fair? Should Christians talk openly about their faith when they are at work or when they are in a social setting? Give reasons to support your answer.

REVIEW

Practice Exam Questions

Try these practice questions. You could:

» write plans for each of them, to practise your skills in structuring an essay

» use them for practice in writing introductions and/or conclusions

» write the whole essay, perhaps against the clock.

1. How fair is the claim that the Scriptural Reasoning Movement relativises Christian belief?

2. Discuss critically the view that Christians should seek to convert people who belong to other faith communities.

Use page 9 to review your essay and make sure you have met the assessment objectives. See pages 242–243 for a mark scheme.

Chapter 3.9 : Gender and society

Christianity has traditionally taken the view that God created two distinct genders, each with their own skills and complementary natures, both equally valuable to God and made in God's image.

Contemporary secular society questions whether traditional views of gender and family life are appropriate or whether they are repressive.

Biological sex and gender

- Biological sex is determined by physical attributes. Most people are born clearly male or female, but some people have physical characteristics of both male and female and have an ambiguous biological sex.

- Gender is a more sophisticated concept combining:

Gender biology: physical characteristics	**Gender identification:** the gender in which a person feels most comfortable, which is not necessarily distinctly male or female	**Gender expression:** the ways in which a person chooses to behave (such as clothing and speech), which might be traditionally associated with a gender

- People are born with a biological sex but gender is heavily influenced by society.

- Socialisation is the lifelong process by which we learn the norms of our society. Socialisation tells us how people of different genders are expected to behave in society, with both spoken and unspoken rules.

- Traditionally in the UK we are socialised to think in gender-binary terms, in other words that there are two distinct genders, male and female, and people should belong to either one or the other depending on their biological sex. These ideas are beginning to be challenged by some.

Changing views of gender and gender roles

- There are many different attitudes to gender and gender roles:

  There is the view that men and women are not equal and that men are superior to women; this view dates back at least as far as Plato and Aristotle. Plato believed that souls were reborn as women if they had failed as men. Aristotle thought that women were 'defective' males who were naturally inferior and more inclined to weak behaviour. Aquinas wrote that women are inferior to men in physical strength and intelligence, although he did think that there was a special place in heaven for the Virgin Mary and the women who stayed at the foot of Jesus' cross.

There is the view that men and women are equally valuable to God but they have different, complementary characteristics and are suited to different roles in domestic and public life. Some Churches take this view and use it to argue that women should not become priests, on the grounds that Jesus chose only men to be his closest disciples, and that a woman cannot represent Christ when celebrating the Eucharist.

Some people, such as the feminist theologian Mary Daly and many separatist feminists, take the view that women are superior to men.

An increasingly popular view is that the idea of 'masculine qualities' and 'feminine qualities' is misguided. According to this perspective, society encourages people to conform to binary gender roles but this is learned behaviour rather than natural tendency. In this view there is no sense in saying that men are better than women or women are better than men because everyone is different: there is no such thing as male nature or female nature.

- Changes in societies as they become more multicultural and diverse lead to a wider range of beliefs and attitudes about the roles of men and women in society.
- During the twentieth century, changes were made in laws that enabled women to have more freedom. Some significant changes were:

Women were allowed to vote on an equal footing with men in 1928.

Reliable birth control became available from the 1960s, at first only for married women who had completed their families.

Abortion was legalised in the UK (excluding Northern Ireland) in 1967.

The Equal Pay Act of 1970 legally entitled women to be paid the same as men for doing the same job.

From 1974 single women could obtain the contraceptive pill, enabling women to have more control over their sexual activity both within and outside the context of marriage.

Patriarchy

- A patriarchal society is one in which men have more power than women, dominating social structures, domestic life and government.
- Patriarchal societies tend to be organised in ways that benefit men more than women.
- In patriarchal societies, men's history tends to be recorded more than women's, men's art is more celebrated than women's and men are encouraged into higher levels of education than women.
- In patriarchal societies men are usually seen as stronger than women, and men make the measure of what counts as 'stronger'.

Feminism

- Feminism is not a single ideology but the name given to a wide range of views sharing the aim of improving rights and opportunities for women. Feminists do not all agree with each other.

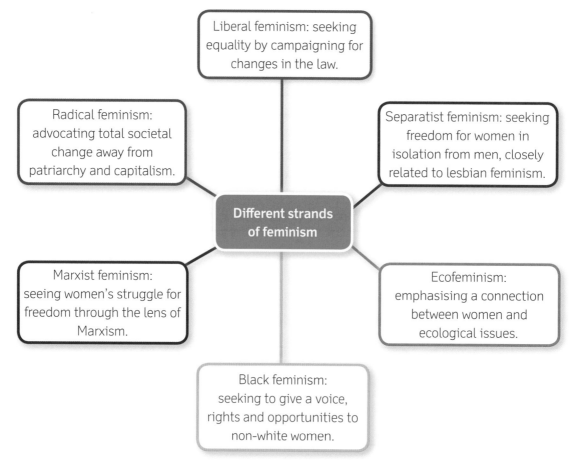

Liberal feminism: seeking equality by campaigning for changes in the law.

Radical feminism: advocating total societal change away from patriarchy and capitalism.

Separatist feminism: seeking freedom for women in isolation from men, closely related to lesbian feminism.

Different strands of feminism

Marxist feminism: seeing women's struggle for freedom through the lens of Marxism.

Ecofeminism: emphasising a connection between women and ecological issues.

Black feminism: seeking to give a voice, rights and opportunities to non-white women.

- One of the best-known early feminist texts was *A Vindication of the Rights of Women* by Mary Wollstonecraft in 1792. She advocated educating girls to the same standard as boys.
- Sometimes feminism is identified as having three 'waves':

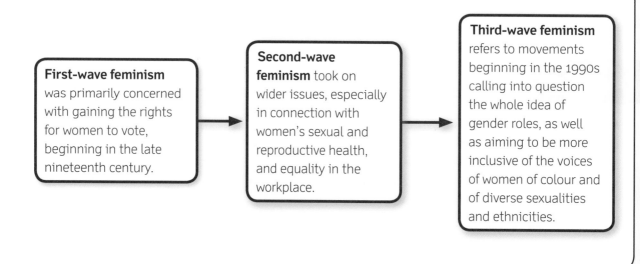

First-wave feminism was primarily concerned with gaining the rights for women to vote, beginning in the late nineteenth century.

Second-wave feminism took on wider issues, especially in connection with women's sexual and reproductive health, and equality in the workplace.

Third-wave feminism refers to movements beginning in the 1990s calling into question the whole idea of gender roles, as well as aiming to be more inclusive of the voices of women of colour and of diverse sexualities and ethnicities.

Traditional Christian views about men and women

- There is a wide range of views within Christianity about the roles of men and women in the family and in society.
- Traditional Christian teaching, based on the Bible, presents men and women as being created by God to have different, complementary roles.

The book of Genesis teaches that:

- men and women are both made in the image of God
- the man is created first, and the woman second to be a 'helper' and companion for the man
- the woman was the first to succumb to temptation from the serpent in the Garden of Eden.

Letters to new Christian Churches in the New Testament (first century) teach that:

- an orderly household has the man as the head of the house
- husbands should love their wives in the way Christ loves the Church
- the wife should accept the authority of her husband
- women should not teach or speak in Church.

- Christian teaching developed in a particular social context. Some argue that biblical teaching has authority as the word of God and should be accepted as authoritative for all times and cultures, whilst others argue that social rules (such as rules about gender roles) need to be reconsidered given that society has changed.
- Traditional Christian gender roles have been challenged by some as 'biblical patriarchy' – written by men, led by men's interests, to reinforce male dominance. Others respond by saying that the Bible comes from God, not from one gender, and that God has decided to create two distinct genders with distinct purposes.

Key terms

Gender biology: the physical characteristics that enable someone to be identified as male or female

Gender identification: the way people perceive themselves in terms of masculine, feminine, both or neither

Gender expression: the ways in which people behave as a result of their gender identification

Socialisation: the process by which people learn cultural norms

Patriarchal society: a society that is dominated by men and men's interests

Feminism: the name given to a wide range of views arguing for, and working for, equality for women

Christian responses to contemporary secular views about gender roles

- Christian views about the contemporary role of women in the home, in society and in the Church vary widely.
- *Mulieris Dignitatem* ('On the dignity of women') was written in 1988 as an open letter by Pope John Paul II, on the subject of the dignity and rights of women, to clarify the Catholic position on issues raised by feminism.

The main points of *Mulieris Dignitatem*

- Men and women have different, complementary characteristics given by God.
- Women have particular skills and qualities, as exemplified by many European saints.
- No one would be here at all unless women fulfilled their unique role in bringing the next generation into the world.
- A woman's role as a Christian is to be respected.
- Women are naturally more capable than men of attending to the needs of others, as well as being better at coping with pain.
- Jesus' incarnation was made possible by a woman.
- Both virginity and motherhood are admirable.
- Women are naturally disposed to motherhood both physically and psychologically, and this disposition is a gift from God.

- This letter was criticised by some, especially on the grounds that women cannot achieve dignity and respect unless they have access to artificial contraception, which the Catholic Church does not allow.
- Contemporary Christian teaching from many sources reminds people that women should be treated with respect.

Christian views about different types of family

- The concept of an 'ideal family' of two parents and their children is traditional, but there are and always have been families and households of different kinds.
- 'Family' as a concept is difficult to define. Sociologists and anthropologists see it as a social unit, usually made of people who are related to each other, where tasks are shared and members protect each other.
- Christianity traditionally sees the ideal family as one with two married, heterosexual parents and their children.
- Christianity teaches that marriage is the best context for raising children. Some Christians understand this to be heterosexual marriage but some are supportive of the idea of children being raised by same-sex couples.
- Divorce is an issue for Christians. The Catholic Church does not recognise divorce, and so if people separate and then want to marry a new partner, the Catholic Church regards this as adultery because God has already joined them to the first partner for life as a sacrament which cannot be undone. Many other Christian denominations recognise divorce and allow divorced people to marry in church, emphasising the importance of forgiveness in Christian morality.

- Same-sex marriage is an issue for Christians – some welcome it as a celebration of God-given human love in all its variety, and see it as an opportunity to support couples in committed relationships regardless of their sexuality. Others see marriage as a sacred institution given by God and intended to be between a man and a woman.

- Homosexuality is an issue for Christians – some see it as unnatural and believe that homosexual people should live celibate lives. Others accept homosexuality but do not think 'marriage' is the right word for same-sex partnerships, whilst other Christians think that same-sex couples should be treated in the same way as heterosexual couples.

Different views of motherhood

- In Christianity, motherhood is seen as a role with special dignity and value. In the Catholic Church, the supreme example is the Virgin Mary, the mother of Jesus.

- Christianity teaches that children are a gift from God. In Catholic teaching, following the principles of natural law, artificial contraception should not be used and sex between a husband and wife should always allow for the possibility of the creation of new life.

- Many non-Christians, both secular and from non-Christian religions, agree that motherhood can be one of life's most profound experiences.

- Some thinkers have taken a different view. Simone de Beauvoir wrote in the 1940s that motherhood forces women to crush their own personalities so that they can care for others.

- The sociologist Ann Oakley wrote about the negative side of motherhood, saying that it often leaves women powerless and restricted.

APPLY

Test yourself on key knowledge (AO1)

1. What is meant by the term 'patriarchal society'?
2. What is the difference between gender biology and gender identification?
3. In which book of the Bible does God create men and women in his own image?
4. Who wrote *A Vindication of the Rights of Women* in 1792?
5. What is 'second-wave feminism'?
6. What is 'liberal feminism'?
7. In which year did the UK allow women to vote on an equal footing with men?
8. When did the UK introduce the Equal Pay Act for men and women?

9. In which century were the New Testament letters to early Christian Churches written?
10. What was the name of the letter written by Pope John Paul II about the dignity of women?
11. What is the name given to the processes by which we learn the norms of our society?
12. What is the Catholic position on divorce?

If you are unsure about any of the questions, look back over the key points on pages 180–185. You can check your answers on page 220.

Develop your skills in critical argument and evaluation (AO2)

For high marks in AO2, you need to think about the ideas in this chapter and develop your own perspective, so that you can produce critically evaluative arguments rather than just describing and presenting the views of others. At AS level, 50% of your marks are awarded for your skills in critical evaluation, and at A level, 60%.

Use the following questions to help you formulate your own views.

» Discuss them with friends, making sure you articulate your own view and listen to the views of others.

» Try writing your answers to these questions, to familiarise yourself with expressing your ideas in an academic style.

» Remember to give reasons for your views.

» Think about counter-arguments – what might someone say who held a different view from your own, and why do you think they are wrong?

1. **Do you think that differences between men and women are primarily biological, or primarily social (or something else)? Some people argue that modern thinking fails to recognise that there are important differences in the way men and women think, in their interests and in their needs; they might argue that religious teachings about gender distinction have authority and should not be ignored in favour of current fashions of thinking. Would you agree with this criticism?**

Here is an example of the kinds of ideas you might explore in formulating your analysis and evaluation:

You might want to argue that the 'nature versus nurture' question is impossible to answer because we cannot experiment with people, taking them out of society at birth to see how they grow up without societal influence. Or you might think that there are fundamental biological differences that make men naturally more inclined to have different talents and interests from those of women; you might be able to give examples and you might want to use the letter Mulieris Dignitatem in support of your view. Perhaps you would argue that traditional religious teaching about differences between men and women should not be ignored and that modern thinking about gender fluidity is going too far. Or perhaps you think that a distinction between genders is a way in which patriarchal societies maintain the dominance of men and that such distinctions are purely social constructions which should be discarded. Give reasons for your point of view and try to support it with examples.

Now use your critical and evaluative skills to explore these questions on your own.

2. Some Christians argue that biblical teaching has authority as the word of God and should be accepted as authoritative for all times and cultures, including teaching about traditional gender roles. They might argue that if these rules are discarded, then other rules are also called into question and people will end up just choosing the moral rules they happen to like. Others argue that biblical social rules such as those governing gender roles need to be reconsidered, given that society has changed and a binary division between male and female has been called into question. Which point of view do you find more convincing, and for what reasons?

3. Do you think Christian Churches should aim to adapt to changes in societal norms in order to keep themselves relevant and up-to-date, or should they resist changes when they seem to be going in a different direction from traditional Church teaching? Are there some circumstances where adaptation is best and others when resistance is best? How might a Christian know when is the right context to adapt and when is the right context to resist? Should Christians adapt to, or resist, secular changes in views about gender roles?

4. The New Testament is quite consistent in the teaching that wives should submit to the authority of their husbands. Some Christians argue that in a

relationship, it is important to have someone who is in charge so that they can have the casting vote in disagreements and prevent them from going on and on. How far would you agree with this point of view? Are there better reasons for claiming that husbands should have authority over wives? Should domestic relationships have the same kind of rules as working relationships or are the two contexts entirely different? Give reasons for you answer.

5. Some people argue that the whole idea of 'family' is a social construct. People choose to live with their relations for practical reasons, such as so that one can go out and earn money whilst another looks after the home and children. Others, including many Christians, argue that family life is ordained by God and is a gift from God, given because of its many benefits for human well-being. How far would you agree with the idea that the family is nothing more than a social construct, and how would you defend your opinion?

6. How far would you agree with the view that women can only achieve dignity, respect and equal rights with men when they are allowed access to artificial contraception and abortion? Does motherhood restrict women or does it enable them to fulfil their potential, or is the situation different for different women? Do you think fatherhood is equivalent to motherhood or are they two entirely different experiences? Give reasons and examples to support your point of view.

REVIEW

Practice Exam Questions

Try these practice questions. You could:

» write plans for each of them, to practise your skills in structuring an essay

» use them for practice in writing introductions and/or conclusions

» write the whole essay, perhaps against the clock.

1. 'Secular views of gender equality have undermined Christian gender roles.' Discuss.

2. How convincing is the claim that the idea of family is entirely culturally determined?

Use page 9 to review your essay and make sure you have met the assessment objectives. See pages 243–244 for a mark scheme.

Chapter 3.10

Gender and theology

RECAP

Feminist thought has presented Christianity with serious challenges.

Christianity is accused of allowing itself to be shaped by patriarchal views, framing its concepts, doctrines and morality in terms of male dominance and promoting the interests of men over women.

Christianity is also accused of being to blame for enabling and encouraging patriarchy in society.

Feminist theology

- Feminist theology questions:

Whether there is any justification in theology for male dominance.	The view that only men and not women can represent God as leaders in the Church and in society.
Why language used of God always depicts God as male.	The view that women have a religious duty to be subordinate to men.
The view that men are more closely in the image of God than women.	Why theology is dominated by male writers and male voices.

- Feminist theology draws attention to what it sees as the patriarchal nature of Christian teachings, beliefs and practices.

- Not all feminists see feminist theology as having the same goals. Some suggest that there needs to be a reinterpretation of Christianity in order to make it less sexist. Some suggest that the patriarchal elements of Christianity need to be removed and replaced, rather than just reinterpreted. Others suggest that Christianity is intrinsically sexist and so needs to be rejected altogether.

Key terms

Post-Christian theology: religious thinking that abandons traditional Christian thought

Reform feminist theology: religious thinking that seeks to change traditional Christian thought

Davidic Messiah: a Messiah figure based on the kingly military images of the Hebrew scriptures (the Old Testament)

Servant king: an understanding of the Messiah that focuses on service rather than overlordship

Sophia: Greek for 'wisdom', personified in female form in the ancient world

Mary Daly

The thinking of Mary Daly

- Mary Daly is an American post-Christian radical feminist and writer of *Beyond God the Father: Toward a Philosophy of Women's Liberation* (1973).

- She argued that the idea of a Father-God sustains and creates a patriarchal view of society and of spirituality which results in oppression of women and violence towards women: 'If God is male then the male is God.'

- She suggests that religion has been, and still is, used as a tool to enforce the oppression of women.

- She said that the cultural impact of Christianity on society creates an 'unholy trinity' of rape, genocide and war.

- The patriarchal view of God combines sexism, racism and classism to create a three-headed monster.

- Daly criticised the biblical imagery of a male God in heaven who dominates and rewards and punishes. She saw this as a distortion and a limitation of the spirituality of nature.

- She said that Christian ideas about the incarnation of God in Jesus Christ were symbolic ways of legitimising 'rape of all women and all matter'.

Daly's criticisms of Christian thinkers

- Daly criticised the so-called 'fathers' of Christian doctrine, pointing out how they were responsible for traditional views of women as primarily responsible for the Fall, a temptation for men, and destined to be men's helpers and to be mothers. She criticised:

> Tertullian for saying that women were 'the devil's gateway': women had brought sin into the world.

> Augustine for suggesting that women were not made in the image of God.

> Martin Luther for saying that Eve spoiled God's plans for Adam.

> Aquinas for saying that women were 'misbegotten' men.

- She also criticised modern theologians, including:

> Pope Pius XII for saying that true liberation for women comes from motherhood, not from feminism or from equality with men.

> Bonhoeffer for insisting that women should be subject to their husbands.

> Barth for saying that a woman is subordinate to a man.

> Joseph Fletcher and situation ethics as part of a patriarchal way of thinking, devised by a man to look at ethics in an individualistic way rather than acknowledging the need for communal ethics, which she saw as essential for the liberation of women.

Daly's unholy trinity of rape, genocide and war

Rape

- Daly wrote of 'rapism', a word that she used to signify a culture of rape and a symbol of violent oppression.
- She wrote emotively of how rapism is part of a culture which represses and imprisons women through culture, professions and the media.
- She wrote of women as 'patriarchally possessed', where they become so entrenched in male-dominated society that they stop seeing how imprisoned they are and become divided against each other.
- She turned attention to systematic acts of physical violence towards women including FGM, foot binding and rape. She saw a connection between rapism and war, where rape is used as a weapon of war.
- She drew attention to passages in the Bible where women are raped in the context of war or as revenge for male acts of war.
- She thought that rape was not just a physical act but that there are 'arm-chair rapists' who enjoy pornography and watching entertainment that includes violence against women.

Genocide

- Daly described how in her view there is a gender 'caste system', giving men an unequally large share of power. This inequality is reinforced through socialisation so that men and women accept it as normal.
- She thought that male sexual violence underlies military conflicts and that there is a strong link between rape and genocide.
- This is because both rape and genocide objectify the victims, so that they are no longer seen as people but as objects that can be violated.
- Daly found similarities between the groupthink used by the Nazis and the groupthink of the Catholic Church. Both concentrated on their own sameness and saw different people as 'other', which she thought contributed to male oppression.
- She also highlighted Jewish belief that the Jews are a separate and holy nation chosen by God, apart from other people. This was highly controversial as she seemed to be suggesting that the Jews had some responsibility for their own genocide during the Holocaust.

War

- Daly argued that war is an inevitable result of male-dominated society and politics.
- She said that men try to disguise the horrors of war by using euphemisms like 'collateral damage' to describe the deaths of civilians. Men justify wars by using what she called a 'phallic morality'.
- Women need to seek liberation from men and their morality by completely demolishing the expectations society places on women.

Daly and spirituality in nature

- Daly argued that Christianity needs to be left behind because it is tightly interwoven with male oppression.
- Men have taken over religion and placed themselves in positions of authority, trapping and imprisoning women.

- Traditional religious buildings are built and managed by men and so are unsuitable places for women to find spiritual fulfilment.
- Instead of worshipping God the Father, Daly wrote in terms of 'quintessence', the most supreme essence of nature, life and vitality in the universe. Quintessence can be blocked by male dominance and by poverty but can be rediscovered in the natural world.
- Daly's ideas about quintessence reflect the interest in pagan culture and nature worship popular in the 1970s. She encouraged women to embrace paganism and witchcraft and connect with their wild sides.

Possible criticisms of Daly

- Simon Chan in *Christianity Today* (2013) argues that seeing God as Father, Son and Holy Spirit is a symbol for the unity of God in three persons, and not meant to be an emphasis on maleness.
- Chan argues that Daly glosses over the important symbolism of the idea of God the Father as creator of all, dwelling only on negative aspects but not recognising the richness that the concept of a Father God offers.
- Chan also points out parts of the Bible where God, even though depicted as male, exhibits qualities such as compassion which are not stereotypically male.
- Elisabeth Schussler Fiorenza, a feminist theologian, argues that Daly's understanding of the Bible is too narrow and fails to recognise biblical passages that directly challenge patriarchy.

Rosemary Radford Reuther

The thinking of Rosemary Radford Reuther

- Rosemary Radford Reuther is a reform feminist theologian and author of *Sexism and God-Talk: Toward a Feminist Theology* (1983).
- Reuther argues that patriarchy has had a profound and damaging effect on Christianity, but believes that the Church needs to reform rather than be totally abandoned.
- Reuther describes herself as an eco-feminist. She is in favour of women in the Catholic priesthood and argues that the Catholic Church needs to rethink its teaching on abortion.
- Reuther argues that patriarchy in society has distorted the Christian message and has shaped Christian thought about God in a way that needs to be challenged.

Jesus and the male warrior expectation

- At the time of Jesus, many Jews expected the coming of a Messiah who would be a military king like King David of the past. He would lead his people to victory and restore power to Israel. This is known as the Davidic Messiah.
- The Messiah is chosen by God and is the Son of God, as well as representing people before God. Therefore, Reuther argued, 'the Messiah can only be imagined as male'.
- However, Reuther does not argue that the idea of Jesus as Messiah needs to be discarded. Instead she points out that Jesus himself rejected the male-warrior stereotype.

- She thought that the idea of Jesus as a military Messiah was something invented by the early Church rather than Jesus' own understanding of himself.
- Jesus took on the role of servant king, serving rather than dominating, seeking out the poor and the oppressed and arguing against people who claimed positions of religious authority. He called God 'Abba' in a familiar way rather than speaking of an authoritarian God.
- Reuther argues that in placing himself as the servant Messiah, Jesus connected the role of Messiah with female as well as male characteristics and images.

Jesus and the female wisdom principle

- Reuther drew attention to the principle of wisdom, personified as female in Greek culture as 'Sophia'.
- She notes that the biblical idea of wisdom would have emerged from Greek culture and the feminine idea of wisdom.
- She makes links between Jesus as the Word of God and the idea of God's wisdom, saying that Jesus is God's wisdom in human form and therefore has both masculine and feminine aspects.

Reuther and using feminine language of God

- The Christian Church traditionally uses male pronouns of God, and male imagery for God, such as Father, King and Son.
- Reuther challenges the use of exclusively masculine terms for God and refers to God using the Greek term Gaia, which was the name of the ancient Greek goddess of the earth. She argues that she is recovering an ancient notion of God in the feminine, a notion that has been covered up by patriarchy, rather than inventing a new way of talking about God.
- She argues that this terminology gives a much better reflection of the relationship of all of humanity, whatever gender, in the image of God.

Possible criticisms of Reuther

- Some critics of Reuther claim that she goes too far in trying to reform Christianity to suit a feminist agenda, and others claim that she does not go far enough.
- Chan argues that Reuther is wrong to try to rewrite Christianity to give more prominence to women because beliefs in doctrines such as that God is Father, Son and Holy Spirit are central to Christian tradition. He thinks it would be wrong to try to downplay the masculinity of Christian liturgy.
- Chan points out that many religions have had goddesses as well as gods, celebrating the feminine in deities as well as the masculine, but the societies holding these beliefs have nevertheless been patriarchal societies. He argues that therefore changing ideas of God to feminine as well as masculine would make no difference.
- Daphne Hampson, a modern post-Christian theologian, argues that Christianity and feminism are essentially incompatible. Christianity is too tightly interwoven with patriarchy to be reinterpreted with a feminist agenda. She thinks that trying to carry out a radical feminist transformation of Christianity, in the way Reuther is attempting, is impossible.

Is Christianity essentially sexist?

Many feminist theologians and other people argue that Christianity is sexist and promotes sexist attitudes:

- Hampson and Daly both argue that it is impossible to be a Christian and a feminist.

- Hampson says that some of the stories of the Bible are inherently sexist (such as the story of Adam and Eve) and some of the morality of the Bible is sexist (such as the teaching about how to run an orderly household).

- Hampson argues that it is better to interpret ideas about the love of God in new ways and to leave Christianity behind.

- Daly argues that religion as an institution needs to be discarded as it imprisons women.

Others argue that Christian theology can be read through a more feminist lens:

- Fiorenza argues that the Bible is a mixture of a revelation of timeless truth and a reflection of the culture in which it was written.

- She says that the moral messages of the Bible present a challenge to sexism and a requirement for treating all individuals with respect and equality, ignoring their differences of gender.

- The Bible is consistent in its messages of freeing the oppressed and giving a voice to those who have been silenced.

- Jesus breaks sexist customs such as ignoring the cultural rules not to touch women.

- Reuther also argues that there is scope for change towards a more feminist theology without the need to abandon Christianity altogether.

APPLY

Test yourself on key knowledge (AO1)

1. Which early Christian father said that women were 'the devil's gateway' and had brought sin into the world?

2. Which Christian thinker called women 'misbegotten' males?

3. Which Pope said that women should find their true liberation in motherhood rather than in feminism?

4. On what grounds did Daly criticise Fletcher's situation ethics?

5. Did Daly think the Church needed to be reformed from within, or did she think it needed to be abandoned altogether?

6. How did the feminist theologian Fiorenza criticise Daly's interpretation of the Bible?

7. Did Reuther think the Church needed to be reformed from within, or did she think it needed to be abandoned altogether?

8. What did Daly mean by the term 'quintessence'?

9. Who wrote *Sexism and God-Talk: Toward a Feminist Theology*?

10. What is meant by the term 'Davidic Messiah'?

11. Who was Sophia in Greek thought?

12. Who was Gaia in Greek thought?

If you are unsure about any of the questions, look back over the key points on pages 188–193. You can check your answers on page 220.

Develop your skills in critical argument and evaluation (AO2)

For high marks in AO2, you need to think about the ideas in this chapter and develop your own perspective, so that you can produce critically evaluative arguments rather than just describing and presenting the views of others. At AS level, 50% of your marks are awarded for your skills in critical evaluation, and at A level, 60%.

Use the following questions to help you formulate your own views.

» Discuss them with friends, making sure you articulate your own view and listen to the views of others.

» Try writing your answers to these questions, to familiarise yourself with expressing your ideas in an academic style.

» Remember to give reasons for your views.

» Think about counter-arguments – what might someone say who held a different view from your own, and why do you think they are wrong?

1. **Do you think that feminist critics of Christianity are right to accuse it of being patriarchal in its language, beliefs and practices? Are they right to blame Christianity for having a significant effect on the development of a patriarchal society – is Christianity part of the problem of gender equality? Give reasons for your answer.**

Here is an example of the kinds of ideas you might explore in formulating your analysis and evaluation:

You might want to agree that Christianity is patriarchal. You could use examples such as rules about leadership in the Church, where some Churches allow women equality in leadership but many others do not, and where equal leadership for women is only conceded after long battles. You could use examples of biblical teaching and symbolism to support the view that Christianity is patriarchal, such as the creation stories or moral teaching about husbands and wives and about divorce. You might think that Church teaching on ethics, such as natural law, involves men making decisions about issues that affect women's bodies and reproductive health. Or you might disagree: you might argue that the Bible promotes the interests of women even though it was written in an era when women were hardly recognised except as the possessions of men. You might point to stories of strong women in the Bible, such as Ruth and Esther and Lydia. You might argue that Christianity gives special dignity to women in their own roles, especially as mothers, and that it encourages unconditional love for everyone regardless of gender.

Now use your critical and evaluative skills to explore these questions on your own.

2. Christianity traditionally uses male pronouns and imagery in its language of God. Do you think that this matters? Should people understand that 'he' is being used as an all-gender pronoun and leave the language as it is, or is it important for the language to change? If the language changes, will this have the effect of changing attitudes towards patriarchy in Christianity? Give reasons for your answer.

3. Daly believes that Christianity is irretrievably patriarchal and misogynistic and needs to be left behind by feminists. Reuther, in contrast, believes that Christianity needs reforming from within, to uncover feminine ideas about God and Messiahship that have been hidden by years of patriarchy. Which of these ideas do you prefer, if either? Give reasons for your preference or for your rejection of both.

4. It could be argued that Daly goes too far in her descriptions of a patriarchal society as one led by rape, war and genocide. Perhaps, in stating her case so extremely, she undermines it by making a caricature of it rather than being more measured in her objections to male dominance. How far would you agree with this point of view? Should Daly have expressed her views less extremely? Is she exaggerating in order to make a point, or is patriarchal society just as bad as she says it is? Give reasons and examples to support your answer.

5. Daly argues that a male saviour-figure cannot be a saviour for women, because the whole imagery surrounding a male God carries with it male oppression and female submission. How might her view be defended? Christians disagree and argue that Jesus is a saviour for all, not just for one gender. What counter-arguments could they offer to Daly?

6. Daly argues that women's spirituality can only flourish outside Christianity, and suggests that true spirituality is only possible for women because men are entrenched in ideas about their own superiority and power, and these ideas block a genuine connection with the divine. Others might draw attention to the spirituality of female saints of the Middle Ages, such as Teresa of Avila, and claim that female spirituality has a special quality which male spirituality could never have. How far would you agree with this perspective?

7. If Christianity is patriarchal, expressing and promoting views that men should have more power than women, is there anything wrong with that? Could a case be made for saying that the Bible is the word of God and if the Bible says that men should have control over women, then men should have control over women? How might this point of view be supported and how might it be challenged?

Mary Daly (1928–2010)

REVIEW

Practice Exam Questions

Try these practice questions. You could:

» write plans for each of them, to practise your skills in structuring an essay

» use them for practice in writing introductions and/or conclusions

» write the whole essay, perhaps against the clock.

1. 'Rosemary Radford Reuther's feminist theology is more acceptable than the thinking of Mary Daly.' Discuss.

2. Discuss the view that using feminine terms of God is unnecessary.

Use page 9 to review your essay and make sure you have met the assessment objectives. See pages 244–245 for a mark scheme.

Chapter 3.11 | The challenge of secularism

RECAP

Secularisation is a term broadly used to describe a society becoming less religious in its outlook. José Casanova describes three ways the term can be understood:

1. A decline in religious belief in modern society.

2. Religion becoming something that should be done in private rather than in public.

3. The separation of Church and State, where the country is governed without reference to religious authorities and teachings.

The question of whether the UK is a secular country depends on which understanding of secularisation is being used.

Freud's ideas of God as an illusion

- The psychologist Freud offered an explanation of religion in terms of psychology. He rejected the view that religious feelings and experiences come from God, and instead claimed that they come from within the individual's own mind.

- Freud said that religion is infantile and a 'mass delusion'.

- Freud thought religion is a product of wish fulfilment. People experience vulnerability as children, and those who remain infantile in adult life invent a God as a kind of imaginary friend because they feel unable to cope with life on their own.

- Freud related religious belief to his ideas about the Oedipus complex. He thought that male children secretly wanted to kill their fathers so that they could have their mothers all to themselves. They know, however, that it is wrong to want to kill their fathers, so they over-compensate by inventing a cosmic father-figure God to worship.

- He thought that religious believers invent the idea that there are absolute morals and a purpose to life and a goal at the end, because they wish that life could be like that. They transfer these wishes into beliefs.

- Religious believers invent a God who seems stern but is actually loving and forgiving. They invent a life after death that will begin a new existence, where the good will be rewarded and the wicked punished, to compensate for the injustices of real life.

- Religion represses human desires such as sexual violence, theft and murder.

- Religious beliefs and teachings gain authority because they are passed down through generations.

- Freud thought that religion is fundamentally unhealthy. It discourages people from having normal, healthy adult reactions to the world, and from taking on responsibility for their own actions and their consequences. It also represses people and causes conflicts.

Possible strengths and weaknesses of Freud's views on God

- Freud could be right that religion has a particular appeal for vulnerable and lonely people.

- A non-supernatural explanation of religious feelings and experiences could be viewed as more plausible than a supernatural one.

- There is evidence to support Freud's idea that people depict God as a kind of super-human. For example, feminists argue that men have given God male characteristics.

- Many religious people have been particularly strong and courageous in standing up for their beliefs in the face of danger.

- The demands of leading a Christian life are difficult rather than comfortable (see Bonhoeffer's 'costly grace').

- Religious beliefs might be said to be more uniform than would be expected if different individuals made them up.

The struggle and sacrifice of Christians such as Mother Teresa suggests that belief can give people strength or purpose

Dawkins' critique of religion

- Dawkins is a scientist who often criticises religion. He criticises traditional arguments for the existence of God and gives scientific explanations of phenomena that are sometimes used as evidence for God.

- In his book *The God Delusion* (2006), he concentrates on explaining why belief in God is damaging for society and for intellectual progress.

- He argues that human life is meaningful without reference to religious ideas. People do not need the idea of God in order to find meaning in their lives.

- He argues that religion is responsible for division, war and conflict in society, both in the modern world and throughout history.

- He argues that religious belief discourages scientific enquiry by allowing a lazy mindset that says 'it's a divine mystery' rather than looking for answers.

- He claims that religions are repressive, and singles out religious dress codes as an example of the repression of women.

- Dawkins is particularly concerned about the indoctrination of children into religion, citing examples of where babies are initiated into religious faiths before they can understand what is happening, and also giving examples of abuse of children by Christian priests and nuns. Dawkins considers bringing up children to be religious as a form of psychological abuse. He says that children have a right not to have their minds confused by other people's nonsense.

Possible strengths and weaknesses of Dawkins' critique of religion

- Some Christians do see science and religion as opposites and oppose the teaching of evolution in schools, which could lend support to Dawkins' views.
- Dawkins is right to say that some acts of war and terrorism have been the result of disagreements over religious beliefs.
- There is evidence to support his view that religion can be repressive for some groups; many feminists would agree with the claim that religion can be repressive for women.
- Dawkins could be criticised for taking isolated, extreme examples and using them to draw general conclusions.

- He glosses over the many positive contributions religion has made to societies, such as the founding of schools, the campaigning for civil rights, the work for the poor and the pressure for social change.
- He does not take account of the many scientists who have also held religious beliefs and have been motivated by their faith to continue their scientific exploration.
- It could be argued that keeping children away from learning truths about God is abusive.

Jo Marchant, a view contrasting with Freud and Dawkins

- Marchant is a science journalist. In her book *Cure: A Journey into the Science of Mind Over Body* (2016) she argued that religious belief can be psychologically helpful rather than damaging.
- She does not seek to demonstrate that religion is true, but uses interviews and gathers data to question the view that religion is psychologically harmful.

- She suggests that there is compelling evidence that religious practices, such as meditation, social gatherings and belief in a loving God, bring about measurable benefits for religious believers.
- She argues that belief in God and hope for life after death can help people overcome loneliness and fears, allowing people to live happier and longer lives.

Christianity and public life

- Some secular traditions see a separation between the Church and the State as essential. France became secular after the French Revolution abolished the monarchy and took power away from the Church. In France the Government is separate from the Church and religious influence over public matters is not allowed. There are no state-funded religious schools and people are not allowed to wear religious symbols in public. Marriages take place in civic institutions and any religious celebrations of a marriage happen separately. The French separation of Church and State is known as *laïcité*.
- Other countries such as the USA and Turkey also have constitutions that separate religion

from the State. The idea is that government should be democratic and fair for all rather than based on a religious foundation that not everyone shares.
- Not all countries follow the French model. In the Netherlands in the twentieth century there was a policy of 'pillarisation' where each different Christian denomination had its own schools, newspapers, political parties and so on.
- People in the UK disagree about the place of religion in public life. There have been legal disputes over the wearing of religious symbols at work and the extent to which people's religious beliefs should be protected.

Education and schools

- Many schools in the UK have Christian foundations, often because they date back to times when the only free education was provided charitably by the Church. There are also 'faith schools' for the children of other religious traditions in the UK.

Many schools in the UK have Christian foundations

- Church schools usually have state funding as well as sponsorship from the Church. When schools have Church funding, they are expected to have a 'Christian ethos' with an emphasis on Christian moral principles and assemblies of Christian worship. Preference might be given in the admissions policy to children of families who go to church, and teachers might be recruited on the understanding that they are sympathetic to the Christian character of the school. Larger Church schools might employ a chaplain to act as a counsellor and to conduct acts of worship.

- Some organisations such as the British Humanist Association campaign against 'faith schools' for the following reasons:

> a diversity of faith and belief is better for children educationally

> school time should be for lessons, not worship and prayer

> separating children into faith groups encourages division, intolerance and conflict

> faith schools give unfair privileges to children because of the religion of their families

> children should not be recruited into a religion whilst they are at school

- Dawkins argues against religious fundamentalism (such as taking the Bible literally) in schools because:

> religious fundamentalism is anti-scientific and harmful to young minds

> religious fundamentalism replaces scientific, evidence-based enquiry with superstition

> religious schools teach children that unquestioning faith is a virtue, whereas they should be educated to believe that questioning and open-mindedness are good

- Those in favour of retaining faith schools argue differently:

Churches originally built schools for the poor and own a lot of the land they are built on, so the schools cannot just be 'taken away' from the Church.

Parents have the right to want their children to be educated in a way that reflects the family's morality and beliefs.

James Conroy argued that religious schools have a 'liminal function' in a liberal democratic state, giving children the sense that they are not just being prepared for a place in a capitalist world of work and that human flourishing is defined by more than just market value.

A plural, diverse society should have plural, diverse schools to reflect the many different groups in society.

Arguments in favour of faith schools

Replacing faith schools with secular schools can be seen as indoctrinating children into atheism. In his essay 'The Challenge of Secularism', Christopher Dawson argues that secular education has a consciously atheist agenda.

There is no evidence to suggest that children educated at faith schools are less tolerant or open-minded or unscientific than children educated at secular schools.

Critics of Dawkins suggest that his arguments are directed at a fundamentalist and extreme kind of religion which is not prevalent in Church schools in the UK.

Religion, government and State

- The ruling British monarch is also Head of the Church of England and Defender of the Faith.
- There are Anglican bishops in the House of Lords, serving as part of the process of UK government. There are also religious leaders of other faiths, but the Church of England has the most seats in the House of Lords.
- In the UK, religious places of Christian worship are licensed to legalise marriages.
- The UK largely has a culture of 'inclusive secularity', where people's religious beliefs are respected up to a point. Medical staff, for example, may opt out of participating in some

medical procedures if participation would compromise their religious principles. Religious dress is allowed in public if it does not impact someone's ability to do their job or compromise security. People are allowed to make speeches in public about their religious views.

- When political leaders have firm religious beliefs, this can cause controversy, for example if an MP's personal religious beliefs could influence a vote on abortion, people might object and say that the MP should be representing the constituency and not allow religious beliefs to determine the vote.

- Rowan Williams, the former Archbishop of Canterbury, distinguished between 'programmatic secularism' and 'procedural secularism':

> **Programmatic secularism** assumes religious belief in public is offensive and assumes religious people want to drown out opposing views. It equates a non-religious forum with a 'neutral' forum.

> **Procedural secularism** allows public voices from all kinds of beliefs and none, without privileging any of those voices, which ensures a balanced discussion.

Secularisation as a theory

- Sociologists of the mid- and late-twentieth century, such as Peter Berger, argued that the world was becoming less and less religious. This position was supported by evidence such as the decline in church attendance and the growing number of people who registered as having no religion on surveys such as the UK census.

- It was assumed that there would be a decline in religion until it simply disappeared. Reasons given to explain this included the rise of science, globalisation and increased diversity in society.

- The secularisation theory has since been discarded. Berger's later work revisits his earlier conclusions and retracts them. He no longer argues that a modern world is inevitably a secular world.

- Modernity has had effects on religion. Fewer people attend church in Western Europe but other religions have a strong presence. In the rest of the world, religion is as strong as ever. Many people describe themselves as 'spiritual' without wishing to associate closely with a particular religious group.

- Ford argues that it is too simplistic to think of religion as growing or being in decline in a linear way. He also rejects the idea that a religious mentality belongs to an unscientific age and is gradually being replaced with a better, secular, enlightened mentality. He says that the growth and decline of religious belief is unpredictable and can go in many different directions at the same time.

- Ford and Casanova question the idea that secular society is better than religious society. They draw attention to times when ideologies have tried to enforce atheism, sometimes brutally, and have been unsuccessful.

Key terms

Secularism: a term that is used in different ways. It may mean a belief that religion should not be involved in government or public life. It may be a principle that no one religion should have a superior position in the State. It often entails a belief in a public space and a private space, and that religion should be restrained from public power

Secularisation: a theory developed in the 1950s and 1960s from Enlightenment thinking, arguing that religious belief would progressively decline as democracy and technology advanced. Sociologists now doubt such a linear decline

Secular: not connected or associated with religious or spiritual matters. Used colloquially in widely differing ways by atheists, pluralists and those who are anti-religion. Historically, the term was used to distinguish priests who worked in the world (secular priests) from those who belonged to religious communities such as monasteries

Wish fulfilment: according to Freud, wish fulfilment is the satisfaction of a desire through a dream or other exercise of the imagination

APPLY

Test yourself on key knowledge (AO1)

1. What is meant by 'wish fulfilment'?
2. Which psychologist called religion a 'mass delusion'?
3. Which modern atheist holds the view that indoctrinating children into religion is a form of child abuse?
4. What is the name given to the system in the Netherlands of having different schools, political parties and newspapers for different Christian denominations?
5. Who wrote an essay entitled 'The Challenge of Secularism' in which he argued that secular education is atheist education?
6. Who argued that religious schools have a 'liminal' function in a liberal democratic society?
7. What is the meaning of the French term 'laïcité'?
8. What did Williams mean by 'procedural secularism'?
9. When Berger changed his views about the secularisation of society, what did he change them from and what did he replace them with?
10. Who is Head of the Church of England?
11. Give two examples to support the view that Christianity is beneficial for modern society.
12. Give two examples to support the view that secular society is the best option for everyone in it.

If you are unsure about any of the questions, look back over the key points on pages 196–201. You can check your answers on page 220.

Develop your skills in critical argument and evaluation (AO2)

For high marks in AO2, you need to think about the ideas in this chapter and develop your own perspective, so that you can produce critically evaluative arguments rather than just describing and presenting the views of others. At AS level, 50% of your marks are awarded for your skills in critical evaluation, and at A level, 60%.

Use the following questions to help you formulate your own views.

» Discuss them with friends, making sure you articulate your own view and listen to the views of others.
» Try writing your answers to these questions, to familiarise yourself with expressing your ideas in an academic style.

» Remember to give reasons for your views.
» Think about counter-arguments – what might someone say who held a different view from your own, and why do you think they are wrong?

1. **The British Humanist Association and individual thinkers such as Dawkins argue that the UK should get rid of faith schools, because they are damaging to children and bad for their education. How far would you agree with this point of view? If you have been educated at a faith school, how far does their critique of faith schools match your own experience? What counter-arguments might be put forward? Give reasons to support your responses.**

Here is an example of the kinds of ideas you might explore in formulating your analysis and evaluation:

You might agree with the view that there should not be faith schools. You could support this view by arguing that faith schools discourage children from mixing with children from other backgrounds, depriving them of an educationally enriching experience. You might argue that faith schools discourage an inclusive, tolerant attitude towards others. You might argue that schools are chosen by parents and that the children themselves might not want to be confined to being educated within a single faith group. You could argue that faith schools present children with the assumption that their religious tradition is right, which is indoctrination and closes down questioning. Or you might think that people have the right to educate their children in whatever way they think is best, and that there is a lot to be gained culturally and morally from learning in a school with a religious ethos. You might argue that a faith school is preferable to having the children home-schooled by parents who might teach them extremism or just be poor teachers. You could argue that Church schools are part of the heritage of the UK and should not be discarded.

Now use your critical and evaluative skills to explore these questions on your own.

2. Freud argues that religion is invented by infantile people because they find it hard to cope with adult life. How far would you agree or disagree with his point of view, and what reasons would you give to support your opinion?

3. It could be argued that Freud's account of religion is inaccurate, and that Christianity does not promise people that they will be looked after and given rewards in heaven, but instead calls on them to make difficult, courageous choices, be self-sacrificial and put themselves in danger for the sake of Christ. How far would you agree with this criticism of Freud's opinions?

4. Dawkins argues that life is meaningful for atheists and there is no need for people to adopt religious beliefs in order to give life meaning. How far would you agree with this view, and what reasons might be offered on different sides of the argument?

5. Marchant finds evidence to support the view that religious beliefs and practices have psychological and physical benefits for believers. How might Freud or Dawkins respond to such findings? How convincing is the claim that if a belief makes you live a longer and happier life, it is worth holding on to even if it is false? Give reasons to support your view.

6. What do you think of the view that religion should be a private matter and not be seen in public? Should people be allowed to wear religious symbols and religious dress in public? What harm might it be seen to cause? Should wearing political symbols be viewed in the same way as wearing religious symbols? Is having a non-religious public life the same thing as having a public promotion of atheism? Give reasons to support your views.

7. Some people argue that a non-religious upbringing allows children to make up their own minds about religious issues as they mature, rather than forcing a particular set of beliefs on them from a young age. Others argue that a non-religious upbringing forces atheism on children from a young age, giving them the impression that religion is an optional add-on to life, but unnecessary. Do you think that a non-religious upbringing for children is the same as a 'neutral' upbringing, or do you think that any kind of upbringing carries its own agenda? Give reasons to support your answer.

8. Some people argue that Christian values are just normal, sensible human values, and that the values can be continued without any need for all the beliefs and religious practices of Christianity as a religious institution. How far would you agree? Do you think that Christian values are distinctive or are they no more than the values that any responsible human adult is likely to adopt?

9. On balance, do you think that a country is better when it is secular or when it has some kind of religious foundation? Is Christianity of benefit to public life or is religious belief something that should only be practised in private? What reasons and examples could you give to support your answer?

REVIEW

Practice Exam Questions

Try these practice questions. You could:
» write plans for each of them, to practise your skills in structuring an essay
» use them for practise in writing introductions and/or conclusions
» write the whole essay, perhaps against the clock.

1. 'Christianity should continue to be a significant contributor to values and culture.' Discuss.

2. How fair is the claim that Christianity is a major cause of personal and social problems?

Use page 9 to review your essay and make sure you have met the assessment objectives. See pages 245–246 for a mark scheme.

Liberation theology and Marx

 RECAP

Liberation theology is a theological movement about action for the poor.

It is primarily a practical movement but it also has theories behind it. Liberation theologians stress that action is more important than academic theology.

Liberation theology links to Marxist criticisms of capitalism. It looks at the ways in which unequal societies affect the poor, and takes action to work for justice in the world.

What is liberation theology?

- Liberation theology is a practical movement that began in Latin America in 1964. It is about doing the right thing for the poor.

- The aim of the movement was to find ways in which the truth of the Christian message could work in the poverty of Latin America.

- Latin America had and still has a lot of problems, including: a sharp distinction between rich and poor, with extreme poverty; corruption in the government and in the police force; gang warfare; and drug dealers taking power. Latin America was used as a battleground during the Cold War between the USA and the USSR. The competing claims of capitalism and communism caused violence.

- Jon Sobrino and Gustavo Gutiérrez were two leading liberation theologians involved with the movement from the beginning.

- Liberation theology was inspired by the work of Paulo Freire and his book *Pedagogy of the Oppressed* (1970).

- Freire used the term 'conscientisation' to describe the ways in which a person becomes aware of the power structures in society.

- Freire believed in the transformative effect of education. He thought education was essential to enable people to ask the right questions about injustice, and so bring about change.

- Followers of liberation theology hold that action must come first, rather than abstract theorising:

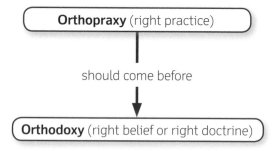

Orthopraxy (right practice)

should come before

Orthodoxy (right belief or right doctrine)

- The concept of the Kingdom of God is central to liberation theology. They stress that the Kingdom of God is not just something Christians should hope for after they die. It is something they should try to bring about in this world. The Kingdom of God grows through the liberation of the poor.

- Gutiérrez wrote that liberation happens in two ways and both must happen if there is to be true freedom:

Liberation from social and economic oppression

Liberation from sin

- In his book *A Theology of Liberation* (1973), Gutiérrez described how sin can be not just personal but also institutional. He meant that there can be whole methods of doing things that wrong God and disobey his commandments, so sin is not just done by individuals but can be done by society as a whole, as 'structural sin'.

- Liberation theology is a theology of hope, seeing possibilities that the world will overturn oppression, not just after death but in this life.

- As part of the liberation theology movement, Christians formed 'base communities', which were discussion groups for people to share their challenges and think about practical solutions supported by Christian faith.

Key biblical texts for liberation theologians

- The Exodus story. God sends Moses to Pharaoh with the demand that people are liberated from slavery: 'Let my people go' (Exodus 9.1, New International Version).

- The Magnificat (the song of Mary when she finds out she is expecting Jesus). Mary sings about how God will bring down the mighty and lift up the poor and oppressed: 'He has brought down rulers from their thrones but has lifted up the humble. He has filled the hungry with good things but has sent the rich away empty' (Luke 1:52–53, New International Version).

- Jesus' teaching about wealth: 'it is easier for a camel to go through the eye of a needle than

for someone who is rich to enter the kingdom of God' (Matthew 19:24, New International Version).

- Jesus' Resurrection, seen as the ultimate expression of freedom: 'I will raise them up at the last day' (John 6:40, New International Version).

- The Beatitudes, which list examples of groups who are singled out for the grace of God, for example: 'Blessed are the poor in spirit, for theirs is the kingdom of heaven' (Matthew 5:3, New International Version).

Marx, alienation and exploitation

- Karl Marx's works helped to inspire liberation theologians.

- Marx lived in the nineteenth century at a time of great social change, due in part to the Industrial Revolution.

- His best-known works are *The Communist Manifesto* (1848) and *Das Kapital* (1867). He was a philosopher, economist and political theorist whose ideas laid the foundations of socialism and communism.

- Marx argued that the development of technology means that people become less immediately connected to the results of their work.

- Production becomes more mechanised. Many people's working lives focus on only one part of a process, so that people feel less pride in the finished outcome.

- Labour itself is bought and sold, not just the finished products of labour.

- People also feel at the mercy of things they cannot control as individuals, such as governments, climate change or fear of war.

- People become 'alienated' – they feel powerless. They are forced to work because they need wages in order to survive, but they have no control over the goods they are working to produce.

- In a capitalist society, private individuals own the 'means of production', for example factories and businesses. The workers have to rely on these private owners who are their employers if they are to survive. Employees feel as if they are part of a machine. They are unable to lead fulfilling lives because they are being exploited by private ownership of the means of production.

- Marx thought that capitalist society alienates workers and creates a divide between those who own the means of production and those who work for the owners. This class divide, he thought, leads to conflict and injustice. Eventually the people who are at the bottom of the heap will turn to violence as the only way of resisting the social structures that alienate them.

- Marx was an atheist. He famously called religion 'the opiate of the people', by which he meant that religion is like a drug that makes people sleepy. He thought that the ruling classes (the owners of the means of production) used religion to keep social classes divided so that they could stay in power. Marx thought Christianity teaches that God chooses what sort of lives people have, encourages the poor to be meek, and makes false promises of rewards in heaven to compensate for injustice in this world, as a way of dampening down any ideas about revolution.

Liberation theology and Marxism

- Latin America in the second half of the twentieth century was in a state of tension. The Cold War between the USA and USSR offered competing ideologies. The USA believed in a capitalist system of government and the USSR followed communism.

- Latin America was at a crossroads, with some people wanting a capitalist system and others wanting communism. Many people lived in poverty.

- Socialist governments were overthrown with the support of the USA, and rebel movements developed. The violent revolutions predicted by Marx seemed to be a real danger.

- Gutiérrez used many of Marx's ideas in the development of his liberation theology. He agreed that the poor were alienated from society and that they were exploited by capitalism. He thought that the poor had a deep desire to overturn the current social system and be liberated.

- Gutiérrez did not endorse every aspect of Marxism, but he saw the task of Christianity through a Marxist lens and used Marxist terminology when writing about theological ideas.

- He argued that Christians have a duty to involve themselves in politics, otherwise injustice just stays as it is.

- He thought it was the responsibility of the Church in Latin America to speak out against injustice, alienation and exploitation, because these things are dehumanising. The Church should take political action to promote brotherhood, justice and liberty. Orthopraxy should be more important than orthodoxy. Gutiérrez thought that the Church should be working with the aim of building a classless, socialist society.

- Other liberation theologians pointed out that their views use Marxism as a means to understand the situation of the poor and the oppressed, but they do not follow Marxism in the way that they follow the teachings of the Bible and the Church.

Structural sin

- Liberation theologians take many of the ideas of Marx but reinterpret them in the context of Christian belief.
- 'Structural sin' is a theological term used to convey the idea that a system can embrace inequality, oppression, alienation and exploitation, and so the whole system can be sinful (disobeying the will of God).
- Liberation theologians saw structural sin in capitalist society. They thought that capitalism has failed to meet the needs of the poor and has pushed them into greater poverty. Socialism is seen not as an ideal but as a better and fairer system.

The preferential option for the poor

- The phrase 'preferential option for the poor' was first used by Pedro Arrupe, Superior General of the Jesuits (a scholarly organisation within the Catholic Church) in 1968.
- It refers to biblical ideas about God having a special preference for people who are poor, outcast or on the margins of society.
- The Jesuit theologian Juan Segundo made the 'preferential option for the poor' a key feature of his liberation theology.
- Segundo wrote that Christians should not remain neutral when there is obvious human misery and injustice. The crushing effects of poverty do not allow for the kind of peace, justice and love that are central to the Christian message.
- Segundo did not entirely agree with Gutiérrez. Gutiérrez thought that people needed to be freed from poverty and exploitation before they could be freed from sin, but Segundo thought that liberation from sin should come first, as freedom from poverty might be unachievable.
- Christians should give priority to helping the poor and should stand in solidarity with them.
- The idea of a preferential option for the poor started out as a motto of liberation theology but later gained wider acceptance by the Catholic Church. Pope John Paul II used the phrase in an encyclical in 1991, although he made it clear that the concern was for those in spiritual poverty as well as those in social and economic poverty. The Pope thought that those who relied too heavily on material goods could be in spiritual poverty even if they had plenty of money.
- Pope Francis took on the idea of solidarity with the poor when he began his papacy in 2013. He rejected extravagance in the Vatican and challenged Catholics to live more simply in solidarity with the poor.

'Preferential option for the poor' refers to the bibilical ideas about God having a special preference for people who are poor or on the margins of society

Liberation theology and the Catholic Church

- The Christians of Latin America are mostly Catholics, and liberation theology emerged within the Catholic tradition of Christianity.

- When liberation theology first began, the leaders of the Catholic Church were concerned about the extent to which it embraced Marxist theories, because Marx was well-known as an atheist and countries with Marxist ideologies were not sympathetic towards Christianity.

- In 1984, Cardinal Ratzinger (who later became Pope Benedict XVI) gave reasons why the Church was uncomfortable with the messages of liberation theology:

It is dangerous to adopt some of Marx's theories because Marxism contains intolerant aspects and can emphasise class and community at the expense of the individual.

Saying that the Eucharist is about a power struggle is a perversion of the Christian message.

Only God can remove human suffering.

Catholic concerns about liberation theology

Violent revolution should not be given more importance than Christian mission.

Christian liberation should primarily be seen as liberation from sin.

- Bonaventure Kloppenburg argued that practical opposition to oppression should not be emphasised even more than the teaching of the gospels because it sidelines the spiritual message of Christianity. It emphasises structural sin over personal sin, whereas the Bible emphasises personal sin and reconciliation through God's forgiveness and grace. Kloppenburg argued that only God can deliver liberation and salvation.

- Richard McBrien argued that liberation theology takes some biblical themes but ignores others completely, and it only sees oppression in economic terms.

- Although the Catholic Church initially viewed liberation theology with suspicion, the election of the first Latin American Pope (Pope Francis) has brought about a more sympathetic attitude. Pope Francis invited Gutiérrez to be a keynote speaker at the Vatican. However, the Church's official position of opposing Marxism has not changed.

Key terms

Capitalism: an economic system in which the means of production are privately owned and operated for profit, in contrast with communism where trade and industry is controlled by the state

Conscientisation: the process by which a person becomes conscious of the power structures in society

Structural sin: the idea that sin is not just a personal action but something that can be brought about through unjust organisations and social structures

Alienation: the process of becoming detached or isolated

Exploitation: treating someone unfairly in order to benefit from their work or resources

Preferential option for the poor: the idea that Jesus Christ stood with the poor and oppressed, and that the Church should focus on the poor and oppressed and stand in solidarity with them

Base Christian communities: Christian groups that gather together to try to directly resolve difficulties in their lives

 APPLY

Test yourself on key knowledge (AO1)

1. What was the name of the book by Freire that inspired the liberation theology movement?

2. What did Freire mean by the term 'conscientisation'?

3. What do the terms 'orthopraxy' and 'orthodoxy' mean?

4. Gutiérrez wrote that liberation happens in two ways. One is liberation from sin – what is the other?

5. Jesus said, 'it is easier for a camel to go through the eye of a needle than...' – what?

6. What are base communities, in the context of liberation theology?

7. What did Marx mean by the term 'alienation'?

8. Who first used the phrase 'a preferential option for the poor'?

9. What is meant by the expression 'structural sin'?

10. Who called religion 'the opiate of the people'?

11. Which Cardinal, later to serve as Pope, in 1984 explained reasons why the Catholic Church viewed liberation theology with suspicion?

12. Which critic of liberation theology said that it put a lot of emphasis on some biblical themes, but ignored others completely?

If you are unsure about any of the questions, look back over the key points on pages 204–209. You can check your answers on page 220.

Develop your skills in critical argument and evaluation (AO2)

For high marks in AO2, you need to think about the ideas in this chapter and develop your own perspective, so that you can produce critically evaluative arguments rather than just describing and presenting the views of others. At AS level, 50% of your marks are awarded for your skills in critical evaluation, and at A level, 60%.

Use the following questions to help you formulate your own views.

» Discuss them with friends, making sure you articulate your own view and listen to the views of others.

» Try writing your answers to these questions, to familiarise yourself with expressing your ideas in an academic style.

» Remember to give reasons for your views.

» Think about counter-arguments – what might someone say who held a different view from your own, and why do you think they are wrong?

1. It could be argued that Christian theology should keep itself distinctive and unique, and not engage with secular or atheist ideologies such as Marxism. How far would you agree with this point of view? Give reasons for your answer.

Here is an example of the kinds of ideas you might explore in formulating your analysis and evaluation:

You might want to argue that the role of the Christian is to live a Christian life and share the message of Christianity, with a focus on agapeic love and the example of Jesus. You might think that Christians should focus on the salvation offered by Jesus through the grace of God. You could argue that adopting aspects of another ideology, such as Marxism, wrongly suggests that there is something incomplete or lacking in Christianity that needs to be supplemented with extra ideas. You could argue that Christianity and Marxism have very different perspectives that cannot readily be merged, for example Marxism emphasises economic oppression and the prospect of violent revolution, whereas Christianity emphasises the oppression of personal sin and the chance of spiritual salvation. Alternatively you could argue that Christianity has always had an emphasis on the poor and the weak, and the insights of Marxism serve to remind Christians of this important focus in their own faith. You might argue that engaging with different ideologies helps Christians to remember what they stand for, and that liberation theologians themselves were well aware that their commitment to Christ was primary.

Now use your critical and evaluative skills to explore these questions on your own.

2. Followers of liberation theology often argue that Christians in the modern world get very angry about sexuality, arguing about the ethics of divorce and same-sex marriage, even though there is very little said on the topic in the Bible; but many make hardly any fuss about poverty, inequality and oppression of the poor. Do you think this is a fair comment? If you think it is true, what do you think might explain why poverty does not seem to be a burning issue for many Christians in developed countries?

3. It could be argued that liberation theology is mistaken in trying to put action before theorising, because you have to have a theoretical way of judging what is the right thing to do, before you can be active in the right way. Do you think this is a fair criticism of liberation theology? Give reasons for your answer.

4. Many Christians argue that it is the will of God that all people should be equal, on the grounds that everyone is made in the image of God and all are equally valuable to God. However, others argue that God chooses different paths and purposes for different people: some are chosen to be male and others female, God chooses different ethnicities for people and gives them different abilities. They argue that God does not intend people to be equal, even though they

are all equally valuable. Do you find this point of view persuasive? What arguments could be offered in support of it? What arguments could be offered in support of the view that equality is God's will?

5. Marx called religion 'the opiate of the people', saying that it was a tool used by those in power to keep themselves in power. Was he right? Give reasons to support your opinion.

6. How might a Marxist criticise liberation theology? Might Marxism offer a better, more practical response to issues of poverty, exploitation and oppression than the response offered by liberation theology? Could the Christian emphasis on self-giving love and spiritual salvation get in the way of making society fairer for everyone? Give reasons to support your answer.

7. Do you think that it is possible for humanity to work together to overcome poverty and social injustice? Give reasons for your answer.

Karl Marx (1818–1883)

REVIEW

Practice Exam Questions

Try these practice questions. You could:

» write plans for each of them, to practise your skills in structuring an essay

» use them for practice in writing introductions and/or conclusions

» write the whole essay, perhaps against the clock.

1. 'Christian thinkers should not engage with the ideologies of atheists such as Marx.' Discuss.

2. Discuss critically the view that liberation theology would be more successful if it became more Marxist in its outlook.

Use page 9 to review your essay and make sure you have met the assessment objectives. See pages 246–247 for a mark scheme.

Sample student answers

1. **'There is no such thing as a distinctive human nature.'
Discuss.**

Augustine thought that there was a distinct human nature, and he thought that it was created by God but that it had been spoiled by human sin. When God created Adam and Eve, he created Adam first 'out of the dust of the ground', and breathed into him to make him into a living being. Then God realised that Adam was lonely and needed a helper, so when Adam was asleep, God took one of Adam's ribs and used it to form a woman. Adam called the woman Eve. They lived in the Garden of Eden and the Bible says that they walked with God. Augustine thought that they must have lived in a spirit of friendship, which he called concordia. He thought that this was the purest kind of relationship and that was why he thought they must have lived as friends, because this was the time when they were pure.

This introduction shows that the writer understands the question and can relate the issues raised in it to the thinking of Augustine, but there is no suggestion that there is going to be an argument. If the essay is going in one particular direction, the reader has no idea what direction that is.

Adam and Eve were told not to eat the fruit from the middle of the garden, but the serpent tempted them to eat it. Eve took it first, and then she offered it to Adam and he took it as well. This incident is known as the Fall, because Adam and Eve fell away from good and brought sin into the world. Augustine said that after the Fall, human nature changed and Original Sin entered the world. The Fall also brought about natural disasters and made the world a harsher place to live in.

This is factually accurate but the writer did not need to spend quite so long retelling the story of the Garden of Eden. The story could have been used to make points in an argument, rather than just presented.

Augustine said that human nature was damaged for ever by the Fall. People have become obsessed with cupiditas. Cupiditas is a love of material wealth and worldly pleasure such as eating and drinking. People are unable to live without sin following the Fall, even when they become Christians. Augustine was interested in Paul's writing in Romans 7, where Paul writes about his struggles to avoid sin once he has become a Christian. Augustine's view is that human nature can never escape sin because of the Fall. He did think, however, that people can be saved by the grace of God, through the sacrifice made by Jesus on the cross.

This is an accurate if rather basic presentation of Augustine's thought on human nature.

Other thinkers agree with Augustine in saying that there is a distinct human nature, although they do not always agree with him about what that nature is. Hobbes, for example, thought that human nature was selfish and that people only work together and co-operate for selfish reasons, because they know it will be for their own benefit, otherwise they wouldn't do it. Rousseau thought that there is a distinctive nature and that nature is good, so he agreed with Augustine up to a point.

Other thinkers disagree with Augustine. Some, such as John Locke, think that people are born with a tabula rasa, which means a blank slate. They do not have a nature when they are born but form their own natures through the experiences they have and the choices they make. Jean Paul Sartre was an existentialist philosopher from France. He thought that people make their own natures and are free to become whatever kind of people they want to become. So he would not think there is a distinctive human nature because people might make different choices and develop different natures.

In conclusion, there are arguments for Augustine's view and arguments against it. But neither side has proved that it is right. In the end it is up to individuals to decide for themselves because the range of different opinions shows there is not one right answer.

The essay has a sensible structure, in that one possible opinion is presented and then alternatives are presented, so that the essay has a clear sense of direction. However, the points of view are merely described, and nothing else is done with them. There is no evaluative comment or opinion given at all.

This conclusion does not tie up the argument of the essay because the essay does not have an argument. The writer should give us an opinion – if they think it is impossible to form a judgement, they should say so and explain why with reasoned comments.

The examiner says:

This is a weak essay because of the lack of argument in it. The candidate has presented points of view that differ, but these points of view have been presented without being used to form an argument. It is not a critical argument if the candidate simply says on the one hand there are these views and on the other hand, there are different views. The conclusion is weak and says little more than that there are different points of view.

- The essay scores reasonably well for AO1 because there is factually accurate material that the candidate clearly understands. The material selected is relevant to the question and it ranges over a good selection of different points of view. However, the essay does not score in the top band for AO1 because the material has been presented rather than 'used' (as the level descriptors require).

- For AO2, the essay scores hardly anything, because there is no argument. We never find out what the candidate thinks about the different points of view they present; we never find out which are considered to be more persuasive than others, or what the implications might be of holding one view rather than another. The conclusion is entirely inconclusive. The fact that there are different opinions on the issue does not demonstrate that there is no right answer, as one could be right and the others wrong.

To achieve a better mark, the candidate needs to:

» think through the essay title in terms of what they plan to argue, rather than just in terms of the information they want to present

» decide whether or not they agree with the statement in the question, and give reasons for or against supporting it

» consider counter-arguments, rather than just describing them, and say whether they are strong or weak points of view

» reach a conclusion that summarises the arguments given.

2. 'Bonhoeffer's teaching has little relevance for Christians today.' Discuss.

Dietrich Bonhoeffer lived at a time of great danger and social conflict. In Germany in the 1930s, the Nazi regime came to power, and as a Protestant Christian minister Bonhoeffer had to decide what was an appropriate response for a Christian to make to Nazism. His teaching and his life focused on 'costly discipleship', the suffering of Christ and the call to solidarity. This teaching could seem to be much more appropriate for life in Nazi Germany than it is for Christians today. However, I will argue that Bonhoeffer's teaching is just as relevant today as it was when he was teaching and writing.

Bonhoeffer's teaching about costly discipleship included the idea that people should be absolutely obedient to the will of God in a single-minded way, just as Jesus' disciples were. Jesus called them, 'Come, follow me' and immediately they dropped what they were doing and became his disciples. They did not try to fit Jesus' teachings around their lives to make things convenient for themselves. Bonhoeffer said that true discipleship is costly. People have to give things up, make changes and sacrifice things they might have wanted in order to lead a Christian life. This contrasts with 'cheap grace' which is when people accept God's grace towards them but make no changes in their own lives as a result.

This is a very good introduction. The candidate has given a confident and concise summary of Bonhoeffer's context in history, a quick note of the key themes in his teaching and a clear indication of where the essay is going in terms of an argument.

The candidate is making good use of quotations. Rather than memorising long lines of text, they have learned little phrases that capture the essence of what is being said, and the quotations are used as part of the argument rather than simply presented.

Bonhoeffer said that this kind of attitude was the 'deadly enemy' of the church.

It could be argued that if Christians live in countries and at times when there is peace, and where Christianity is accepted and encouraged, they have no need to put their lives on the line in order to be disciples. They could just seek change through the way they use their votes or through peaceful protest such as petitions. Perhaps Bonhoeffer's teaching applies only when Christianity is threatened. However, in my view he was right to say that true discipleship is costly. Obeying the will of God can be costly on a personal level, such as deciding not to have an affair with a married man even if you are deeply in love, or deciding to give a large part of your income to the poor even if it means you have to live in a smaller house.

Bonhoeffer also wrote about the suffering of Christ. At the time he was writing, people were being tortured and killed by the Nazis for all kinds of reasons, such as for being gay or for being Jewish. Bonhoeffer knew that he was putting himself in danger of suffering torture or death when he opposed the Nazis so openly. He wrote about sharing the suffering of Christ and 'taking up the cross', but said that this was not a terrible thing but an invitation to 'communion with God'. It might seem that this kind of suffering is only appropriate for times when people are under attack. Usually, in Christian countries in the developed world, Christians do not have to suffer in this kind of way, and so it could be seen that Bonhoeffer's teaching is relevant only during times of war and persecution. However, Bonhoeffer said that sharing in Christ's suffering involves things like self-denial, resisting temptation and having to forgive others even when we don't feel like it. It does not have to be just danger of physical pain that brings Christians to share in the suffering of Christ. Perhaps 'suffering' is the wrong word as it suggests physical pain, whereas Bonhoeffer was talking about being prepared to give yourself up for Jesus, whether it was giving yourself up to be killed by the Nazis or giving yourself up as the price paid for helping other people and possibly being rejected because of your beliefs.

This is a very good paragraph – the candidate obviously has a good understanding of Bonhoeffer's thinking, and is using it to address the question. The candidate has thought of some examples to illustrate the points, showing personal engagement with the topic rather than just learning class notes. It would be good to see the points developed further.

The candidate is taking Bonhoeffer's key themes one by one and commenting on them in relation to the question, showing awareness of possible counter-arguments. This is a solid structure and manages to combine knowledge and understanding with critical comment.

The other key theme in Bonhoeffer's teaching is solidarity. He meant by this, 'existing for others'. He did not just say, helping other people out when you can, but 'existing for', showing that he thought a Christian's whole life and reason for existence should be concerned with other people.

Unfortunately, the candidate seems to have run out of time. The exam script shows that they spent a long time on another essay before beginning this one. The candidate had made a detailed plan before beginning writing, and this probably contributed, as the plan must have taken fifteen or twenty minutes. It would have been better if they had made just quick, brief notes before beginning, rather than adding so much detail to the plan. It was, however, worth doing some planning, as the essay has a clear structure that really helps to form a lucid account, but the candidate should have been stricter about planning concisely.

The examiner says:

Although the candidate ran out of time, this has the potential to be a strong essay. The candidate knows and understands the material, has grasped exactly what the question is asking and has a clear structure and consistent line of argument.

- For AO1, the essay scores quite well, although it would have scored higher marks if the candidate had finished, because there are some key features of Bonhoeffer's thinking that are left unexplored, and some of the points made are rather superficial; they would have benefited from deeper exploration. However, the information given is accurate and it has been used in the process of furthering an argument rather than just being described.

- For AO2, the essay also scores quite well, although it would have scored higher marks if the candidate had finished. The third point about solidarity has barely been introduced before time is up. There is no conclusion to pull the threads of the argument together and give a clear and conclusive answer to the question.

To achieve a better mark, the candidate needs to:

» be very strict about timing, by allowing only a few minutes to read the question carefully and sketch a very brief plan. The plan is only for the candidate's own use and will not be marked, so it does not matter if the candidate wants to use abbreviations or memory-jogging words: there is no need to write out a plan in full sentences.

» make sure that each essay is given the same amount of time in the exam and that enthusiasm for one topic does not overrun and spoil a later essay. Keep a close watch on the clock and start the next essay on time rather than going back to the previous one and adding extra quotations and comments to it.

» **Practice** writing timed essays during revision, as much as possible, until the skill is as near to perfect as it can be.

Answers to Test Yourself questions

1.1 Ancient philosophical influences

1. *Republic*/**2.** It means he thought knowledge was primarily obtained through reason/**3.** It means he divided reality into two distinct categories/**4.** Because the Forms are unchanging, but the physical world changes all the time/**5.** The Form of the Good/**6.** It represents him being enlightened about the existence of the Forms/**7.** It means he thought knowledge was primarily obtained through sense experience/
8. He means we can explain something in terms of what it is made from – its matter/**9.** He means the Prime Mover must be something which does not depend on anything else for its existence/**10.** He means we can explain something in terms of the activity which brought it about/**11.** The Prime Mover attracts things towards itself whilst remaining unmoved/**12.** Because it cannot change and therefore cannot be corruptible, and because it has no potential and therefore must be already everything that it could be.

1.2 Soul, mind and body

1. He thought it went back to the world of the Forms/**2.** Reason, appetite and emotion/**3.** A slave-boy could work out the answers to geometry problems despite being uneducated, which made Plato think he must have known geometry concepts already, before birth/**4.** It illustrates how the soul is inseparable from the body just as the stamp shape is inseparable from the wax/**5.** The capacities or capabilities of living things; their 'essence'/**6.** The problem of the nature of the mind and the body, whether they are separate and how they interact/**7.** Thought, emotion, memory, etc./**8.** Because he was thinking with it/**9.** Property dualism/**10.** Because they do not think there is any part of a person which is non-physical and so there is nothing to survive physical death/
11. *The Concept of Mind*/**12.** He means two distinct beliefs about the soul. One is the belief in the soul as a separate part of the person, capable of surviving death, and two is the belief that the soul is the essence of a person in terms of their individuality and personality.

1.3 Arguments based on observation

1. An argument which uses sense experience to draw conclusions about which explanation provides the best fit/
2. A priori arguments/**3.** Attempts to use human reason to work out truths about God/**4.** Because they look at the end results (the world) to draw conclusions about God/**5.** Aquinas/**6.** *Natural Theology*/**7.** He thought the care and detail that God put into creation shows how much he cares for us/**8.** Gottfried Leibniz/**9.** He thought it was a weak analogy and that the world is not much like a watch/
10. It might have come about by chance, or the universe might be its own cause. It might have been made by a stupid God, or one copying ideas from another, or by a committee of gods or angels or demons/**11.** Ockham's razor/**12.** It is the principle that says the universe seems to be perfectly fine-tuned for the existence of human life.

1.4 Arguments based on reason

1. A priori/**2.** That than which nothing greater can be thought/**3.** There is no God/**4.** Existence that depends on other things/**5.** The first looks at the idea of an actual God surpassing an imaginary one, whilst the second looks at the nature of necessary existence/**6.** A proposition that does not need any sense experience to support its truth/
7. He said that if we replace 'God' in the argument with 'island' then it becomes plain that we cannot bring something into existence just by our description of it/**8.** He said that just as three angles adding up to 180 degrees are inseparable from a triangle, so existence is inseparable from God/**9.** A term which describes something and tells us about its characteristics/**10.** Eighteenth/**11.** He didn't think that we all share a concept of what God is; he thought that God is beyond understanding/**12.** Bertrand Russell.

1.5 Religious experience

1. Rudolf Otto/**2.** E.g. Paul on the road to Damascus, or any other/**3.** An experience impossible to describe, invoking feelings of awe, worship and fascination/**4.** The principle that we should trust our own experience unless we have good reason not to/**5.** Feeling that something has been learned/
6. Ineffability, transience and passivity/**7.** It could be seen as valid if it had good long-lasting effects, like a medicine/
8. It means he thought something was true if it worked on a practical level/**9.** A religious experience involving several people together/**10.** He thought God is an infantile neurosis for people who cannot cope with adult life/**11.** He was trying to discover if the feelings of religious experience could be created artificially using magnetism/**12.** It might be understood as the effect of hormones produced by the body in a state of crisis.

1.6 The problem of evil

1. The beliefs that God is omnipotent and omnibenevolent and that evil exists/**2.** The evil and suffering not caused by human actions/**3.** Irenaeus/**4.** Fourth/**5.** An absence or lack of goodness/**6.** Because God created things with variety/
7. He said that sin was so catastrophic that it disrupted the natural order of the universe/**8.** He thought it was part of God's loving plan to help us grow and develop/**9.** A distance in knowledge/**10.** John Keats/**11.** He thought we had to be able to choose between genuine good and bad options, otherwise it is not real freedom/**12.** We continue with our spiritual journeys.

1.7 The nature or attributes of God

1. All-goodness or all-loving/**2.** Descartes/**3.** God can do everything that is within his nature and does not imply a contradiction/**4.** Anselm/**5.** Schleiermacher/
6. Boethius/**7.** That God is everlasting and moves along the same timeline that we do/**8.** The incarnation and sacrifice of Christ/**9.** Because omnipotence suggests God can do anything but omnibenevolence suggests God can't do anything bad/**10.** Because if God knows the future with certainty, we have to do the things God knows we will do/

11. E.g. Peter Vardy/**12.** Because a God outside time cannot interact with the world in time; because an eternal God could not have emotions and could not love; because an eternal God could not respond to prayer; because an eternal God could not have relationships; because the Bible does not consistently give a picture of an eternal God (or other valid answers).

1.8 Religious language: negative, analogical or symbolic

1. The *via negativa*/**2.** Pseudo-Dionysius the Areopagite/**3.** Moses Maimonides/**4.** Because it can say things which are literally true of God and avoids making God too small/**5.** The cataphatic way/**6.** A comparison made between one thing and another in an effort to aid understanding/**7.** Language which is used in the same way in different contexts/**8.** When there is a causal relationship between the two analogous things/**9.** When there is a difference of proportion or scale between the two analogous things/**10.** Paul Tillich/**11.** Many possibilities, such as Father, judge, rock, bread of life, shepherd, fire, light/ **12.** E.g. that symbols require interpretation which might be misled, that symbols can have different connotations in different times and cultures, or any other valid response.

1.9 Religious language: twentieth-century perspectives and philosophical comparisons

1. Antony Flew/**2.** Form of life/**3.** Both have rules which are understood properly only when involved with the game, or any other reasonable response/**4.** A partisan in wartime/**5.** Logical positivism/**6.** It does not have factual content but is a tool for achieving something/**7.** A statement that is true by definition/**8.** A blik/**9.** E.g. neither dismissed religious language as meaningless, or any other reasonable response/**10.** Wittgenstein (amongst others)/**11.** *Language, Truth and Logic*/**12.** Testing using the five senses.

2.1 Natural law

1. To live in an ordered society/**2.** Doing good and avoiding evil/**3.** Happiness in the sense of human flourishing; living well/**4.** Prudence, temperance, fortitude, justice/**5.** Divine law/**6.** Some actions have more than one effect. If the intention is to do good then other unintentional effects do not make the action bad/**7.** Tail, or end result, or final purpose/**8.** Pleasures which seem tempting but which do not accord with the primary precepts/**9.** Fundamentally good/**10.** Focused on action and duty/**11.** Reason/**12.** Being in God's presence (beatific vision).

2.2 Situation ethics

1. 1966/**2.** Primarily considering the individual rather than any rules/**3.** Ethics which look at the end result in order to determine the morality of an action/**4.** Practicality; the action chosen has to be practically applicable/**5.** Agapeic love/**6.** Love distributed/**7.** Being without and opposed to having rules or laws/**8.** Conscience/**9.** Each situation should be judged according to its own circumstances rather than according to rules already set/**10.** If love is the end result then any means are justified /**11.** Yes/**12.** Nothing should be completely ruled out – euthanasia might be the most loving action in some situations.

2.3 Kantian ethics

1. A priori/**2.** A posteriori/**3.** The good will/**4.** Hypothetical imperative/**5.** So that justice can be done/**6.** The kingdom of ends/**7.** Through reason/**8.** People should act as if their actions are setting the standards for laws in an ideal kingdom/**9.** Never/**10.** Deontological/**11.** The highest good, in which happiness and virtue are combined/**12.** It should be a law suitable to be applied to everyone.

2.4 Utilitarianism

1. The greatest happiness (and the least harm) for the greatest number/**2.** Jeremy Bentham/**3.** Consequentialist, or teleological/**4.** Seeking pleasure or happiness/ **5.** Nearness – how far in the future will the happiness be experienced/**6.** Fertility – will the happiness give rise to other happinesses/**7.** Whether it will bring about only happiness, or happiness with some harm too/**8.** He talked about the quality of the happiness as higher and lower pleasures/ **9.** *Utilitarianism*/**10.** An act utilitarian/**11.** Not at all/ **12.** Mainly relativist.

2.5 Euthanasia

1. Non-voluntary is when people cannot make the decision for themselves (e.g. in a persistent vegetative state, or newborn) and involuntary is when it is against their will/**2.** Because of beliefs about the sanctity of human life in comparison with other animal life/**3.** Jonathan Glover/**4.** If the main aim of the treatment is to relieve pain but the side-effect is shortening life then this is acceptable/**5.** The argument that if something is allowed in a few cases, soon it will become unstoppable/**6.** Because able-bodied people have the choice to commit suicide but some disabled people are not physically able to make that same choice without help/**7.** Joseph Fletcher/**8.** Agape/**9.** To protect life, live in society and love God/**10.** That life is holy, sacred and special/**11.** Aquinas/ **12.** It contrasts with a real good – it seems to be good at first sight but there are hidden problems with it.

2.6 Business ethics

1. Having money invested in it and taking a share of its profits/**2.** Being affected in some way by the business and the ways it operates/**3.** Kantianism/**4.** E.g. when there is bullying or discrimination against employees, when health and safety is being ignored, when the company is being dishonest to the public, or many other situations/**5.** Corporate social responsibility/**6.** A set of social beliefs that puts a high value on acquiring possessions/**7.** Act utilitarianism/**8.** Rule utilitarianism/**9.** Crane and Matten/**10.** Friedman/**11.** Capitalism./**12.** Businesses taking a wider responsibility for the community and/or the environment.

2.7 Meta-ethical theories

1. It is a mistake to think that good can be defined in terms of anything else/**2.** Stevenson/**3.** An 'ought' cannot be derived from an 'is'/**4.** *A Treatise of Human Nature*/**5.** The view that there are fixed, eternal, universal moral facts and truths/**6.** Yes/**7.** Relativism/**8.** Someone who believes that meaning and truth can be found only in that which is available to be observed using the five senses/**9.** Because they cannot be subjected to empirical testing/**10.** MacIntyre/**11.** E.g. Ross, amongst others/**12.** Something that seems, on the face of it at first glance, to be a duty.

2.8 Conscience

1. Following the good and avoiding evil/**2.** Reason is given by God and distinguishes human beings from other animals, to be used to make moral judgements for the purpose of progress/**3.** Natural law/**4.** Vincible ignorance is a lack of knowledge where someone should have informed themselves: they should have known better. Invincible ignorance is a lack of knowledge where someone could not be expected to have known any better and is not blameworthy/**5.** Id, ego and super-ego/**6.** The part of the mind that contradicts the id/**7.** John Henry Newman/**8.** No role at all – Freud thought God was imaginary/**9.** It mediates between the id and the super-ego/**10.** E.g. Butler and Newman, amongst others/
11. Fromm/**12.** Because he thought that conscience is the operation of reason, and it would be wrong to choose to do something irrational.

2.9 Sexual ethics

1. Cohabitation/**2.** John Stuart Mill/**3.** Catholicism/
4. Sex before marriage, usually between two people who are intending to marry each other/**5.** 2014/**6.** It does not recognise same-sex marriage as in any way equivalent to heterosexual marriage/**7.** The sealing of a relationship, usually a marriage relationship, with sexual intercourse/
8. It is based around the idea of duty/**9.** Relativist/
10. Explaining that man leaves his parents and joins with a wife in marriage/**11.** Forbidding sexual relationships between two men/**12.** Natural law.

3.1 Augustine's teaching on human nature

1. Manichees/**2.** Concordia/**3.** Caritas/**4.** They were not to eat the fruit of the tree from the middle of the garden/**5.** Rationality, freedom of choice and a moral nature/**6.** Uncontrollable desire for physical pleasure and material things/**7.** Dominated by desire for worldly pleasures and material goods/**8.** Romans (chapter 7)/**9.** E.g. Hobbes, amongst others/**10.** A blank slate/**11.** E.g. Sartre, amongst others/**12.** Any of: love and mercy, reaches the human heart and will, gives moral guidance, helps the soul understand sin, encourages the soul to praise God, transforms the will to want to please God, calms the soul with forgiveness and hope, is demonstrated in the sacrifice of Christ and in the Holy Spirit at work.

3.2 Death and the afterlife

1. Being able to exist as purely mental and spiritual without having a body/**2.** Original Sin/**3.** A tent, and clothing/**4.** Universalism/**5.** The opportunity to see God face-to-face in a timeless vision/**6.** Pope Gregory/**7.** Because it is not in the Bible, and because in the Middle Ages it was used by Catholics as a means of getting money from people/**8.** Election/**9.** He held a view of limited election/
10. He believed in unlimited election: God offering salvation to all/**11.** He said it made Christ's death on the cross seem pointless/**12.** When the Son of Man comes in all his glory.

3.3 Knowledge of God's existence

1. The eye of the flesh/**2.** John Calvin/**3.** A theatre/
4. Teleological or design arguments/**5.** Epistemic distance/
6. In favour/**7.** Immediate revelation is direct, whereas mediate revelation is reported and interpreted/**8.** Unveiling or uncovering/**9.** God's freely given, unconditional gifts to humanity/**10.** He thought people could not learn about God through their own effort, they could only learn when God chose to reveal himself/**11.** Athens/**12.** Calvin.

3.4 The person of Jesus Christ

1. John Hick/**2.** E.P. Sanders, amongst others/**3.** A Jewish political group opposed to Roman rule/**4.** Suetonius, Tacitus, Pliny the younger, Josephus/**5.** C.S. Lewis/**6.** David Hume/
7. An 'infused' knowledge/**8.** Examples include Samaritans, women, tax collectors, people with leprosy/**9.** Dietrich Bonhoeffer/**10.** Reza Aslan/**11.** Having the same substance or the same essential nature/**12.** No (in the records we have).

3.5 Christian moral principles

1. 1 Corinthians/**2.** E.g. historical facts, facts about animal species, inconsistent accounts of a single event, amongst others/**3.** The line of priests and bishops from Peter to the present day/**4.** Natural law/**5.** MacIntyre and Hays, amongst others/**6.** Bultmann/**7.** Tillich/**8.** It is overwhelmingly a men's tradition without female voices or experiences/**9.** Justice, love and wisdom/**10.** Because Church tradition in the Middle Ages did not always live up to biblical standards/**11.** Love God and love your neighbour as yourself/**12.** Catholic.

3.6 Christian moral action

1. The Confessing Church/**2.** Deliberately disobeying certain laws put in place by the government/**3.** From the Sermon on the Mount in Matthew 5–7/**4.** E.g. people of non-Aryan descent were not allowed in the ministry, young people who joined Church youth groups had to belong to Hitler Youth, amongst others/**5.** Because he was openly critical of Nazism/**6.** Existing for others/**7.** Grace of God which is accepted without the recipient making any changes in their lives/**8.** Finkenwalde/**9.** The Gestapo, under Himmler, closed it down/**10.** He disguised them as military intelligence and got them across the border into Switzerland/**11.** To share in the suffering of Christ and become closer to God/**12.** Hitler.

3.7 Religious pluralism and theology

1. Christian thinking about how its relationship with other world religions should be understood/**2.** Those who believe that only some people will be saved/**3.** E.g. Augustine and Calvin, amongst others/**4.** Those who believe that all can be saved but only by means of Christianity/**5.** Karl Barth/
6. No salvation outside the Catholic Church/**7.** Karl Rahner/
8. Because religions are entire systems of belief, not collections of different threads that can be unpicked/
9. Noumena are things as they really are, and phenomena are things as they appear to us/**10.** Just as Copernicus moved the earth out of the centre of understanding of astronomy and recognised that the planets orbit the sun, so people should move Christianity out of the centre and recognise that all religions orbit 'the Real'/**11.** Panikkar/**12.** E.g. John 14:6, 1 Timothy 2:3–6, amongst many others.

3.8 Religious pluralism and society

1. Worshipping together with people from other faith traditions/**2.** The Holocaust, resulting in *Dabru Emet*, and the letter from the Muslim community in 2007/**3.** Dialogue of mutual understanding/**4.** 'A Common Word Between Us and You'/**5.** Speak the Truth/**6.** An open letter to more than one recipient/**7.** The Mission of the Redeemer/**8.** John Paul II/**9.** 2010/**10.** Actively engage with people of other faiths/**11.** Yes/**12.** Yes.

3.9 Gender and society

1. Society where men have the power and where decisions are made with men's interests primarily in mind/**2.** Gender biology is to do with physical gender characteristics whereas gender identification is to do with the gender expression people choose to adopt for themselves/**3.** Genesis/**4.** Mary Wollstonecraft/**5.** The feminism of the 1960s and 1970s, primarily concerned with women's sexual health and reproductive rights and also with equal pay and discrimination issues/**6.** Feminism that tries to change views within the law and the current social system/**7.** 1928/**8.** 1970/**9.** First century/**10.** *Mulieris Dignitatem*/**11.** Socialisation/**12.** The Catholic Church does not recognise divorce.

3.10 Gender and theology

1. Tertullian/**2.** Aquinas/**3.** Several, including Pope Pius XII/**4.** It is a male perspective recommending male ideas about love appropriate for male-dominated circumstances, serving the interests of men/**5.** Abandoned altogether/**6.** She said Daly ignores the parts of the Bible which do not suit her feminist agenda/**7.** Reformed from within/**8.** The vital spirit that permeates nature/**9.** Rosemary Radford Reuther/**10.** A military, political, warrior-type Messiah/**11.** The personification of wisdom/**12.** The personification of the earth and the natural world.

3.11 The challenge of secularism

1. The satisfaction of desire through dreams or imagination, according to Freud/**2.** Sigmund Freud/**3.** Richard Dawkins/**4.** Pillarisation/**5.** Christopher Dawson/**6.** James Conroy/**7.** A concept in the French Constitution that states France is a secular nation/**8.** A situation where the voices of all people of whatever religious belief and non-belief can be heard, without preference being given to any one opinion/**9.** He thought that religion was in a kind of linear decline and would gradually disappear, but then changed his view and thought that things do not work as neatly as that and are unpredictable/**10.** The monarch/**11.** E.g. charitable organisations, pressure for acceptance of homosexuality, campaigns against slavery, Samaritans, amongst others/**12.** E.g. indoctrination is bad, religion can be divisive, examples related to terrorism and conflict, examples related to science and religion, amongst others.

3.12 Liberation theology and Marx

1. *Pedagogy of the Oppressed*/**2.** The process by which people come to be aware of the power structures of their society/**3.** Orthopraxy means right action and orthodoxy means right doctrine/**4.** Liberation in socio-economic terms/**5.** For a rich man to enter the kingdom of God/**6.** Christian communities that meet to discuss practical ways of dealing with their difficulties/**7.** A sense of separation and distance from the results of labour/**8.** Father Pedro Arrupe/**9.** Sin that is endemic in institutions and societies because of the way they are set up/**10.** Karl Marx/**11.** Ratzinger/**12.** Bonaventure Kloppenburg (amongst others).

Mark schemes for practice questions

The following points are 'indicative content' only, showing the sort of thing candidates are likely to write. If you have taken a different approach then you will be credited as long as you have taken a reasonable interpretation of the question. You are expected to make use of the views of well-known thinkers, scripture or other sources of wisdom and authority to support your line of argument.

Chapter 1.1

1. Discuss critically the philosophical views presented by Plato in his Analogy of the Cave.

AO1 Essays might demonstrate knowledge and understanding through the use of some of the following ideas. This list is not prescriptive (you may have used other ideas instead) or exhaustive (you may have included valid ideas that are not listed here).

- Description and explanation of why Plato gave his Analogy of the Cave, such as to explain the differences between knowledge of the physical world and knowledge of the Forms, and the superiority of knowledge gained through reason over knowledge gained through the senses.

- Description and explanation of the key features of Plato's cave analogy, such as the prisoners, the chains and the shadows.

- Description and explanation of the key philosophical ideas Plato demonstrates in his cave analogy, such as his dualist understanding of the nature of reality and his belief that the Form of the Good illuminates all knowledge.

AO2 Essays might demonstrate skill in critical evaluation, analysis and coherent argument through the use of some of the following:

- Leaners might argue that Plato is right to make a distinction between knowledge gained through reason and knowledge gained through sense experience; or they might argue that this distinction is not as clear in real life.

- They might argue that he is right to give superiority to rationalism, as this gives certain and logical answers; or they might argue that he is wrong and that empiricism is superior because it provides evidential support even if it cannot be certain.

- They might argue that Plato successfully shows the importance of having a critical and philosophical attitude to knowledge as it is essential in a quest for the truth; or they might argue that Plato is elitist in suggesting that only the intellectually gifted can understand goodness.

- They might argue that Plato is right in comparing those who are ignorant of philosophy with prisoners, because they are missing the opportunity to gain deeper understanding of truths; or they might argue that Plato overstates the value of philosophy and that people can live very happy lives whether or not they question their sense experiences.

2. 'Aristotle is wrong to think worthwhile knowledge can be gained through sense experience.' Discuss.

AO1 Essays might demonstrate knowledge and understanding through the use of some of the following ideas. This list is not prescriptive (you may have used other ideas instead) or exhaustive (you may have included valid ideas that are not listed here).

- Description and explanation of what it means to be an empiricist and what it means to be a rationalist.

- Description and explanation of how Aristotle thought knowledge was to be obtained, including Aristotle's understanding of reality.

- Description and explanation of the contrast between Aristotle's thought and that of other thinkers such as Plato.

AO2 Essays might demonstrate skill in critical evaluation, analysis and coherent argument through the use of some of the following:

Learners might support the view that Aristotle is wrong by using some of the following arguments:

- Plato and other rationalists argued that reason is the primary source of knowledge because reasoning can lead us to certain answers and proofs.

- Sense experience can lead us only to probabilities because the physical world is always changing, so the knowledge gained is not worth having because it is provisional.

- When reason and sense experience conflict, for example when we think we see something but reason tells us it is impossible, then reason overrides, showing that reason is superior to sense experience.

- Sense experience can often be misleading as our senses are not 100 per cent reliable.

- Our senses are limited, for example there are sounds we cannot hear, and relying on sense experience makes us think we know the full picture when this is not necessarily the case.

Learners might reject the view that Aristotle is wrong by using some of the following arguments:

- Sense experience is readily available to people and does not depend on them being particularly intellectually gifted.

- Sense experience provides a way of knowing that is testable by others and open to peer review.

- Without sense experience, there would be little to reason about.

- Even if the world is changing all the time, we can still have useful knowledge about this changing world.

- We can use both reason and sense experience, we do not have to reject the one in order to be in favour of the other, although the question still remains about which has priority.

Answers and mark schemes

Chapter 1.2

1. How convincing is Plato's view that the soul is distinct from the body?

AO1 Essays might demonstrate knowledge and understanding through the use of some of the following ideas. This list is not prescriptive (you may have used other ideas instead) or exhaustive (you may have included valid ideas that are not listed here).

- Description and explanation of Plato's dualist understanding of the soul as distinct from the body, the spiritual as distinct from the physical.
- Description and explanation of Plato's understanding of the soul as tripartite with reason in control of appetite and emotion.
- Description and explanation of Plato's understanding of the soul as immortal and capable of existence outside the body in the realm of the Forms.
- Description and explanation of other substance dualist positions, such as that of Descartes.
- Description and explanation of views which contrast with those of Plato.

AO2 Essays might demonstrate skill in critical evaluation, analysis and coherent argument through the use of some of the following:

Learners might support the view that Plato is convincing by using some of the following arguments:

- We often experience feelings of being a soul or mind inside a body, like a driver in a vehicle.
- Plato's views are supported by the holy scripture of some religions, including Christianity, which many believe to be authoritative sources.
- Descartes' hyperbolic doubt experiment led him to support the view that the mind and body are distinct.
- The view that the soul is distinct from the body allows for the possibility of life after death.
- Some people claim to have out-of-body experiences, suggesting that there is something separate from the body that is capable of leaving the body.

Learners might support the view that Plato is unconvincing by using some of the following arguments:

- Materialists argue that there is no more to the person than physical matter; there is no such thing as the soul.
- Ryle argued that drawing a distinction between the soul and the body involves making a category error.
- There is no convincing evidence for the existence of the soul as distinct from the body.
- Substance dualism does not have a convincing account of how a soul and body are attached to each other.

2. 'People are no more than complex physical matter.' Discuss.

AO1 Essays might demonstrate knowledge and understanding through the use of some of the following ideas. This list is not prescriptive (you may have used other ideas instead) or exhaustive (you may have included valid ideas that are not listed here).

- Description and explanation of a materialist point of view, perhaps using examples such as Aristotle or Dawkins.
- Description and explanation of how a materialist position might contrast with dualist positions.

AO2 Essays might demonstrate skill in critical evaluation, analysis and coherent argument through the use of some of the following:

Learners might support the view that people are no more than complex physical matter by using some of the following arguments:

- There is no evidence to suggest that people have souls or minds distinct from the body.
- Neuroscience is developing in sophistication and showing how different parts of the brain are responsible for different aspects of human behaviour.
- Ryle argues that imagining people have souls that operate like a 'ghost in a machine' involves making a category error.

Learners might reject the view that people are no more than complex physical matter by using some of the following arguments:

- Descartes argues that we can doubt the existence of our bodies but not our minds so there must be a fundamental difference between them.
- The mind and the body have very different properties so they cannot be identical substances.
- Rejecting belief that we are more than physical could have a profound effect on our ethics because of the way we view other people – the idea of sanctity of life loses meaning.
- Rejecting belief in the soul is pessimistic and removes hope of life after death.
- There is no evidence that we do not have souls. 'Absence of evidence is not evidence of absence'.

Chapter 1.3

1. 'Hume presents insurmountable challenges to a posteriori arguments for the existence of God.' Discuss.

AO1 Essays might demonstrate knowledge and understanding through the use of some of the following ideas. This list is not prescriptive (you may have used other ideas instead) or exhaustive (you may have included valid ideas that are not listed here).

- Description and explanation of Hume's criticisms of a posteriori arguments, for example his suggestions of other possible causes of apparent design in the world.
- Description and explanation of some examples of a posteriori arguments for the existence of God, such as the teleological and cosmological arguments and perhaps the use of religious experience as evidence for God's existence.
- Description and explanation of some defences of a posteriori arguments for the existence of God in the face of criticism.

AO2 Essays might demonstrate skill in critical evaluation, analysis and coherent argument through the use of some of the following:

Learners might support the view that Hume's challenges are insurmountable by using some of the following arguments:

- Hume successfully shows that God might not be the best explanation for the things we observe.
- He presents other alternative explanations which are equally plausible, such as that the world might have been designed by a committee of gods.
- He is right in saying that it is wise to proportion your belief to the evidence.
- Other, scientific explanations for the existence of the world and its apparent design have been produced since Hume's lifetime, showing that he was right to question the idea that the best explanation is God.

Learners might reject the view that Hume's challenges are insurmountable by using some of the following arguments:

- Hume's alternative explanations are not more plausible than the belief that God created the world, as there is nothing to support his alternative hypotheses whereas belief in God has the support of the Bible and of years of Christian belief.
- Counter-arguments to Hume might include the idea that there is plenty of evidence to suggest the existence of God.
- Scientific explanations do not rule out the possibility that God works through natural physical methods in creating and designing the world.

2. Discuss critically the view that the existence of God is the best explanation for the existence of the universe.

AO1 Essays might demonstrate knowledge and understanding through the use of some of the following ideas. This list is not prescriptive (you may have used other ideas instead) or exhaustive (you may have included valid ideas that are not listed here).

- Description and explanation of the cosmological argument, perhaps with reference to Aristotle, Aquinas and/or Leibniz.
- Description and explanation of other possible explanations of the existence of the universe, such as chance or the view that it does not require an explanation (Russell).
- Description and explanation of the nature of a posteriori arguments and the need to find a 'best fit' explanation for observable features of the world.

AO2 Essays might demonstrate skill in critical evaluation, analysis and coherent argument through the use of some of the following:

Learners might support the view that the existence of God is the best explanation for the existence of the universe by using some of the following arguments:

- The universe must have been created by an uncaused, necessary being, and that can only be God.
- The existence of God is a simpler explanation than some of the alternatives, using the principle of Ockham's razor.
- The question of why there is something rather than nothing cannot be explained in any other way.
- Russell's view that the universe does not require an explanation dodges, rather than answers, the issue.

Learners might reject the view that the existence of God is the best explanation for the existence of the universe by using some of the following arguments:

- There is not enough evidence for the existence of God to make God a reasonable explanation for the existence of the universe.
- The cosmological argument fails because there are other, better explanations for the existence of the universe.
- The universe could be part of an infinite regress and be its own explanation.

Chapter 1.4

1. 'The ontological argument fails because it rests on a logical fallacy.' Discuss.

AO1 Essays might demonstrate knowledge and understanding through the use of some of the following ideas. This list is not prescriptive (you may have used other ideas instead) or exhaustive (you may have included valid ideas that are not listed here).

- Description and explanation of Anselm's two forms of ontological argument.
- Description and explanation of Descartes' version of the ontological argument.
- Description and explanation of the a priori nature of ontological arguments and their dependence on logical reasoning.
- Description and explanation of counter-arguments such as those of Gaunilo, Aquinas and Kant.

AO2 Essays might demonstrate skill in critical evaluation, analysis and coherent argument through the use of some of the following:

Learners might support the view that the ontological argument fails because it rests on a logical fallacy by using some of the following arguments:

- Gaunilo's argument using the analogy of a lost island successfully highlights the differences between describing something and that thing existing in reality.
- Aquinas points out the flaw that Anselm assumes we all share an understanding of what God is, but that premise might be false.
- Kant asserts that existence is not a predicate, showing the logical flaw that God's existence cannot be demonstrated simply by describing his attributes.

Learners might reject the view that the ontological argument fails because it rests on a logical fallacy by using some of the following arguments:

- The intention of the argument was to support faith seeking understanding, so it has not failed in that aim as it encourages reflection on the nature of God.
- Existence could be a predicate of God because although contingent existence is not a predicate, a case could be made to say that necessary existence is.
- It could be argued that the ontological argument does fail, but for a different reason; not because of its internal logic, but because belief in God does not arise through reasoned debate.

2. How persuasive are ontological arguments for the existence of God?

AO1 Essays might demonstrate knowledge and understanding through the use of some of the following ideas. This list is not prescriptive (you may have used other ideas instead) or exhaustive (you may have included valid ideas that are not listed here).

- Description and explanation of the persuasiveness of a priori arguments as opposed to a posteriori, for example that if their internal logic is consistent and the premises are true, they can lead to certainty.

- Description and explanation of ontological arguments, such as those of Anselm and Descartes.

- Description and explanation of the thinking of critics of ontological arguments, such as Gaunilo, Aquinas and Kant.

AO2 Essays might demonstrate skill in critical evaluation, analysis and coherent argument through the use of some of the following:

Learners might support the view that ontological arguments are persuasive by using some of the following arguments:

- As an a priori argument, the ontological argument can give certainty, which makes it persuasive.

- Necessary existence is a predicate which can be ascribed to God, which successfully shows that God exists.

- The ontological argument sets out to seek understanding for those with faith and it is persuasive in doing this.

Learners might reject the view that ontological arguments are persuasive by using some of the following arguments:

- The ontological argument fails to persuade because we do not all agree what God is.

- The ontological argument fails to persuade because existence is not a predicate.

- The ontological argument fails to persuade because arguments against the existence of God, such as the problem of evil, are more persuasive on balance.

- Rational arguments of any kind do not tend to lead people to religious belief, as faith is not solely an intellectual choice.

Chapter 1.5

1. 'Conversion experiences present powerful evidence for the existence of God.' Discuss.

AO1 Essays might demonstrate knowledge and understanding through the use of some of the following ideas. This list is not prescriptive (you may have used other ideas instead) or exhaustive (you may have included valid ideas that are not listed here).

- Description and explanation of conversion experiences, perhaps with reference to reputable thinkers.

- Description and explanation of examples of conversion experiences, with reference to sources of wisdom and authority.

- Description and explanation of the views of thinkers who claim that conversion experience is, or is not, evidence for the existence of God. Reference might be made to thinkers such as William James, Richard Swinburne or Sigmund Freud.

AO2 Essays might demonstrate skill in critical evaluation, analysis and coherent argument through the use of some of the following:

Learners might support the view that conversion experiences provide powerful evidence for the existence of God by using some of the following arguments:

- The existence of God is the best explanation for a dramatic change in someone's way of thinking.

- The principles of credulity and testimony put forward by Swinburne successfully make the case that people's experiences of God should be taken at face value.

- Conversion experience is supported by the Bible, which could be seen as authoritative.

- William James successfully argued that a conversion experience can be tested for validity by its long-lasting positive effects.

Learners might reject the view that conversion experiences provide powerful evidence for the existence of God by using some of the following arguments:

- There might be better, more plausible explanations of conversion experiences than the explanation that they came from God.

- Psychology and neurophysiology offer some natural explanations for religious experience which are more persuasive than the belief that they arise from encounters with God.

- Swinburne's principles only apply to everyday sense experience but are not appropriate for religious experience.

- James' test of religious experience is unconvincing, as long-lasting effects could occur without them being attributable to God.

2. How convincing are William James' conclusions about religious experience?

AO1 Essays might demonstrate knowledge and understanding through the use of some of the following ideas. This list is not prescriptive (you may have used other ideas instead) or exhaustive (you may have included valid ideas that are not listed here).

- Description and explanation of James' conclusions about religious experience, including his ideas about the characteristics of religious experience and the ways it can be tested for validity through a pragmatic approach, and his conclusions that religious experience deserves to be taken seriously as a part of the human experience.

AO2 Essays might demonstrate skill in critical evaluation, analysis and coherent argument through the use of some of the following:

- Learners might give critical evaluation of James' characteristics of religious experience, discussing whether he is right to characterise it in these ways and whether his list needs additions.

- They might give critical evaluation of his pragmatic test of religious experience, considering whether it is a reliable test, whether other kinds of tests might be better or whether religious experience can be tested at all.

- They might evaluate his conclusion that religious experience should be taken seriously, and discuss whether it can be dismissed as an infantile neurosis or whether it is a worthwhile subject for further enquiry.

Chapter 1.6

1. How convincing is the claim that it is necessary for there to be evil in the world if we are to have genuine free will?

AO1 Essays might demonstrate knowledge and understanding through the use of some of the following ideas. This list is not prescriptive (you may have used other ideas instead) or exhaustive (you may have included valid ideas that are not listed here).

- Description and explanation of 'free-will defence' theodicies, such as those of Irenaeus, Augustine and Hick. For high marks, learners should demonstrate knowledge and understanding of the differences in approach between different theodicies.
- Description and explanation of the concept of free will and its necessary conditions.

AO2 Essays might demonstrate skill in critical evaluation, analysis and coherent argument through the use of some of the following:

Learners might support the view that free-will defence theodicies are convincing by using some of the following arguments:

- Free will is an essential part of what it means to be human. Without free will, we would be like puppets and not in the image of God.
- It is impossible to have free will without genuine opportunities to make wrong choices. God cannot be expected to do the impossible.
- We could not develop as mature people and could not make a free choice for God without living through a 'vale of soul-making'.

Learners might reject the view that free-will defence theodicies are convincing by using some of the following arguments:

- If God is omnipotent, he ought to have been able to design a world in which we could freely choose to do what is right despite God being in control of everything.
- God could have given us more limited free will and limited our abilities to do harm. The opportunities for people to cause mass suffering are disproportionate.
- God should have anticipated our misuse of free will before he made us, if he is omniscient.
- Not everyone suffers the same amount, and yet everyone has free will, so clearly more limited suffering would not impinge on our freedom.
- Free will is an illusion – we suffer but we do not have genuine free will because we live in a deterministic universe.
- If God could only give us free will if he also gave us evil and suffering, he could have chosen not to create the world at all.
- Allowing evil and suffering for the sake of free will is taking an 'ends justify the means' approach, which many ethicists reject.

2. 'Irenaeus' theodicy gives a more satisfactory response to the problem of evil than Augustine's theodicy.' Discuss.

AO1 Essays might demonstrate knowledge and understanding through the use of some of the following ideas. This list is not prescriptive (you may have used other ideas instead) or exhaustive (you may have included valid ideas that are not listed here).

- Description and explanation of the key features of Irenaean theodicy, for example the ideas that we are made in the image of God but have to grow into his likeness, and that challenges are necessary for us to exercise free will and to help us mature into a relationship with God.
- Description and explanation of the key features of Augustinian theodicy, for example the ideas that God made the world perfect but it has been corrupted by misuse of free will, that variety is a good part of creation, and that evil is a privatio boni.

AO2 Essays might demonstrate skill in critical evaluation, analysis and coherent argument through the use of some of the following:

Learners might support the view that Irenaeus' theodicy is preferable to Augustine's by using some of the following arguments:

- Irenaeus does not expect us to believe literally in stories of angels and the Fall, which might be difficult for modern people.
- He avoids suggesting that God did not anticipate the misuse of free will, which would threaten the idea of God's omniscience.
- He gives an optimistic theodicy in which bad things happen for the best and there is hope for the afterlife.
- He places emphasis on personal autonomy and choice, which can be appealing.

Learners might reject the view that Irenaeus' theodicy is preferable to Augustine's by using some of the following arguments:

- Augustine does not suggest that God deliberately put evil in the world, which could suggest a God who is not omnibenevolent.
- Augustine avoids suggesting that evil is in some way good, which would cast doubt on ideas about morality, sin and salvation.
- Augustine places the blame firmly on the misuse of free will, which could be seen as preferable to the suggestion that God made evil.
- Learners might suggest that neither view is acceptable, or that both are equally helpful.

Chapter 1.7

1. How fair is the claim that an omnipotent God should be able to do absolutely anything, even the logically impossible?

AO1 Essays might demonstrate knowledge and understanding through the use of some of the following ideas. This list is not prescriptive (you may have used other ideas instead) or exhaustive (you may have included valid ideas that are not listed here).

- Description and explanation of different understandings of the concept of omnipotence, for example from Descartes, Aquinas, Swinburne or Hartshorne.

- Description and explanation of the key issues arising from different understandings of the omnipotence of God, for example the idea that God can do anything whether or not it is logically possible, and the idea that God is limited by his own nature or deliberately self-limits his own omnipotence.

AO2 Essays might demonstrate skill in critical evaluation, analysis and coherent argument through the use of some of the following:

Learners might support the view that an omnipotent God should be able to do even the logically impossible by using some of the following arguments:

- Descartes argued that omnipotence should mean power to do absolutely everything; learners might agree that limited omnipotence is not omnipotence at all.

- Anselm claims that God is that than which nothing greater can be thought; it could be argued that a God with limited omnipotence would be surpassed by a God with unlimited omnipotence.

- Descartes' argument that God created the laws of logic and is therefore not subject to them might be considered a strong argument.

- It could be argued that we should not expect to reach a rational understanding of the power of God given that we have finite minds, and so if we cannot comprehend the idea of total omnipotence, this does not rule it out.

Learners might reject the view that an omnipotent God should be able to do even the logically impossible by using some of the following arguments:

- Total omnipotence is incompatible with the concept of an omnibenevolent God.

- Total omnipotence is incompatible with many theodicies.

- Aquinas' understanding of the power of God is the best way of capturing the nature of divine omnipotence.

- Swinburne argued that logically impossible things are not things at all – God can still do everything even if not the logically impossible.

- God can do absolutely anything but self-limits his power for human benefit so that we have an orderly world and epistemic distance.

- Hartshorne suggested that total omnipotence is not as impressive as great power which is not total.

2. Discuss critically issues arising from the belief that God is omniscient.

AO1 Essays might demonstrate knowledge and understanding through the use of some of the following ideas. This list is not prescriptive (you may have used other ideas instead) or exhaustive (you may have included valid ideas that are not listed here).

- Description and explanation of different understandings of omniscience.

- Description and explanation of the reasons why omniscience might be seen to present a challenge to human free will.

- Description and explanation of why omniscience might be seen to present a challenge to theodicies.

- Description and explanation of how God's relationship with time might relate to issues of omniscience.

As the question asks for 'issues arising', for high marks you should aim to consider a range of ideas rather than just one.

AO2 Essays might demonstrate skill in critical evaluation, analysis and coherent argument through the use of some of the following:

- Consideration of whether concepts of God's omniscience do present a serious challenge to ideas of human free will, or whether these have been successfully addressed.

- Consideration of whether God's omniscience is compatible with theodicies relating to free will, for example whether God should have foreseen the Fall of Adam and Eve.

- Consideration of the relative merits of ideas of God as eternal or everlasting.

Chapter 1.8

1. How effective is analogy in communicating religious ideas and beliefs?

AO1 Essays might demonstrate knowledge and understanding through the use of some of the following ideas. This list is not prescriptive (you may have used other ideas instead) or exhaustive (you may have included valid ideas that are not listed here).

- Description and explanation of what an analogy is, with examples of its use in religious and non-religious contexts.

- Description and explanation of Aquinas' thinking about religious language as analogical, including his ideas about analogy of attribution and analogy of proportionality.

- Description and explanation of the views of other thinkers on the issue of religious language as analogical, for example Ian Ramsey.

AO2 Essays might demonstrate skill in critical evaluation, analysis and coherent argument through the use of some of the following:

Learners might support the view that analogy is effective by using some of the following arguments:

- Analogy is used in many contexts to aid explanation, which suggests that it is found to be effective.

- Analogy can help understanding by finding examples with which the listener is familiar, in order to support understanding of the unfamiliar.

- Analogy can provide vivid examples which aid memory and give insights.

- The Bible uses analogy to communicate religious ideas, suggesting that it is appropriate for Christians to do the same.

Learners might reject the view that analogy is effective by using some of the following arguments:

- Analogy can encourage people to imagine God or other theological ideas in terms of the limited and imperfect physical world; they might make God too small and the *via negativa* might be preferable.

- Analogy does not necessarily work well if the listener has no sense of the ways in which the unfamiliar object is similar to the familiar object.

- Some analogies only work well in a particular cultural context or a particular era.

- It could be argued that analogy is effective but that it needs to be used alongside other methods of conveying religious ideas rather than in isolation.

2. 'Symbol is too often misleading for it to be useful in religious language.' Discuss.

AO1 Essays might demonstrate knowledge and understanding through the use of some of the following ideas. This list is not prescriptive (you may have used other ideas instead) or exhaustive (you may have included valid ideas that are not listed here).

- Description and explanation of what symbolism is and how it is used in religious and everyday contexts; learners might give examples of visual symbols or other religious symbols such as dress and food.

- Description and explanation of what it means to interpret religious language as symbolic.

- Description and explanation of the contribution of Paul Tillich to discussions of symbolism in religious language.

- Examples of symbolic language in religious texts or in the context of religious worship will probably enhance an answer.

AO2 Essays might demonstrate skill in critical evaluation, analysis and coherent argument through the use of some of the following:

Learners might support the view that symbols can be too misleading to be useful by using some of the following arguments:

- Symbols can mean different things in different times or cultures and therefore are open to misinterpretation. (Examples would enhance the strength of this line of argument.)

- Symbols require interpretation and there is no means of telling whether the individual's interpretation of the symbol is what was intended by the author.

- It can be difficult to know what is meant to be taken symbolically and what is meant to be taken literally; examples would be useful here, such as the creation stories.

- Differences of opinion about whether language is meant to be symbolic or literal can cause serious divisions.

Learners might reject the view that symbols can be too misleading to be useful by using some of the following arguments:

- Symbols can be a powerful and memorable visual aid.

- Symbols can have meaning for people who cannot speak the same language or who cannot read.

- Symbols allow individuals to bring their own meaning to religious ideas, making it more personal and appropriate for different people in their own circumstances.

- Symbols can give a sense of belonging and connection across times and cultures.

- People can find different levels of meaning in a symbol, so that it can mean something new to them and lead them to new ways of thinking.

Chapter 1.9

1. To what extent can Wittgenstein's theory of language games help to resolve the issues raised by religious language?

AO1 Essays might demonstrate knowledge and understanding through the use of some of the following ideas. This list is not prescriptive (you may have used other ideas instead) or exhaustive (you may have included valid ideas that are not listed here).

- Description and explanation of the issues of religious language that Wittgenstein's theory of language games might seek to address.

- Description and explanation of Wittgenstein's theory of language games. Higher-level answers will include details such as examples and an explanation of Wittgenstein's understanding of Lebensforms.

AO2 Essays might demonstrate skill in critical evaluation, analysis and coherent argument through the use of some of the following:

- Learners might argue that Wittgenstein's theory of language games helps to a large extent because it recognises that meaning does not happen in a vacuum, but that people in their contexts find words and concepts meaningful or meaningless.

- They might argue that the analogy between language and games is useful because it highlights features such as understanding rules, practical applications and sharing goals.

- They might argue that the theory is not completely successful because it does not take into account important issues of the factual quality of religious truth-claims, concentrating on meaning rather than on truth.

- They might argue that Wittgenstein ignores the importance of empirical evidence for supporting religious and other truth-claims.

- They might argue that Wittgenstein overstates the problems of understanding the language games of belief systems that are different from one's own.

2. 'A non-cognitive approach to religious language provides valuable insights into the interpretation of religious texts.' Discuss.

AO1 Essays might demonstrate knowledge and understanding through the use of some of the following ideas. This list is not prescriptive (you may have used other ideas instead) or exhaustive (you may have included valid ideas that are not listed here).

- Description and explanation of non-cognitive approaches to religious language in the context of sacred texts, and explanation of how they differ from cognitive approaches.
- Description and explanation of examples of non-cognitive approaches to sacred texts. Higher-level answers will probably give specific examples of thinkers and/or books which have taken non-cognitive approaches to the interpretation of sacred texts.
- Description and explanation of the kinds of insights non-cognitive approaches might give, such as opportunities to make existential decisions.

AO2 Essays might demonstrate skill in critical evaluation, analysis and coherent argument through the use of some of the following:

Learners might support the view that insights offered by non-cognitive approaches to sacred texts are valuable by using some of the following arguments:

- Non-cognitive approaches are more appropriate for modern people who might find it impossible to believe things like miracle stories as having a factual, cognitive basis.
- Non-cognitive approaches allow the individual to make personal decisions and develop their own attitudes and responses to the challenges offered by sacred texts.
- They allow readers to interpret symbolism in a way which is subjectively meaningful.
- They might reduce conflicts and divisions of belief by allowing that different approaches to sacred texts are valid.
- They might open new possibilities for inter-faith dialogue and understanding.

Learners might reject the view that insights offered by non-cognitive approaches to sacred texts are valuable by using some of the following arguments:

- They might argue that sacred texts were written with the intention of being taken at face value.
- They might argue that non-cognitive approaches reduce sacred texts to little more than advice to be nice to other people.
- It could be argued that non-cognitive approaches allow people to pick and choose which parts of a sacred text they like, and ignore the parts which challenge them to make changes.
- Non-cognitive approaches might be seen to go too far in rejecting the cognitive value of central doctrines such as Jesus as God incarnate, the Virgin Birth or the Resurrection stories.

Chapter 2.1

1. Discuss critically the use of the concept of 'telos' in natural law ethics.

AO1 Essays might demonstrate knowledge and understanding through the use of some of the following ideas. This list is not prescriptive (you may have used other ideas instead) or exhaustive (you may have included valid ideas that are not listed here).

- Description and explanation of 'telos' as the idea of an end or purpose.
- Description and explanation of the main features of natural law ethics, its basis in the thinking of Aquinas and the idea that the universe and humanity were created by God with a purpose.
- Description and explanation of the dependence of natural law ethics on the thinking of Aristotle and his idea of a final cause.
- Description and explanation of the concept of telos as it underpins natural law ethics, with its focus on moral decision-making around the idea of fulfilling potential and becoming whatever we are supposed to become, using our reason alongside Christian teaching.

AO2 Essays might demonstrate skill in critical evaluation, analysis and coherent argument through the use of some of the following:

- Learners might argue that the concept of telos is helpful in encouraging people to be the best they can be and gives a sense of purpose to being good.
- They might argue that it is difficult for us to know what our telos is, except in very general terms, which could be difficult to apply in a specific moral dilemma.
- They might argue that the concept of telos fits well with Christian morality but might be more difficult as a moral system for people without religious belief.
- They might argue that people disagree about what people ought to become, for example some argue that a woman is fulfilling her potential if she is a mother and homemaker, whereas others argue that these roles prevent her from fulfilling her potential, making the idea a difficult one to use in practice.

2. 'One of the greatest strengths of natural law is that it provides an absolute and universal standard for judging right and wrong.' Discuss.

AO1 Essays might demonstrate knowledge and understanding through the use of some of the following ideas. This list is not prescriptive (you may have used other ideas instead) or exhaustive (you may have included valid ideas that are not listed here).

- Description and explanation of natural law as an absolutist ethical system – knowledge and understanding of the main principles of natural law ethics.
- Description and explanation of what absolutist means in contrast with relativist ethics.
- Description and explanation of the different strengths of natural law ethics, such as its dependence on reason and the clarity it offers on several ethical issues.
- Description and explanation of the views of different thinkers and sources of wisdom and authority, such as the views of Aquinas and the teaching of the Catholic Church.

AO2 Essays might demonstrate skill in critical evaluation, analysis and coherent argument through the use of some of the following:

Learners might argue that absolutism is one of the greatest strengths of natural law ethics:

- Absolutism gives the same rules for everyone, which can be seen as fair if everyone has the same standards to maintain.
- Natural law relates to a fixed set of rules which can be worked out by people using their reason and observation of the world.
- Using natural law, standards of social morality cannot slip because the same standards apply across different times and cultures.
- Natural law often gives a clear answer about the right thing to do, regardless of individuals and personal circumstances.

Learners might argue that absolutism is not one of the greatest strengths of natural law ethics:

- It could be argued that natural law does not take sufficient account of individual circumstances or needs. Learners might contrast natural law with other systems of ethics such as situation ethics.
- Natural law might be seen as too rigid and inflexible for changes in society, for example an absolute ban on artificial contraception did not anticipate the spread of HIV and Aids.
- Other features of natural law ethics might be selected as being greater strengths, for example the emphasis on human reason and responsibility.

Chapter 2.2

1. How useful is situation ethics as a guide to moral decision-making?

AO1 Essays might demonstrate knowledge and understanding through the use of some of the following ideas. This list is not prescriptive (you may have used other ideas instead) or exhaustive (you may have included valid ideas that are not listed here).

- Description and explanation of Fletcher's situation ethics, probably with reference to the principle of agape, the six propositions, the four working principles and conscience.
- Description and explanation of different contexts in which situation ethics might be useful or less useful.
- Description and explanation of the views of thinkers who support or criticise situation ethics, for example Fletcher, the Catholic Church and thinkers who propose more absolutist ethics.

AO2 Essays might demonstrate skill in critical evaluation, analysis and coherent argument through the use of some of the following:

Learners might argue that situation ethics is a useful guide by using some of the following arguments:

- It allows individual circumstances to be taken into account rather than keeping to a rigid set of rules.
- It does not require knowing a set of rules or trying to apply a complicated formula.
- The principle of agape is easy to understand and might be considered easy to apply in a wide range of moral dilemmas.

- Acting in a loving way could be undertaken by people of any religious persuasion or none.
- It encourages people to develop a loving moral character as individuals.

Learners might argue that situation ethics is not a useful guide by using some of the following arguments:

- Not everyone agrees on what the most loving action or outcome would be, especially when there are a lot of people involved and different needs conflict.
- It can often be difficult to guess the outcomes of particular actions; it requires people to know a lot about the details of the circumstance.
- The conscience can be unreliable as it can be heavily influenced by upbringing and society.
- It might lead people into actions which are contrary to the teachings of the Bible or the law of the land.
- It could be argued that a set of rules makes decision-making a faster process as well as a more secure process.

2. 'An action is good if it produces the most loving result.' Discuss.

AO1 Essays might demonstrate knowledge and understanding through the use of some of the following ideas. This list is not prescriptive (you may have used other ideas instead) or exhaustive (you may have included valid ideas that are not listed here).

- Description and explanation of Fletcher's situation ethics, probably with reference to the principle of agape, the six propositions, the four working principles and conscience.
- Description and explanation of different understandings of what makes an action 'good', such as the good will, the categorical imperative, the greatest happiness for the greatest number or the aim of promoting human flourishing.
- Description and explanation of the views of a range of supporters and critics of situation ethics.

AO2 Essays might demonstrate skill in critical evaluation, analysis and coherent argument through the use of some of the following:

Learners might agree that the most loving result is the defining characteristic of a good action by using some of the following arguments:

- Love is identified as the 'greatest' of the three things that last for ever: faith, hope and love (1 Corinthians 13).
- Jesus' life and teaching had a focus on love.
- It could be argued that an action that lacks compassion or causes harm cannot be morally good.

Learners might disagree that the most loving result is the defining characteristic of a good action by using some of the following arguments:

- Ethics should be deontological rather than teleological, supporting this point of view with reasoning.
- The most loving outcome might be impossible to identify.
- Ethics should have a different goal, such as eudaimonia or the greatest happiness for the greatest number.

Chapter 2.3

1. To what extent should ethical judgements about right and wrong be based on the extent to which duty is served?

AO1 Essays might demonstrate knowledge and understanding through the use of some of the following ideas. This list is not prescriptive (you may have used other ideas instead) or exhaustive (you may have included valid ideas that are not listed here).

- Description and explanation of deontological ethics in contrast with teleological ethics; the concept of duty.
- Description and explanation of Kant's ethical system, including reference to the good will, the *summum bonum*, the categorical and hypothetical imperatives.
- Description and explanation of alternative views for contrast, for example situation ethics with the view that agape rather than duty is of prime importance, or utilitarianism with the view that the greatest happiness for the greatest number should be the basis for ethical judgements.

AO2 Essays might demonstrate skill in critical evaluation, analysis and coherent argument through the use of some of the following:

Learners might argue that ethical judgements about right and wrong should be based on the extent to which duty is served by using some of the following arguments:

- Kant argued that we all know where our duties lie and this makes ethical judgements easy to reach by intuition.
- Deontological ethics avoid the practice of finding ways to justify actions to suit oneself.
- Duty-based ethics help people to resist external pressures.
- Ethics based on duty rather than on emotions such as love or happiness are more secure judgements because they do not rely on how someone happens to be feeling.

Learners might argue that ethical judgements about right and wrong should not be based on the extent to which duty is served by using some of the following arguments:

- Duties can sometimes conflict, making it difficult to reach an ethical judgement.
- It might be unrealistic to expect people to act according to duty when there are strong emotions connected with the decision.
- Sometimes it is not clear where our duties lie.
- People do not always know when they are being influenced by external pressures and may not be able to distinguish their intuition for duty from the pressures of society.
- Trying to do an action which has entirely pure motives can be impossible; there might be no course of action available at all which has no self-interest involved.

2. 'Kantian ethics do not give enough importance to human emotions such as sympathy and compassion.' Discuss.

AO1 Essays might demonstrate knowledge and understanding through the use of some of the following ideas. This list is not prescriptive (you may have used other ideas instead) or exhaustive (you may have included valid ideas that are not listed here).

- Description and explanation of Kant's ethical system, including reference to the good will, duty, the *summum bonum*, the categorical and hypothetical imperatives.
- Description and explanation of absolutist ethics in contrast with relativist ethics.
- Description and explanation of alternative normative ethical views which give greater importance to human emotion, such as utilitarianism and/or situation ethics.

AO2 Essays might demonstrate skill in critical evaluation, analysis and coherent argument through the use of some of the following:

Learners might agree that Kantian ethics do not give enough importance to human emotions such as sympathy and compassion by using some of the following arguments:

- Emotions such as love and compassion are morally valuable and to be encouraged; it could be morally wrong to see injustice and not feel the emotion of anger.
- A Christian point of view is important: Jesus demonstrated love and compassion.
- It is impossible for people to separate themselves from their emotions, especially when the ethical decision involves loved ones.
- Emotions do not always work in opposition to reason but enhance reason and are reasonable things to feel, therefore they should not be ignored.
- Different systems of ethics which place emphasis on maximising happiness or on bringing about agape are better alternatives.

Learners might disagree that Kantian ethics do not give enough importance to human emotions such as sympathy and compassion by using some of the following arguments:

- Emotions should be kept out of moral decisions as far as possible because they can cloud reasoned judgement, just as doctors are not allowed to treat members of their own family.
- Emotions run high at times of stress and can be unreliable, whereas duty and reason are more stable and secure.
- It can often be difficult or even impossible to judge which actions will give rise to which emotions, whereas deontological ethics do not concern themselves with outcomes.
- Emotions are often private and subjective, whereas rules and reason are equally available to everyone.

Chapter 2.4

1. How useful is utilitarianism as a guide to moral decision-making?

AO1 Essays might demonstrate knowledge and understanding through the use of some of the following ideas. This list is not prescriptive (you may have used other ideas instead) or exhaustive (you may have included valid ideas that are not listed here).

- Description and explanation of the key features of utilitarianism, including teleology and the greatest happiness principle.
- Description and explanation of different kinds of utilitarianism, including act and rule, showing awareness of their different approaches as well as their similarities.
- Description and explanation of the views of different thinkers who support or criticise utilitarian ethics.

AO2 Essays might demonstrate skill in critical evaluation, analysis and coherent argument through the use of some of the following:

Learners might argue that utilitarianism is useful as a guide to moral decision-making by using some of the following arguments:

- It does not depend on people holding religious beliefs or all believing the same thing.
- Everyone knows and recognises happiness and it is something everyone wants.
- It allows different decisions to be made in different personal circumstances, which can be useful because people are not trying to force a result which does not work.
- It treats everyone equally rather than trying to give preferential treatment to some over others, which can be complicated to apply.
- It can work as well for big organisations such as businesses as it does for personal relationships.

Learners might argue that utilitarianism is not useful as a guide to moral decision-making by using some of the following arguments:

- It is often not easy to measure the amount of pleasure or pain that a course of action will create. Often we do not know enough about the other people involved and their circumstances.
- It is not easy to know in many circumstances which people should be included in the calculation, for example whether the impact on society at large or on future generations should be part of the consideration.
- It does not give enough consideration to the needs of the minority of people.
- It might be argued that rule utilitarianism is more useful than act utilitarianism because it gives rules of thumb to speed up and unify the decision-making process.

2. 'Utilitarianism fails because it is impossible to measure happiness and harm.' Discuss.

AO1 Essays might demonstrate knowledge and understanding through the use of some of the following ideas. This list is not prescriptive (you may have used other ideas instead) or exhaustive (you may have included valid ideas that are not listed here).

- Description and explanation of the nature of utilitarianism as a teleological normative ethical system. Reference to Bentham and Mill might be expected.
- Description and explanation of the greatest happiness principle in utilitarianism, especially the hedonic calculus and the factors that should be taken into consideration when applying it: intensity, duration, certainty, propinquity, fecundity, purity and extent.

- Description and explanation of the views of some of those who support and criticise utilitarianism and the hedonic calculus in particular.

AO2 Essays might demonstrate skill in critical evaluation, analysis and coherent argument through the use of some of the following:

- Learners might not agree that utilitarianism fails and might instead defend it and the hedonic calculus as a fair, democratic and secular way of making ethical decisions.
- Learners might argue that utilitarianism fails, but for different reasons; for example they might argue that it fails because happiness is an inadequate goal for ethics, rather than because it is difficult to measure.
- Learners might argue that happiness is indeed difficult to measure and that it is a failing of utilitarianism; they might suggest that happiness can be transient and that people are quite bad at predicting what will make them happy, and/or that we can never know enough about all the people involved in a situation to make an accurate judgement, and/or that decisions can often have unforeseen consequences.
- Learners might argue that happiness is indeed difficult to measure but that on balance, despite this difficulty utilitarianism still provides very useful guidance in ethical decisions.

Chapter 2.5

1. 'Natural law provides excellent moral guidance for people making decisions about euthanasia.' Discuss.

AO1 Essays might demonstrate knowledge and understanding through the use of some of the following ideas. This list is not prescriptive (you may have used other ideas instead) or exhaustive (you may have included valid ideas that are not listed here).

- Description and explanation of the main features of natural law, including its moral absolutism, its basis in the thinking of Aquinas based on Aristotelian ideas about eudaimonia, and its influence on the ethical teaching of the Catholic Church.
- Description and explanation of the primary precepts of natural law, especially the precept of the preservation of life.
- Description and explanation of the idea of sanctity of human life and its basis in Christian teaching.
- Description and explanation of euthanasia as an issue, perhaps delineating voluntary, involuntary and non-voluntary euthanasia, and ideas about autonomy.
- Description and explanation of views that support, criticise or offer an alternative to natural law ethics in relation to euthanasia.

AO2 Essays might demonstrate skill in critical evaluation, analysis and coherent argument through the use of some of the following:

Learners might agree that natural law provides excellent moral guidance for people making decisions about euthanasia by using some of the following arguments:

- It provides clear guidance in emphasising the sanctity of life and the need to preserve it.

231

- It allows for 'double effect' which can prevent decisions based on natural law from becoming cruel and leaving people to suffer.

- In giving firm guidance, it removes the responsibility from relatives and medical professionals for having to make very painful decisions at times when emotions are running high.

- In forbidding euthanasia, the dangers of misdiagnosis or unnecessarily pessimistic diagnoses are avoided.

- In forbidding euthanasia, the possibility of a miraculous cure remains a possibility.

- Natural law ethics protect vulnerable people from being exploited and pushed towards euthanasia when this is not what they really wanted.

Learners might disagree that natural law provides excellent moral guidance for people making decisions about euthanasia by using some of the following arguments:

- People might be regarded as having the right to autonomy over their own lives.

- Natural law ethics can be seen as cruelly prolonging suffering against the patient's best interests.

- Each person's situation is different and an absolutist ethic does not take this into account.

- Natural law ethics were formulated in the thirteenth century and medicine has moved on significantly.

- Natural law ethics are based on a belief in God and in the sanctity of human life, but not everyone shares these beliefs.

2. How convincing is the claim that decisions about euthanasia should be made according to the principles of situation ethics?

AO1 Essays might demonstrate knowledge and understanding through the use of some of the following ideas. This list is not prescriptive (you may have used other ideas instead) or exhaustive (you may have included valid ideas that are not listed here).

- Description and explanation of euthanasia as an issue, perhaps outlining voluntary, involuntary and non-voluntary euthanasia, and ideas about autonomy.

- Description and explanation of the key features and principles of situation ethics: the work of Joseph Fletcher, the concept of agape and other aspects of the six propositions.

- Description and explanation of the views of some supporters and critics of situation ethics.

- Description and explanation of some alternatives to situation ethics.

AO2 Essays might demonstrate skill in critical evaluation, analysis and coherent argument through the use of some of the following:

Learners might argue that decisions about euthanasia should be made according to the principles of situation ethics by using some of the following arguments:

- Situation ethics looks at each situation individually and allows for a consideration of different circumstances.

- The principle of agape can be extended to everyone involved, such as family members and nurses as well as to the patient.

- Situation ethics allows patients to have autonomy over their own lives.

- Situation ethics might be compared with other ethical systems the learner finds less persuasive.

Learners might argue that decisions about euthanasia should not be made according to the principles of situation ethics by using some of the following arguments:

- Situation ethics does not give a high priority to the principle of the sanctity of life.

- Treating each individual situation according to its own circumstances makes legislation very difficult.

- With situation ethics, there is the possibility of vulnerable patients being exploited if euthanasia is an option.

- It is not always easy to know what the most loving course of action will be, and euthanasia does not allow for a change of mind if the decision turned out to be the wrong one.

Chapter 2.6

1. 'Globalisation makes it impossible for businesses to act ethically.' Discuss.

AO1 Essays might demonstrate knowledge and understanding through the use of some of the following ideas. This list is not prescriptive (you may have used other ideas instead) or exhaustive (you may have included valid ideas that are not listed here).

- Description and explanation of what globalisation means and how it impacts on businesses and their stakeholders.

- Description and explanation of some of the ethical issues facing businesses, such as the difficulties in finding prices which are competitive yet allow for a respectable living wage for employees.

- Description and explanation of different ethical approaches to business ethics in a global world, such as Kantian ethics and utilitarianism.

- Description and explanation of examples of business ethics in practice.

AO2 Essays might demonstrate skill in critical evaluation, analysis and coherent argument through the use of some of the following:

Learners might disagree that globalisation makes it impossible for businesses to act ethically by using some of the following arguments:

- Ethical systems such as Kantian ethics and utilitarianism might be discussed to demonstrate how they could be used in a global business context to establish ethical practices.

- It could be argued that even if businesses cannot act in the best interests of all their stakeholders at once whilst remaining competitive, they can still make efforts not to exploit the poor, to be honest in their dealings and to keep their promises.

- It could be argued that the greatest happiness for the greatest number is a practical guide even with globalisation, because it recognises that 'the greatest number' does not equate to an impossible 'everybody'.

• It could be argued that ethical business is impossible for reasons other than globalisation, for example the nature of competition and consumerism makes self-centred decisions necessary.

Learners might agree that globalisation makes it impossible for businesses to act ethically by using some of the following arguments:

• Making profit for shareholders is an obligation for businesses so this is necessarily at other people's expense, and with globalisation, there could be an argument for using the cheapest labour available in developing countries.

• Globalisation increases competition which makes it harder to do things like pay producers a fair price rather than as little as possible.

• Buying labour from developing countries does harm as well as good, which could be seen to make every possible course of action unethical in some respects.

2. 'Utilitarianism is the most practical way to deal with issues of business ethics.' Discuss.

AO1 Essays might demonstrate knowledge and understanding through the use of some of the following ideas. This list is not prescriptive (you may have used other ideas instead) or exhaustive (you may have included valid ideas that are not listed here).

• Description and explanation of the nature of utilitarianism as an ethical system. Reference to Bentham and Mill might be expected.

• Description and explanation of the greatest happiness principle in utilitarianism, especially the hedonic calculus and the factors that should be taken into consideration when applying it: intensity, duration, certainty, propinquity, fecundity, purity and extent.

• Description and explanation of key issues in business ethics and the ways in which utilitarianism might be applied to them.

AO2 Essays might demonstrate skill in critical evaluation, analysis and coherent argument through the use of some of the following:

Learners might agree that utilitarianism is the most practical way to deal with issues of business ethics by using some of the following arguments:

• In offering the principle of utility, utilitarianism does not aim for an impossible ideal but looks for the best outcome in real practical terms.

• Utilitarianism does not require people to hold religious beliefs which can make it more practical in a diverse company.

• Utilitarianism relies on calculation rather than on something more subjective such as instinctive sense of duty.

• Utilitarianism allows flexibility as a relativist ethic, so it can keep up with a rapidly changing world and changing business practices.

• It could be argued that although utilitarianism is the most practical, ethics should be about goodness not practicality.

Learners might disagree that utilitarianism is the most practical way to deal with issues of business ethics by using some of the following arguments:

• The extent of happiness can be impossible to measure, especially in the context of a large business operating in different countries.

• Decisions can have far-reaching effects that businesses could not have anticipated.

• A lack of firm rules in act utilitarianism could make it unwieldy to apply, if every decision needs to be made on its own in a large and busy organisation.

• Rule utilitarianism might be seen to be more practical, especially in a big company that needs a coherent and consistent ethos.

Chapter 2.7

1. 'Statements such as "stealing is wrong" are no more than expressions of emotion.' Discuss.

AO1 Essays might demonstrate knowledge and understanding through the use of some of the following ideas. This list is not prescriptive (you may have used other ideas instead) or exhaustive (you may have included valid ideas that are not listed here).

• Description and explanation of emotivism as an approach to meta-ethics, with reference to thinkers such as Ayer and Stevenson.

• Description and explanation of the views of critics of emotivism.

• Description and explanation of alternative points of view to emotivism, such as naturalism.

AO2 Essays might demonstrate skill in critical evaluation, analysis and coherent argument through the use of some of the following:

Learners might agree that statements such as 'stealing is wrong' are no more than expressions of emotion by using some of the following arguments:

• Ethical statements are not cognitive statements.

• Hume said that an 'ought' cannot be derived from an 'is', which shows that ethical statements have to be about something other than facts.

• The subjective elements of ethical decision-making, such as reliance on intuitive feelings, demonstrates that ethics have an emotional basis rather than being based on anything empirically observable.

Learners might disagree that statements such as 'stealing is wrong' are no more than expressions of emotion by using some of the following arguments:

• Although ethics cannot be defined, we know by intuition what is right and wrong (intuitionism).

• There are observable facts about morality (perhaps referring to thinkers such as Philippa Foot to support their arguments).

• Reducing ethics to the level of emotion makes it impossible to claim that acts such as rape, torture and genocide are intrinsically wrong: they become just matters of personal taste.

2. How convincing is the view that moral statements refer to facts that can be observed?

AO1 Essays might demonstrate knowledge and understanding through the use of some of the following ideas. This list is not prescriptive (you may have used other ideas instead) or exhaustive (you may have included valid ideas that are not listed here).

- Description and explanation of ethical naturalism as an approach to meta-ethical issues, possibly including the views of F.H. Bradley and theological naturalism such as the views of Thomas Aquinas.
- Description and explanation of the naturalistic fallacy.
- Description and explanation of the views of critics of naturalism such as Hume, and possibly of alternative meta-ethical views.

AO2 Essays might demonstrate skill in critical evaluation, analysis and coherent argument through the use of some of the following:

Learners might agree that moral statements refer to facts that can be observed by using some of the following arguments:

- There are similarities in moral codes between societies that have had little contact with each other, giving references of these.
- Philippa Foot (amongst others) claimed that people of good character can be observed and recognised.
- People seem to be in broad agreement about what is good and what is bad even if they differ about the application of moral rules.

Learners might disagree that moral statements refer to facts that can be observed by using some of the following arguments:

- Hume claimed that an 'ought' cannot be derived from an 'is' – we can see what is the case but we cannot observe what we therefore ought to do about it.
- There are moral facts, but they cannot be observed.
- Moral facts exist and can be accessed through revelation in scripture and in religious experience rather than through observation of the natural world.

Chapter 2.8

1. 'Aquinas' understanding of the conscience is convincing.' Discuss.

AO1 Essays might demonstrate knowledge and understanding through the use of some of the following ideas. This list is not prescriptive (you may have used other ideas instead) or exhaustive (you may have included valid ideas that are not listed here).

- Description and explanation of Aquinas' understanding of the conscience, including reference to his understanding of ratio, synderesis and conscientia.
- Description and explanation of the views of key thinkers and sources of wisdom and authority that support or criticise Aquinas' understanding of the conscience, such as the teaching of the Catholic Church.

- Description and explanation of alternative understandings of the conscience, such as that of Freud.

AO2 Essays might demonstrate skill in critical evaluation, analysis and coherent argument through the use of some of the following:

Learners might agree that Aquinas' understanding of the conscience is convincing by using some of the following arguments:

- The view that conscience is the working of the reason might appeal to those who do not find the 'voice of God' approach convincing; the working of reason would explain why people can conscientiously arrive at different moral conclusions.
- Aquinas' view that the conscience can be improved with education might be convincing.
- Aquinas' views might be considered more convincing than those of people who think conscience is nothing more than socialisation, as Aquinas' conviction that there are absolute rights and wrongs is appealing to many who find relativism does not provide an adequate reason for trying to be good.

Learners might disagree that Aquinas' understanding of the conscience is convincing by using some of the following arguments:

- Aquinas assumes the existence of God, which is not an assumption everyone accepts.
- Aquinas' belief that there are absolute rights and wrongs is something that requires justification; relativists would disagree with him.
- Aquinas' view of human nature as seeking the good could be seen as overly optimistic.
- Other views of the conscience might be seen to be more convincing, for example there are views, such as that of Freud, which understand the conscience to be the result of socialisation rather than a God-given ability.

2. To what extent should the conscience be regarded as a reliable guide to moral decision-making?

AO1 Essays might demonstrate knowledge and understanding through the use of some of the following ideas. This list is not prescriptive (you may have used other ideas instead) or exhaustive (you may have included valid ideas that are not listed here).

- Description and explanation of different views of the conscience, referring to thinkers such as Aquinas, Newman, Freud and Fromm.
- Description and explanation of the extent to which conscience is considered important in making moral decisions, possibly referring to thinkers such as Kant, Bentham, Mill and Fletcher.

AO2 Essays might demonstrate skill in critical evaluation, analysis and coherent argument through the use of some of the following:

Learners might agree that conscience should be regarded as a reliable guide to moral decision-making by using some of the following arguments:

- It could be argued that the conscience is a channel through which to 'hear' the 'voice of God', in which case it should be regarded as more authoritative than any human set of rules or principles.
- Aquinas' view that the conscience should be obeyed because it is the working of reason might be supported.
- It could be argued that conscience is a reliable guide to decision-making only when it is properly informed, and that caution should be taken to avoid mistaking current public opinion for conscience.

Learners might disagree that conscience should be regarded as a reliable guide to moral decision-making by using some of the following arguments:

- Freud is right and conscience is no more than socialisation, so it is only as reliable as the opinions of parents, peer groups and wider society.
- It is very difficult for people to make a distinction between what their consciences are saying and what society is telling them.
- The differences of opinion reached by conscientious individuals might suggest that conscience is not reliable, as different consciences reach vastly different conclusions.
- There is no such thing as 'reliable' because there are no absolute moral standards to get right or wrong.

Chapter 2.9

1. To what extent are natural law ethics helpful in guiding decisions about sexual behaviour?

AO1 Essays might demonstrate knowledge and understanding through the use of some of the following ideas. This list is not prescriptive (you may have used other ideas instead) or exhaustive (you may have included valid ideas that are not listed here).

- Description and explanation of the main principles and key features of natural law ethics, including the thinking of Aquinas about primary precepts.
- Description and explanation of the influence of natural law ethics on the teachings of the Catholic Church in relation to issues of sexual ethics.
- Description and explanation of the views of thinkers who support or criticise natural law ethics in relation to sexual behaviour.
- Description and explanation of alternative ethical systems offering different approaches to sexual ethics.

AO2 Essays might demonstrate skill in critical evaluation, analysis and coherent argument through the use of some of the following:

Learners might agree that natural law ethics are helpful in guiding decisions about sexual behaviour by using some of the following arguments:

- They give firm, clear guidelines which are easy to understand and do not need interpretation in order to apply them.
- They are based on biblical teachings and have the support of statements from the Catholic Church to show their relevance to the present day.

- The reasoning behind natural law rules about sexual behaviour is easy to follow.

Learners might disagree that natural law ethics are helpful in guiding decisions about sexual behaviour by using some of the following arguments:

- Some argue that people cannot choose their sexuality, and it is unfair to condemn people for wanting sexual relationships or to prevent them from having any if they are homosexual.
- Natural law ethics might seem to be inconsistent in logic as people who are past the menopause, or for other reasons infertile, are not prohibited from having sex within a marriage.
- Some argue that ethical systems are unnecessary in private relationships and are only needed for issues which involve wider society.
- Other ethical systems are more helpful and appropriate for the modern world than natural law, giving examples.

2. How far might utilitarianism provide useful guidelines in discussions about the ethics of homosexuality?

AO1 Essays might demonstrate knowledge and understanding through the use of some of the following ideas. This list is not prescriptive (you may have used other ideas instead) or exhaustive (you may have included valid ideas that are not listed here).

- Description and explanation of utilitarian key features and principles, including the hedonic calculus and the principle of utility.
- Description and explanation of different variants of utilitarian thought, such as act and rule utilitarianism, with reference to different thinkers.
- Description and explanation of issues surrounding homosexuality, such as whether homosexuality should be considered criminal and issues of same-sex marriage.

AO2 Essays might demonstrate skill in critical evaluation, analysis and coherent argument through the use of some of the following:

Learners might argue that utilitarianism does provide useful guidelines in discussions about the ethics of homosexuality by using some of the following arguments:

- Utilitarianism recognises that legislation should be kept to a minimum.
- It emphasises maximising pleasure and avoiding pain, which is a good rule for sexual relationships, allowing freedom for people to express their sexuality as long as no one else is harmed.
- It avoids involving religious rules that predate reliable contraception and prevention of sexually transmitted diseases.
- It recognises personal autonomy.
- It treats everyone's interests as equal so that the happiness of a homosexual couple is given the same respect and consideration as a heterosexual couple.

Learners might argue that utilitarianism does not provide useful guidelines in discussions about the ethics of homosexuality by using some of the following arguments:

- It ignores the 'telos' of sexual relationships as primarily being for the production of children.

- It disregards the sanctity of heterosexual relationships and the sanctity of marriage.

- It is concerned with pleasure rather than with agapeic love or with the will of God.

- It can be used to justify all kinds of behaviour by the end results, when some behaviours are intrinsically wrong.

Chapter 3.1

1. How fair is the claim that sin means that humans can never be morally good?

AO1 Essays might demonstrate knowledge and understanding through the use of some of the following ideas. This list is not prescriptive (you may have used other ideas instead) or exhaustive (you may have included valid ideas that are not listed here).

- Description and explanation of how sin is understood by Christians.

- Description and explanation of how Paul in Romans 7 struggles with the fact that he still continues to sin even though he has become a Christian.

- Description and explanation of Augustine's teaching that humanity is sinful as a result of the Fall.

- Description and explanation of the idea of Original Sin, cupiditas and concupiscence.

- Description and explanation of Christian teaching about the grace of God.

- Description and explanation of alternative views that do not emphasise humanity's sinful nature, such as the views of Locke or Sartre.

- Description and explanation of ideas about purification after death.

AO2 Essays might demonstrate skill in critical evaluation, analysis and coherent argument through the use of some of the following:

Learners might argue that the claim that humans can never be morally good is fair by using some of the following arguments:

- The Bible teaches that Adam and Eve brought sin into the world and initiated Original Sin.

- There are examples of moral evil in the world (giving some details).

- Human nature is inclined to be savage (following the thinking of people like Hobbes).

- Although people cannot avoid sin by themselves, they can be saved from sin by the grace of God.

Learners might argue that the claim that humans can never be morally good is unfair by using some of the following arguments:

- People are all different and there is not a single thing called 'human nature'.

- Sartre argues that people are free to form their own natures, and Locke claims that we are born with a blank slate.

- The concept of sin can be challenged: human moral behaviour is relative and is determined by social and cultural norms rather than absolute norms.

- Everyone has the opportunity to be free from sin in the afterlife.

2. 'It is impossible for modern people to believe Augustine's teachings about the historical Fall of humanity.' Discuss.

AO1 Essays might demonstrate knowledge and understanding through the use of some of the following ideas. This list is not prescriptive (you may have used other ideas instead) or exhaustive (you may have included valid ideas that are not listed here).

- Description and explanation of biblical accounts of the Fall.

- Description and explanation of Augustine's ideas about the effects of the Fall of humanity on human nature and on the natural world.

- Description and explanation of views influenced by Augustinian thought.

- Description and explanation of alternative views about the origins of humanity, such as the idea that people evolved rather than that they were made as perfect humans by God.

AO2 Essays might demonstrate skill in critical evaluation, analysis and coherent argument through the use of some of the following:

Learners might argue that Augustine's teachings about the historical Fall of humanity are impossible for modern people to believe by using some of the following arguments:

- Many modern people are unlikely to believe that the Genesis stories of the Fall were actual historical events, and are more likely to interpret such stories as myth or as untrue.

- Modern people might believe scientific accounts of the evolution of humanity rather than believing in Adam and Eve.

- Modern people might reject the ideas taught by Augustine of Original Sin, and argue instead that people are a mixture of good and bad, that they do not all share an essential nature, that they are free to develop their own moral natures in an existential way, and/or that people are basically good.

Learners might argue that Augustine's teachings about the historical Fall of humanity are not impossible for modern people to believe by using some of the following arguments:

- A significant proportion of modern people believe that humanity was created as described in the Bible, so clearly it is not impossible.

- People might believe that the story of the Fall teaches important truths about human nature and about humanity's relationship with God, even if it is truth told through myth rather than through an historically accurate account.

- People's experience of sin and of their own internal struggles to live a moral life might be seen as evidence to support Augustine's teachings.

Chapter 3.2

1. How persuasive is the view that God's judgement takes place immediately after death?

AO1 Essays might demonstrate knowledge and understanding through the use of some of the following ideas. This list is not prescriptive (you may have used other ideas instead) or exhaustive (you may have included valid ideas that are not listed here).

- Description and explanation of the concepts of sin and God's judgement.
- Description and explanation of the distinction drawn by some scholars between 'particular judgement' and 'final judgement'.
- Description and explanation of biblical passages which might support each view or which are ambiguous.

AO2 Essays might demonstrate skill in critical evaluation, analysis and coherent argument through the use of some of the following:

Learners might think the belief that God judges each individual at the moment of death is persuasive by using some of the following arguments:

- Some biblical passages suggest that people go to heaven (and therefore must have been judged) as soon as they die. Examples could be used to support this, such as the parable of the Rich Man and Lazarus or Jesus' words to the robber on the cross.
- Christian tradition often supports the idea that the dead are already in heaven, with the wording at Christian funerals echoing this belief.
- The idea of the living praying for souls in purgatory could support the idea that souls are judged immediately after death – otherwise people who died a long time ago would have to spend a lot longer in purgatory before the final judgement.
- It could be argued that there is both individual judgement immediately after death and also a final judgement when the world comes to an end.
- These ideas assume that the Bible and Church tradition are authoritative.

Learners might think the belief that God judges each individual at the moment of death is not persuasive by using some of the following arguments:

- Ideas about life after death in general are not persuasive, for reasons of lack of empirical evidence.
- From a logical positivist perspective, ideas about life after death are meaningless.
- Biblical teachings about God coming in final judgement, such as the parable of the Sheep and the Goats in Matthew 25, could be used to support the view that final judgement is more persuasive.
- Biblical teaching about God's judgement is too ambiguous to give a clear picture.

2. 'Purgatory is a state through which everyone goes.' Discuss.

AO1 Essays might demonstrate knowledge and understanding through the use of some of the following ideas. This list is not prescriptive (you may have used other ideas instead) or exhaustive (you may have included valid ideas that are not listed here).

- Description and explanation of the origins of Catholic teaching about purgatory: its development by thinkers such as Origen and Augustine, based on Matthew 12 and the idea of forgiveness in 'the age to come'.
- Description and explanation of how purgatory could be understood as a place of cleansing of souls, including imagery of fire.
- Description and explanation of alternative views of purgatory such as a metaphorical understanding, with reference to thinkers such as Karl Rahner.
- Description and explanation of Protestant and other objections to the doctrine of purgatory, for example that it is not an idea that has prominence in the Bible and that Protestant reformers objected to the practice of indulgences.

AO2 Essays might demonstrate skill in critical evaluation, analysis and coherent argument through the use of some of the following:

Learners might agree that purgatory is a state through which everyone goes by using some of the following arguments:

- Catholic teaching could suggest that all souls need cleansing before they are fit to come into the presence of God.
- A universalist understanding of salvation could be used to support the view that everyone eventually goes to heaven.
- Hick's view of life after death might be seen as persuasive, with people carrying on their spiritual journeys and learning lessons in a new life before reaching their destination.

Learners might disagree that purgatory is a state through which everyone goes by using some of the following arguments:

- Some people, according to mainstream Catholic and Protestant teaching, go to hell rather than to purgatory.
- Augustine, Calvin and others argued that only some people were elected for heaven; this could be seen as persuasive.
- The Protestant view is usually that purgatory is not a biblical concept; if everyone goes through purgatory, God would have revealed this truth in the Bible.
- Life after death as a concept is unconvincing, as life and death are mutually exclusive states (with reference to Flew and/or others).
- The religious language of life after death is meaningless as it is not empirically verifiable or falsifiable.

Chapter 3.3

1. 'Because of the Fall, people can have no natural knowledge of God.' Discuss.

AO1 Essays might demonstrate knowledge and understanding through the use of some of the following ideas. This list is not prescriptive (you may have used other ideas instead) or exhaustive (you may have included valid ideas that are not listed here).

- Description and explanation of the key features of the Fall.
- Description and explanation of the views of key thinkers in the discussion of whether there can be natural knowledge of God, such as Augustine, Bonaventure, Aquinas, Calvin, Barth and/or Polkinghorne.
- Description and explanation of the concept of natural theology.

AO2 Essays might demonstrate skill in critical evaluation, analysis and coherent argument through the use of some of the following:

Learners might agree that people can have no natural knowledge of God by using some of the following arguments:

- It could be argued that knowledge of God is impossible because human nature has become so tainted through the Fall, following the thinking of scholars such as Barth.
- It could be argued that knowledge of God is impossible but for other reasons, for example because God is beyond human comprehension or because the concept of God is meaningless.
- It could be argued that the Fall is mythological rather than historical and that human nature needs to be understood in the light of this.

Learners might disagree that people can have no natural knowledge of God by using some of the following arguments:

- It could be argued that Aquinas is right in saying that people can use their observation through sense experience and their reason to gain knowledge of God.
- Arguments for the existence of God suggest that God can be known through reason and through sense experience; learners might support the view that these arguments are strong.
- Paul, in his speech at Athens, seems to be arguing that people can be expected to know something of God through observation and reason, and it could be argued that the Bible has authority.

2. Discuss critically the idea that the existence of God can be known through reason alone.

AO1 Essays might demonstrate knowledge and understanding through the use of some of the following ideas. This list is not prescriptive (you may have used other ideas instead) or exhaustive (you may have included valid ideas that are not listed here).

- Description and explanation of natural theology as gaining knowledge of God through reason and observation.
- Description and explanation of the views of thinkers who have suggested that revelation of God can be seen through reason, such as Bonaventure, Aquinas, Calvin and many others.
- Description and explanation of biblical passages that could support the idea that God can be known through reason.
- Description and explanation of examples such as the ontological argument, where it is claimed reason can lead to knowledge of God.
- Description and explanation of views that support the claim humans have an innate sense of the divine, available to reason.

AO2 Essays might demonstrate skill in critical evaluation, analysis and coherent argument through the use of some of the following:

Learners might agree that knowledge of God can be gained through reason alone by using some of the following arguments:

- God gives people reason in order that they can know him.
- The idea of people being made in the image of God has been interpreted by many to refer to rationality.
- People from different religions around the world have knowledge of God and therefore it must be available to all people.
- The Bible supports the idea that God can be known through the things he has made, and that knowledge of God is obvious.

Learners might disagree that knowledge of God can be gained through reason alone by using some of the following arguments:

- Much natural theology requires reason to be combined with the observations of sense experience, such as the observation of the beauty of the natural world or of the way people are made.
- Theologians such as Barth challenge the view that God's revelation can be known by people in any way except when God chooses to reveal himself. He argues that only Christians can receive the revelation of God through the natural world.
- Knowledge of God cannot be gained at all. It might be argued that people cannot gain knowledge of God in a certain way but have to have faith in the teachings of Christianity despite uncertainty.
- Knowledge of God is impossible because of the nonexistence of God; it could be argued that God is a figment of the imagination, or that God is ultimately unknowable.

Chapter 3.4

1. 'Jesus was more than a political liberator.' Discuss.

AO1 Essays might demonstrate knowledge and understanding through the use of some of the following ideas. This list is not prescriptive (you may have used other ideas instead) or exhaustive (you may have included valid ideas that are not listed here).

- Description and explanation of the political situation in Palestine at the time of Jesus and why some of the Jews were expecting a political, Davidic Messiah.

- Description and explanation of the existence of the Zealots and the possibility that Judas was one of the Sicarii.

- Description and explanation of views that Jesus was a political figure involved in the Zealot movement, with reference for example to Reza Aslan.

- Description and explanation of views that Jesus' political activism was exaggerated by the evangelists, with reference to thinkers such as E.P. Sanders.

- Description and explanation of other roles Jesus might be said to fulfil, apart from, or over and above, the role of political liberator, such as Son of God and wisdom teacher.

AO2 Essays might demonstrate skill in critical evaluation, analysis and coherent argument through the use of some of the following:

Learners might agree that Jesus was more than a political liberator by using some of the following arguments:

- Jesus' involvement with the politics of his country was over-emphasised by the evangelists, according to E.P Sanders.

- The person of Jesus as God incarnate is seen by Christians as much more important that anything Jesus might have said about political issues.

- Jesus is understood as the Messiah, as the final revelation of God, as the saviour of people from Original Sin, as a miracle worker and a teacher of wisdom.

- Jesus' teaching about taxes and his relationships with soldiers do not suggest that he was highly political.

Learners might disagree that Jesus was more than a political liberator by using some of the following arguments:

- Aslan argues that Jesus was interested in political liberation, that he associated with disciples who were linked to the Zealots and that actions such as Jesus' entry into Jerusalem were political statements designed to provoke.

- Other scholars such as Horsley and Webb discuss the role of Jesus in 'political banditry'.

- People were looking for a Messiah because of their political situation and attributed a special divine status to Jesus that he never attributed to himself.

- Jesus attempted political liberation but failed at the task.

2. How convincing is the claim that Jesus' relationship with God was unique?

AO1 Essays might demonstrate knowledge and understanding through the use of some of the following ideas. This list is not prescriptive (you may have used other ideas instead) or exhaustive (you may have included valid ideas that are not listed here).

- Description and explanation of the concept of Jesus as God incarnate, sharing a nature with God.

- Description and explanation of events in Jesus' life which suggest his relationship with God was unique, such as the forgiveness of sins and the Resurrection.

- Description and explanation of the views of different thinkers about the uniqueness or otherwise of Jesus, such as Bonhoeffer and Hick.

AO2 Essays might demonstrate skill in critical evaluation,

analysis and coherent argument through the use of some of the following:

Learners might argue that Jesus' relationship with God is not unique by using some of the following arguments:

- Hick and others argue that there are many different paths to God and to salvation, and that Jesus was one of a number of people who have had special relationships with God.

- It might be argued that Jesus' relationship with God was an invention of the early Church and the evangelists, as Jesus did not claim to be the Son of God.

- Jesus prayed to God, which could be used to suggest that although Jesus was a godly man, he was not God himself in human form.

- It could be argued that any historical figure's inner life is not open to investigation and that it is impossible to know what kind of relationship Jesus had with God and what he understood his own nature to be.

Learners might argue that Jesus' relationship with God is unique by using some of the following arguments:

- The earliest Christian writings associate Jesus with God; this does not seem to be an idea that only crept into Christian thinking at a later date.

- If the stories of Jesus' birth, baptism, Transfiguration and Resurrection in the gospels are understood to be authoritative, they all present Jesus in terms of having a unique relationship with God.

- Jesus' actions and words suggest a unique relationship with God, especially in the performing of miracles, the reinterpretation of laws and the forgiveness of sins.

Chapter 3.5

1. How fair is the claim that the principle of love is all that is necessary for Christian ethics?

AO1 Essays might demonstrate knowledge and understanding through the use of some of the following ideas. This list is not prescriptive (you may have used other ideas instead) or exhaustive (you may have included valid ideas that are not listed here).

- Description and explanation of the Christian principle of agape, perhaps in contrast with other kinds of love or referring to the idea that agape encompasses all kinds of love.

- Description and explanation of sources of wisdom and authority, such as biblical teaching that emphasises the importance of love as the nature of God, something that lasts for ever, the two greatest commandments.

- Description and explanation of ethical systems that focus on the principle of love, such as Fletcher's situation ethics.

- Description and explanation of views that put love at the centre of ethics, such as Bultmann's ideas about love and forgiveness and Tillich's ideas about justice, love and wisdom.

AO2 Essays might demonstrate skill in critical evaluation, analysis and coherent argument through the use of some of the following:

Learners might agree that love is all that is necessary for Christian ethics by using some of the following arguments:

*   Jesus taught that loving God and your neighbour as yourself was a summary of the Law.

*   Situation ethics presents an ethical system based around love with principles to demonstrate its practical application.

*   Love is seen as the greatest of the virtues and something that lasts for ever.

*   Other virtues such as compassion and kindness naturally follow from an attitude of love.

Learners might disagree that love is all that is necessary for Christian ethics by using some of the following arguments:

*   It can be difficult to know what is the loving thing to do in an ethical dilemma.

*   Christians also need to be knowledgeable about the circumstances and the people involved; love on its own is not enough without wisdom and reason.

*   Human love is flawed as a result of the Fall and needs to be kept in check with rules.

*   Bultmann wrote about love in conjunction with forgiveness, and Tillich about love in conjunction with justice and wisdom, suggesting that love needs to work alongside other things.

*   Love can be too subjective and emotional and needs to work alongside biblical teaching and Sacred Tradition.

*   Other more absolutist forms of ethics are more reliable for Christians, such as natural law ethics.

2. 'In order to lead a moral Christian life, Christians need more than just the Bible for guidance.' Discuss.

AO1 Essays might demonstrate knowledge and understanding through the use of some of the following ideas. This list is not prescriptive (you may have used other ideas instead) or exhaustive (you may have included valid ideas that are not listed here).

*   Description and explanation of the status of the Bible for Christians, with reference to common and divergent views.

*   Description and explanation of the distinction between propositional and non-propositional revelation.

*   Description and explanation of different ways in which Christians interpret the Bible, for example literally or mythologically.

*   Description and explanation of different kinds of teaching and literature found in the Bible, for example commandments, wisdom and story.

*   Description and explanation of the teaching of different Christian denominations about the relative importance of the Bible, reason and Church tradition.

AO2 Essays might demonstrate skill in critical evaluation, analysis and coherent argument through the use of some of the following:

Learners might argue that the Bible alone is sufficient for Christians to lead a moral life by using some of the following arguments:

*   Church tradition has sometimes been corrupt, for example the Protestant reformers argued that the Church was

too interested in wealth and power; the Bible is needed to form judgements about whether Church teaching is sound.

*   Human reason is faulty as a result of the Fall; the Bible is needed to override human reason.

*   Bible stories of Jesus and his teaching are the full and final revelation of God.

*   The Bible gives commandments, moral exemplars, wisdom literature and advice that is timeless and transcends cultures.

Learners might argue that the Bible alone is insufficient for Christians to lead a moral life by using some of the following arguments:

*   The Bible cannot be read without interpretation; the interpretation needs guidance from the Church and from reason.

*   The Bible was written long ago and there needs to be Church teaching and moral reasoning to see how to apply its teachings to the modern world.

*   Some biblical teaching is not applicable to the modern world at all, such as teachings about how to treat witches.

*   The Bible has some contradictions and inaccuracies which make it an unreliable source.

*   People who rely on biblical teaching tend to 'cherry-pick' particular verses and ignore others; there needs to be a further source of authority to keep a check on this.

*   Biblical teaching has been interpreted by different people to mean entirely different things.

Chapter 3.6

1. Discuss critically the claim that Bonhoeffer's theology puts too much emphasis on suffering.

AO1 Essays might demonstrate knowledge and understanding through the use of some of the following ideas. This list is not prescriptive (you may have used other ideas instead) or exhaustive (you may have included valid ideas that are not listed here).

*   Description and explanation of Bonhoeffer's life and circumstances in Nazi Germany.

*   Description and explanation of Bonhoeffer's teaching about cheap and costly grace.

*   Description and explanation of Bonhoeffer's teaching about the nature of discipleship and the burden of the cross.

*   Description and explanation of Bonhoeffer's teaching about the importance of sharing the suffering of Christ, and the communion this brings with God and with other human beings.

AO2 Essays might demonstrate skill in critical evaluation, analysis and coherent argument through the use of some of the following

Learners might agree that Bonhoeffer puts too much emphasis on suffering by using some of the following arguments:

*   Bonhoeffer was writing at a time of great danger and hardship, meaning that his theology is bleaker than it needs to be for Christians living in peacetime.

- Bonhoeffer does not say enough about the joyful side of Christianity, such as the emphasis in the Bible on praise and thanksgiving.
- He writes about suffering but not enough about the 'blessed' part of the Beatitudes, where people who are suffering have special blessing from God.
- Not everyone suffers a great deal during their lifetime, so Bonhoeffer's teaching might not be something that everyone can easily relate to.

Learners might disagree that Bonhoeffer puts too much emphasis on suffering by using some of the following arguments:

- Spiritual suffering as well as physical suffering are universal human experiences.
- Bonhoeffer is right to concentrate on this area of Christian life as it presents the profoundest struggles for Christians.
- True discipleship should not be comfortable and convenient, and Bonhoeffer is right to draw attention to the need for Christians to take on challenges and risks for the sake of others.
- Although he emphasises suffering, Bonhoeffer also talks about how suffering is not a tragedy but has great spiritual benefits, so his teaching is ultimately optimistic.

2. 'Civil disobedience is never necessary for Christians who live in Christian countries.' Discuss.

AO1 Essays might demonstrate knowledge and understanding through the use of some of the following ideas. This list is not prescriptive (you may have used other ideas instead) or exhaustive (you may have included valid ideas that are not listed here).

- Description and explanation of what civil disobedience means.
- Description and explanation of Christians who have used civil disobedience when they have felt it necessary for their Christian lives, such as Bonhoeffer, liberation theologians, civil rights activists, etc.
- Description and explanation of the views that support civil disobedience in some circumstances, using specific examples.
- Description and explanation of sources of wisdom and authority that might be used in discussion of civil disobedience, such as biblical texts and teachings from the Church.
- Description and explanation of what might be considered a 'Christian country'.

AO2 Essays might demonstrate skill in critical evaluation, analysis and coherent argument through the use of some of the following:

Learners might agree that civil disobedience is never necessary for Christians who live in Christian countries by using some of the following arguments:

- Christians should be loving, even of their enemies, and do good to those who oppose them rather than defying them.
- Jesus praised the peacemakers in the Beatitudes.

- In Jesus' lifetime there was oppressive Roman rule but Jesus did not fight against the Romans.
- Living in an orderly society is one of the principles of natural law, and orderly society demands that people obey its rules.
- The Kingdom of God is promised after death and will compensate for life's injustices.

Learners might disagree that civil disobedience is never necessary for Christians who live in Christian countries by using some of the following arguments:

- Christians have a duty to defend the weak and to challenge injustice.
- Discipleship, according to Bonhoeffer, is always costly and demands Christians should take risks.
- Doing nothing when there is suffering is equivalent to doing nothing for God (the parable of the Sheep and the Goats).
- Christian civil disobedience has been at the root of significant social change, such as civil rights and the work of liberation theologians.
- The Kingdom of God should be seen as an earthly aspiration and not just something for after death.
- Allowing an unjust society to continue unchallenged makes Christianity vulnerable to Marx's accusation that religion is the opiate of the people.

Chapter 3.7

1. 'If different world religions offer different paths to salvation, then Jesus died on the cross for nothing.' Discuss.

AO1 Essays might demonstrate knowledge and understanding through the use of some of the following ideas. This list is not prescriptive (you may have used other ideas instead) or exhaustive (you may have included valid ideas that are not listed here).

- Description and explanation of Christian theology of religion as a discipline.
- Description and explanation of exclusivist, inclusivist and pluralist views in the theology of religion.
- Description and explanation of Christian views about the saving act of Christ on the cross from an exclusivist perspective.
- Description and explanation of the interpretations of the person of Jesus and the nature of salvation given by inclusivists and pluralists.

AO2 Essays might demonstrate skill in critical evaluation, analysis and coherent argument through the use of some of the following:

Learners might agree that if different world religions offer different paths to salvation, then Jesus died on the cross for nothing by using some of the following arguments:

- Jesus' incarnation and sacrifice on the cross are central to the Christian message as the means by which humanity can be reconciled with God after the Fall. If there are also other means of salvation then this makes Jesus' actions superfluous.
- People need to have explicit faith in Christ and be baptised into the Church in order to be saved.

- Other religions can have 'rays of truth' when they agree with the teachings of Christianity but they only have a partial truth.
- People might be 'anonymous Christians' and be saved even if they do not recognise that it was Christ who saved them.

Learners might disagree that if different world religions offer different paths to salvation, then Jesus died on the cross for nothing by using some of the following arguments:

- The story of Christ's incarnation, death and Resurrection might be understood metaphorically rather than literally.
- It does not make sense for a loving God to restrict salvation only to those whose culture happens to belong to the right religion; a loving God would find means of salvation for all.
- If one religion offers truth and salvation, it does not necessarily follow that all other religions must be wrong.
- Religion is a human, social construct rather than the result of divine revelation.
- Christ's death on the cross can be still understood as being true for those who find it meaningful, whereas those operating in a different language game could find meaning elsewhere.

2. 'The best response Christians can make to living in a multi-faith society is to take an inclusivist approach.' Discuss.

AO1 Essays might demonstrate knowledge and understanding through the use of some of the following ideas. This list is not prescriptive (you may have used other ideas instead) or exhaustive (you may have included valid ideas that are not listed here).

- Description and explanation of what a multi-faith society is.
- Description and explanation of what an inclusivist approach is and how it might be justified.
- Description and explanation of how an inclusivist approach compares with other possible positions held in the theology of religion.
- Description and explanation of the key features of inclusivist points of view, such as the view that non-Christian religions might have rays of light or that people could be 'anonymous Christians'.
- Description and explanation of the views of key inclusivist thinkers such as Karl Rahner.

AO2 Essays might demonstrate skill in critical evaluation, analysis and coherent argument through the use of some of the following:

Learners might agree that the best response Christians can make to living in a multi-faith society is to take an inclusivist approach by using some of the following arguments:

- Inclusivism avoids the claim that a loving God would not reject people just because they belong to the wrong religious faith community.
- Inclusivism avoids the accusation of diluting Christianity to the point where its central teachings are sidelined.

- Inclusivism strikes a balance between more extreme views.
- It recognises the truth in other religions in a respectful way whilst staying true to the teachings of the Bible and the Church.
- It allows openness to inter-faith dialogue.

Learners might disagree that the best response Christians can make to living in a multi-faith society is to take an inclusivist approach by using some of the following arguments:

- Inclusivism ignores the fact that religions are whole systems and cannot be viewed in a piecemeal way.
- The idea that some people are 'anonymous Christians' is patronising to those who have chosen a path other than Christianity.
- Inclusivism arrogantly assumes that Christianity is the best religion and that Christians have more knowledge of God than other people.

Chapter 3.8

1. How fair is the claim that the Scriptural Reasoning Movement relativises Christian belief?

AO1 Essays might demonstrate knowledge and understanding through the use of some of the following ideas. This list is not prescriptive (you may have used other ideas instead) or exhaustive (you may have included valid ideas that are not listed here).

- Description and explanation of the Scriptural Reasoning Movement, including its origins in Judaism; its growth; its methods of analysing texts on different subjects from different faiths and discussing their meaning as individuals rather than as representatives of an entire faith; its aims of deepening understanding and offering hospitality and a chance to disagree in a friendly environment without evangelism.
- Description and explanation of what 'relativising' means.
- Description and explanation of why some people might think that relativising is a bad thing.

AO2 Essays might demonstrate skill in critical evaluation, analysis and coherent argument through the use of some of the following:

Learners might argue that the claim that Scriptural Reasoning relativises Christian belief is fair by using some of the following arguments:

- The Movement assumes that there is something to be learned from the scriptures of religions other than Christianity, which suggests that Christianity is not absolute.
- The Movement assumes that there is something to be learned from the way adherents of faiths other than Christianity approach scripture, which assumes that Christian approaches might not always be the best or the only approaches.
- The Movement does not allow people to try to convert others to their own faith during meetings, which suggests that this might not be seen as an urgent task for Christians.

- It might be argued that relativising Christianity is wrong, because Christianity holds the full revelation of God through Jesus and is not just one option amongst many world religions.

- It might be argued that relativising Christianity is right, because it allows openness, inter-faith dialogue and a more inclusivist or pluralist approach to the theology of religion, which could be argued to be better than an exclusivist approach.

Learners might argue that the claim that Scriptural Reasoning relativises Christian belief is not fair by using some of the following arguments:

- Scriptural Reasoning invites religious believers to share their passion for their scriptures and talk to others about its importance but it does not expect people to change their beliefs as a result of the meetings.

- Christians are free to assert that Christianity is the one true religion and this position is not incompatible with Scriptural Reasoning.

- Christians may learn new ways of approaching scripture and gain new insights into the Bible but they are not obliged to treat scriptures from other religions as authoritative.

- Scriptural Reasoning assumes that its members are likely to disagree and has no expectation of a conformity of viewpoint.

2. Discuss critically the view that Christians should seek to convert people who belong to other faith communities.

AO1 Essays might demonstrate knowledge and understanding through the use of some of the following ideas. This list is not prescriptive (you may have used other ideas instead) or exhaustive (you may have included valid ideas that are not listed here).

- Description and explanation of the concept of Christian mission and its place in the Christian faith.

- Description and explanation of key sources of wisdom and authority on the subject of Christian mission, for example biblical texts about mission and Church teachings such as *Redemptoris Missio* and 'Sharing the Gospel of Salvation'.

- Description and explanation of the views of scholars on the subject of whether Christians should seek to convert those of other faiths, for example the thinking of Kraemer, Barth, Hick or Panikkar.

AO2 Essays might demonstrate skill in critical evaluation, analysis and coherent argument through the use of some of the following:

Learners might agree that Christians should seek to convert people who belong to other faith communities by using some of the following arguments:

- Jesus told his followers to 'make disciples of all nations' (Matthew 28:19, New International Version).

- If Christianity is the only means to salvation then Christians have an urgent duty to tell others of the Christian message and the need to be baptised into the Church.

- The teaching of the Pope is that Christian mission is still important for Christians in a multi-faith society.

- Christians do not have to be aggressive in their mission to those of other faiths but can share their beliefs by offering hospitality, working together for the common good and sharing in worship, according to the guidelines of 'Sharing the Gospel of Salvation'.

Learners might disagree that Christians should seek to convert people who belong to other faith communities by using some of the following arguments:

- If an inclusivist position is taken to the theology of religion, people of other faiths could be considered to be 'anonymous Christians' without needing to convert explicitly.

- If a pluralist position is taken, there is no need for people of faiths other than Christianity to be converted as they are on their own path to salvation in a way that is culturally appropriate for them.

- Assuming that others need to share Christian beliefs is arrogant and intolerant.

- Conversion to Christianity from other faiths could cause the convert family difficulties or even danger.

Chapter 3.9

1. 'Secular views of gender equality have undermined Christian gender roles.' Discuss.

AO1 Essays might demonstrate knowledge and understanding through the use of some of the following ideas. This list is not prescriptive (you may have used other ideas instead) or exhaustive (you may have included valid ideas that are not listed here).

- Description and explanation of what 'gender equality' might mean.

- Description and explanation of how ideas of gender roles have changed, for example with the right to vote.

- Description and explanation of traditional Christian gender roles and the justification of these roles in the Bible and from the teachings of the Church, for example *Mulieris Dignitatem*.

- Description and explanation of how gender roles are understood in secular modern society.

AO2 Essays might demonstrate skill in critical evaluation, analysis and coherent argument through the use of some of the following:

Learners might argue that secular ideas about gender equality have undermined Christian gender roles by using some of the following arguments:

- Secular ideas promote gender equality, but the Bible teaches that men have authority over women.

- Secular ideas undermine the role of women as mothers, encouraging women to use artificial contraception, have abortions and divorce their husbands when these practices contravene the teachings of the Catholic Church.

- Secular ideas suggest there are not simply two separate genders created by God but that gender is a social construct, which can put Christians in uncomfortable positions over issues such as transgender rights.

- Secular ideas encourage women to seek positions of authority in the Church even though this contravenes some biblical teaching.

Learners might argue that secular ideas about gender equality have not undermined Christian gender roles by using some of the following arguments:

- Christians do not have to do what secular society does and can continue to have traditional gender roles in the Church and in the home if they want to.

- Secular gender roles and disagreements with traditional Christians might give Christians opportunities to talk about Christian beliefs to friends and neighbours and to the media.

- Christians need to take on board ideas about greater gender equality as the teaching of the Bible also says that everyone is made in the image of God and that there is no 'male or female'. Secular gender roles encourage Christians to think about the position of women in the Church and to make changes for the better. Secular gender roles enhance rather than undermine Christianity because they encourage Christians to rethink old-fashioned cultural viewpoints.

2. How convincing is the claim that the idea of family is entirely culturally determined?

AO1 Essays might demonstrate knowledge and understanding through the use of some of the following ideas. This list is not prescriptive (you may have used other ideas instead) or exhaustive (you may have included valid ideas that are not listed here).

- Description and explanation of different understandings of what a family might be.

- Description and explanation of sociological and anthropological views that the family is a human institution, developed by society for the well-being, protection and division of labour of its members.

- Description and explanation of the view that the family is something designed by God as part of his purposes for human flourishing.

- Description and explanation of biblical teaching about the family.

- Description and explanation of other sources of wisdom and authority about the Christian family.

AO2 Essays might demonstrate skill in critical evaluation, analysis and coherent argument through the use of some of the following:

Learners might argue that the family is culturally determined by using some of the following arguments:

- Family life is different in different cultures, for example in more industrial societies people tend to live in smaller nuclear families, whereas in more agricultural societies people tend to live in wider extended family groups.

- Different people have different views of what a family might consist of, for example there are different views about same-sex marriage, which could suggest that the family is whatever people say it is.

- Living in families has practical advantages which provide a better explanation for the existence of family units than the view that God ordained the family.

Learners might argue that the family is not culturally determined by using some of the following arguments:

- The Bible contains teaching about the importance of families and about how family life should be organised, including relations between husband and wife, parents and children, and masters and servants, showing that family life is part of God's plan for procreation, mutual protection and the education of the young.

- Natural law ethics supports the view that family life with heterosexual married couples raising children is part of God's purposes for humanity.

- People all over the world live in family units, suggesting that there is something universally right about family life.

- It could be argued that relationships within a family are affected by and affect the norms of society, but the existence of the family itself as a unit is ordained by God.

Chapter 3.10

1. 'Rosemary Radford Reuther's feminist theology is more acceptable than the thinking of Mary Daly.' Discuss.

AO1 Essays might demonstrate knowledge and understanding through the use of some of the following ideas. This list is not prescriptive (you may have used other ideas instead) or exhaustive (you may have included valid ideas that are not listed here).

- Description and explanation of the views of Reuther on patriarchy in Christianity and the need to find a significantly feminist response within the Catholic tradition including:
  - rejection of the male-warrior Messianic stereotype
  - the admission of women into the priesthood
  - use of female as well as male language of God
  - emphasis on the female aspect of wisdom.

- Description and explanation of the views of Daly on the need to move away from traditional Christianity and its inextricable links with patriarchy into a more feminine and feminist spirituality including:
  - rejection of Christianity as patriarchal with the unholy trinity of rape, genocide and war
  - rejection of male-built places of worship and male-dominated religious institutions
  - move towards 'quintessence' with nature worship and witchcraft.

AO2 Essays might demonstrate skill in critical evaluation, analysis and coherent argument through the use of some of the following:

Learners might argue that Reuther's feminist theology is more acceptable than the thinking of Daly by using some of the following arguments:

- Reuther proposes radical reforms from within the Church whereas Daly rejects the Church altogether, which is going too far.

- Daly overstates the problems with patriarchy with her extreme 'unholy trinity' and does not make allowances for the cultural context in which the Church grew.
- Reuther makes practical suggestions such as the updating of religious language, whereas Daly's suggestions seem less likely to appeal to ordinary women.

Learners might argue that Reuther's feminist theology is not more acceptable than the thinking of Daly by using some of the following arguments:

- Both criticise patriarchy in the Church, whereas the Bible makes clear that men should have authority over women.
- Neither goes far enough and the best solution would be to abandon any kind of religion and spirituality altogether.
- Daly is right to accuse Christianity of impossibly and irretrievably repressing women.
- Daly is right to want to abandon Christianity in favour of a more feminine spirituality because Christianity is intrinsically patriarchal.

2. Discuss the view that using feminine terms of God is unnecessary.

AO1 Essays might demonstrate knowledge and understanding through the use of some of the following ideas. This list is not prescriptive (you may have used other ideas instead) or exhaustive (you may have included valid ideas that are not listed here).

- Description and explanation of the concept of patriarchy and its application to Christianity.
- Description and explanation of terms currently used of God and concepts about God that might be considered patriarchal, such as 'God the Father' and the idea of a Davidic Messiah.
- Description and explanation of the views of theologians who argue that there is a need for change to more feminine language of God, for example Reuther.
- Description and explanation of the views of those who think the current language should stay.
- Description and explanation of the views of those who think changing the language would not go far enough and Christianity needs to be abandoned altogether.

AO2 Essays might demonstrate skill in critical evaluation, analysis and coherent argument through the use of some of the following:

Learners might argue that feminine terms of God is unnecessary by using some of the following arguments:

- The argument from tradition says that much of the beauty and history of Christian language of worship would be lost if it had to be changed to accommodate feminist ideologies.
- There is nothing wrong with patriarchy as it is ordained by God and supported by some biblical texts.
- Changing the language used by Christians is just papering over the cracks and feminists need to recognise that Christianity should be abandoned altogether.
- People can think of God as being above and beyond the distinctions of gender without needing to be awkwardly politically correct in their language.

Learners might argue that feminine terms of God is necessary by using some of the following arguments:

- Speaking of God and of Christian concepts in male terms all the time alienates women.
- Male language for God reinforces male perceptions of their own importance and encourages patriarchy and inequality.
- Changes to language reflect changes to society in a good way and help to keep Christianity relevant for the modern world.
- Changes to language reflect the true teaching of the Bible and reinstate a concern for equality which has been forgotten and sidelined by men.
- Changes to language are necessary but alongside other equally necessary changes, such as changes in attitude towards abortion and contraception.

Chapter 3.11

1. 'Christianity should continue to be a significant contributor to values and culture.' Discuss.

AO1 Essays might demonstrate knowledge and understanding through the use of some of the following ideas. This list is not prescriptive (you may have used other ideas instead) or exhaustive (you may have included valid ideas that are not listed here).

- Description and explanation of ways in which Christianity has contributed to values and culture in our society; could include a range of ideas such as contribution to moral codes, law, education, art and music, the House of Lords, etc.
- Description and explanation of secularism and secularisation, the decline in church attendance, the growth of multi-faith society, the popularity of relativism.
- Description and explanation of societies in which religion is kept out of public life.
- Description and explanation of the views of those who see religion as damaging to society, such as Sigmund Freud and Richard Dawkins.
- Description and explanation of the views of those who see Christianity as having an important role to play in modern society.

AO2 Essays might demonstrate skill in critical evaluation, analysis and coherent argument through the use of some of the following:

Learners might agree that Christianity should continue to be a significant contributor to values and culture by using some of the following arguments:

- Christianity gives society a moral compass by establishing shared rules of behaviour and a common understanding of the importance of care for others, family life and other Christian values which contribute towards a stable society.
- Christianity is part of the tradition of the country, and tradition is important. We should preserve the heritage of the UK.

- It is good to have religious leaders contributing to the government of the country because they think about people's spiritual well-being and about morality, not just about winning votes or economic wealth.

- Sharing religious festivals such as Christmas and Easter gives people a chance to celebrate together and feel unified.

- Christianity has contributed a great deal to welfare reforms such as the decriminalising of homosexuality, education for all, care for the homeless and prison reform. It should be encouraged to continue.

Learners might disagree that Christianity should continue to be a significant contributor to values and culture by using some of the following arguments:

- In a multi-faith society, all different faiths and those of no religious belief should be given equal opportunity to have a voice. Christianity should contribute but should not be allowed to dominate.

- Christianity is damaging. It encourages people to be infantile and neurotic, relying on an imaginary God instead of pulling together and recognising the strength of human resourcefulness.

- Christianity, as well as other religions, causes divisions, repression and conflict. They should be conducted in private and kept out of public life and the education system.

- Christianity and other religions are damaging to a scientific mindset because they discourage enquiry in favour of blind faith. They should be abandoned in favour of human progress.

2. How fair is the claim that Christianity is a major cause of personal and social problems?

AO1 Essays might demonstrate knowledge and understanding through the use of some of the following ideas. This list is not prescriptive (you may have used other ideas instead) or exhaustive (you may have included valid ideas that are not listed here).

- Description and explanation of Freud's critique of religion, including his argument that religion is an infantile neurosis and the result of wish fulfilment.

- Description and explanation of Dawkins' view that religion is repressive, causes conflict and is anti-scientific.

- Description and explanation of views that religion should be kept out of public life, with description of societies that attempt a secular ethos.

AO2 Essays might demonstrate skill in critical evaluation, analysis and coherent argument through the use of some of the following:

Learners might agree that Christianity is a major cause of personal and social problems by using some of the following arguments:

- Christianity has been repressive of some groups, such as women and the LGBT community.

- Religion has been the cause of conflicts, violence and terrorism.

- Religion has tried to block scientific investigation, for example the condemnation of Galileo or the opposition to genome projects.

- Christian clergy have been found guilty of child abuse.

- Christianity can encourage people to hang on to an infantile mentality and keep them weak.

- Christianity can cause people to feel guilty for being gay.

- Christianity can suppress women and reinforce patriarchal systems.

Learners might disagree that Christianity is a major cause of personal and social problems by using some of the following arguments:

- Although Christianity does not have a spotless record, it has done a great deal of good for people.

- Christianity has helped people overcome alcoholism and bereavement.

- Christianity gives people hope for a better society and a reason to care for others that goes beyond self-interest.

- Christianity has done a great deal of good in terms of advocating social reforms such as education and care for the poor.

- Many conflicts and episodes of violence have more to do with political ideologies than with religion.

- Many Christians are far from infantile and have performed acts of extraordinary heroism or have stood up against injustice despite personal risk.

- Christianity can motivate people to work on scientific exploration, especially when the research is for the good of others.

Chapter 3.12

1. 'Christian thinkers should not engage with the ideologies of atheists such as Marx.' Discuss.

AO1 Essays might demonstrate knowledge and understanding through the use of some of the following ideas. This list is not prescriptive (you may have used other ideas instead) or exhaustive (you may have included valid ideas that are not listed here).

- Description and explanation of the key features of Marxist ideology, such as criticism of private ownership of the means of production, Marxist ideas about alienation and about understanding injustice in terms of class struggle.

- Description and explanation of the views of Christians who have engaged with Marxist ideology, for example leading figures in Latin American liberation theology.

- Description and explanation of critiques of liberation theology from within and outside the Catholic Church.

AO2 Essays might demonstrate skill in critical evaluation, analysis and coherent argument through the use of some of the following:

Learners might agree that Christian thinkers should not engage with the ideologies of atheists such as Marx by using some of the following arguments:

- Christianity should concentrate on the teachings of Jesus, which are full and final.

- There is no need to supplement Christian teaching with additional moral ideals from elsewhere.

- Marx was against religion, calling it the opiate of the people, making Christianity and Marxism entirely incompatible.

- Injustice should be seen not in terms of class struggle but in terms of Original Sin. The need is for salvation in spiritual terms, not action according to a political agenda. .

- Christians should love their enemies and not engage in violent revolution against them. Marxism does not advocate Christian values.

Learners might disagree that Christian thinkers should not engage with the ideologies of atheists such as Marx by using some of the following arguments:

- The religious beliefs of a thinker should not be allowed to cloud the essential truth of their perspective.

- Marxism rightly brings Christian attention to the inequalities of social class.

- Christianity should be prepared to engage with all kinds of ideologies as it does not exist in a vacuum but in a world of many different beliefs and opinions.

- Christians should be prepared to act against injustice in this world, not just wait for everything to be made right in heaven.

- Orthopraxy comes before orthodoxy. Actions are more use to the oppressed than words.

2. Discuss critically the view that liberation theology would be more successful if it became more Marxist in its outlook.

AO1 Essays might demonstrate knowledge and understanding through the use of some of the following ideas. This list is not prescriptive (you may have used other ideas instead) or exhaustive (you may have included valid ideas that are not listed here).

- Description and explanation of the key features of Marxist ideology, such as criticism of private ownership of the means of production, Marxist ideas about alienation and about understanding injustice in terms of class struggle.

- Description and explanation of the views of Christians who have engaged with Marxist ideology, for example leading figures in Latin American liberation theology.

- Description and explanation of different opinions about the extent to which liberation theology should be more Marxist in outlook.

AO2 Essays might demonstrate skill in critical evaluation, analysis and coherent argument through the use of some of the following:

Learners might agree that liberation theology would be more successful if it became more Marxist in its outlook by using some of the following arguments:

- Christianity can sometimes hold back a Marxist recognition of the causes of inequality by attributing spiritual causes such as personal sin, when it should be looking at private ownership of the means of production and alienation of the working class, and adopting a preferential option for the poor.

- Direct action in support of the oppressed needs to come before concerns about Christian orthodoxy of belief.

- Christian emphasis on being meek and peacemaking is of no use in an unjust regime.

- Some of the teachings of Christianity are inappropriate for a post-industrial modern society where power structures inevitably repress the workers.

Learners might disagree that liberation theology would be more successful if it became more Marxist in its outlook by using some of the following arguments:

- Christianity looks for the coming of the Kingdom of God as an eternal reality, not just a worldly reality.

- Spiritual matters are more important than worldly matters.

- It is impossible to right the wrongs of society because of Original Sin, so liberation theology could never be entirely successful whatever it does.

- Marxism is atheist in its outlook and incompatible with Christianity. Societies based on Marxist principles have tried to eradicate religion. It is wrong for theologians to associate with such ideologies as they cannot be Christian.